GUILTY BY REASON OF INSANITY

GUILTY BY REASON OF INSANITY

A Psychiatrist Explores the Minds of Killers

DOROTHY OTNOW LEWIS, M.D.

Fawcett Columbine
The Ballantine Publishing Group | New York

A Fawcett Columbine Book
Published by The Ballantine Publishing Group

http://www.randomhouse.com

Library of Congress Cataloging-in-Publication Data

Lewis, Dorothy Otnow.
Guilty by reason of insanity : a psychiatrist explores the mind of killers /
Dorothy Otnow Lewis. — 1st ed.
p.   cm.
ISBN 0-449-00277-2 (alk. paper)
1. Insane, Criminal and dangerous.   2. Murderers—Psychology.
I. Title.
HV6133.L49   1998
364.15'23—dc21   97-46400
CIP

Designed by Debbie Glasserman

Manufactured in the United States of America
First Edition: April 1998
10   9   8   7   6   5   4   3   2   1

AUTHOR'S NOTE

When defendants rely on the insanity defense, they open up their entire psychological state to public scrutiny. Where a defendant is requesting that the judge or jury show leniency in the trial or sentencing because the defendant claims to be insane, the State (as representative of the general public) is entitled to examine thoroughly the basis for that request. Invariably the request is grounded in a defendant's psychiatric, medical, and family history. Thus, the records of interviews with defendants, their family members, friends, associates, and doctors are all part of the inquiry into the defendant's psychological state. As such, those records are made a part of the public record, and can be used by the prosecution or the defense in support of or in opposition to the defendant's position. Thus they are in the public domain.

Actual names of defendants were used in this book where the defendant's insanity defense or clemency appeal was part of the public record. Pseudonyms, and changes in geographic locale, were used in a limited number of instances, such as cases involving juvenile defendants, or in instances when I felt that privacy interests needed to be respected.

The case studies described in this book are true, and are based upon my own evaluations. In addition to my own records, I have, when available, consulted the public record, including police reports, newspaper accounts, defendants' statements, witnesses' statements, psychiatric and medical records, and reports of other examiners.

ACKNOWLEDGMENTS

Without Jonathan Pincus, my partner in crime, there would be no story to tell. Teacher, colleague, superb clinician, and friend, thank you.

I am indebted to Abby Stein who read through an early draft of this book and, in a lovingly ruthless or ruthlessly loving fashion, got rid of whatever she found to be timorous, extraneous, or less than on target.

I am grateful to Leona Nevler, my editor at Ballantine Books, who gently but firmly forced me to grapple with the Shawcross tale, although she knew it would be a painful case for me to revisit. "It will make it a better book," she insisted, and I think she was right. I was flattered that she made few changes in the rest of the manuscript and thereby, for better or for worse, made sure that my voice was heard.

For the past decade, Catherine Yeager and I have worked together closely, not only at Bellevue, but also in prisons from coast to coast. Cathi and I shared many of the adventures recounted in this book, including the Shawcross case and the visit with an executioner. Cathi recalled certain aspects of cases that I preferred to forget, and she insisted I include them. I am eternally grateful to her not only for her help with this book but also for her courage and friendship.

Vanda Henry has been more than my secretary. True, for the past five years she has typed draft after draft of each chapter. But she has done much more. She has formed cordial relationships not only with our patients but also with our death row inmates (who call her collect) and with each attorney with whom we have worked. I treasure her skills, her graciousness, and her loyalty during especially hard times.

In March of 1997, Cheryl Kissel stole Jonathan Lazear's *New Yorker*. She has confessed. In the "Crime and Punishment" issue she read an article about me and my work and brought it to her boss's attention. When Jonathan Lazear called me to ask if I had ever thought of writing a book about my work, an almost complete *Guilty by Reason of Insanity* lay under Vanda's desk, set aside in favor of more pressing work. I sent the book to him. He liked it. He thought other people would, too. He became my agent. He sold it. All this within eight weeks. Had Cheryl not swiped the *New Yorker*, and had Jonathan Lazear not made that phone call, *Guilty*, would still be stashed under Vanda's desk. Jonathan, am I glad you called!

My husband and children are my biggest fans and severest critics. I am grateful to Luciano, the newest member of our family, for his enthusiasm and encouragement. Eric delights me with his visual take on the book. He sees each chapter as a separate screenplay and shows me possibilities I never before envisioned. Gillian has spent hours with me, listening attentively as I read parts of the manuscript aloud. I have heeded her advice. Thanks to Gillian, rhythms and cadences have been revised and a number of highfalutin phrases were rolled up in yellow paper balls, tossed on the living room floor, and turned into cat toys for Ptolemy.

The years during which this book was written have not always been easy. Without Mel's support, guidance, wisdom, and love the book would not have been completed. I dedicate it to him with love.

PROLOGUE

I never planned to work with violent people, certainly not murderers. I went through medical school in order to become a psychoanalyst. Psychoanalysis, it seemed to me, brought together the most intriguing aspects of art and science; it was the best of two worlds. As a psychiatry resident, when I pictured the future, I saw myself in a private office, seated behind a supine patient, listening and commenting as he struggled to resolve the violent internal conflicts between his id and his superego. That was about as violent as I expected my practice to get.

I never did become an analyst. Instead, a series of unexpected events and serendipitous observations drew me deeper and deeper into the study of violence. And I, neither willing nor able to navigate those depths alone, pulled my dear friend and colleague, Jonathan Pincus, in after me.

Jonathan, a neurologist and my partner in crime for the past twenty-five years, like me, never intended to work with violent patients. When I met him he was a junior faculty member at Yale, dividing his time among teaching, research, and patient care. He had every expectation of continuing his traditional academic way of life. Had anyone told him that twenty years hence he would find himself behind bars at San Quentin in the company of me and a sequence of serial murderers, he would have dismissed the prediction at best as fantasy, at worst, delusion. In fact, when in the late seventies I first convinced Jonathan to examine a group of violent adolescents, I had no idea that the two of us would someday wind up together on death row.

When Jonathan and I began our collaboration, no one thought that neurologic impairment or severe psychopathology contributed significantly to violence. Furthermore, the study of the effects of child abuse was in its infancy. This book tells the story of how Jonathan and I gradually came to recognize the kinds of neuropsychiatric and environmental ingredients that go into the recipe for violence.

Every so often, usually after we have heard that a colleague has pooh-poohed our work, Jonathan will say, "Dorothy, you ruined my reputation."

My response? "I didn't exactly ruin it, Jonathan. I just changed it."

CHAPTER 1

The secret of working with violent people is knowing when to end an interview. Then again, in certain situations that is not an option. Occasionally, in spite of what seem to be adequate precautions, I find myself alone in the company of a very dangerous person. For example, several years ago I was locked in a room with Theodore Bundy. I had not planned it that way.

The very best setting for interviewing a potentially violent prisoner is one where guards can see everything and hear nothing. Indeed, when I began my interview with Mr. Bundy, that was the setup. He and I were locked inside a room, adjoining the administrative area of the Florida State Penitentiary at Starke. One side of the room, the side with the door through which we entered, had a large pane of soundproof glass that looked like a picture window; the other three walls were solid concrete. A guard was posted just outside the glass where we could see him and he could see but not hear us. He stood in a common area, surrounded by two or three administrative offices and another glassed-in interview room. The doors to the offices were open, and I could see people inside, working behind their desks. I was perfectly safe. Every so often someone came into the common area to fill a mug from a coffee urn, which was always full and hot.

The room, small to begin with, was further cramped by the presence of a rectangular wooden table that filled almost the entire space. Mr. Bundy and I sat across from each other, our chairs pushed up against opposite walls. He had taken the chair nearest the door and had managed to angle his seat so that he could keep an eye on me and also keep track of the guard's movements beyond the glass. I was obliged to take the one remaining chair jammed up against the far wall of the cubicle. I would have felt trapped were it not for my clear view of the guard and his clear view of me. There was nothing to worry about. I relaxed and focused my attention entirely on Mr. Bundy and the task at hand. Once an interview is under way, I am oblivious to my surroundings.

We had been talking since nine o'clock and, in spite of the deliberately fat-filled, death row breakfast that I try to consume in order to keep going for hours, my stomach had started to rumble. This tendency of my gastrointestinal tract to make its needs known has been an embarrassment since high school. I looked at my watch. It was a little after twelve noon. Time for a candy break. (Jonathan and I have learned the folly of leaving prisons in order to get lunch. It can take hours to get back inside.) I turned from Mr. Bundy, on whom my attention had been riveted, and tried to catch the eye of the guard to unlock the cubicle so that I could get to a candy machine. The guard was gone. Not only was he gone, but everyone else who worked in the surrounding offices had also disappeared. They had all gone to lunch. It took me a few seconds to realize that I was alone, locked in a soundproof room, with a man who had murdered more than two dozen women. I was not happy.

I turned my attention back to Mr. Bundy. "You were saying?" To this day, I do not recall much of what he was saying; I do remember trying to remain calm and appear attentive. If Mr. Bundy knew the guard had left, he kept the knowledge to himself. I have no idea exactly how long I was alone with Theodore Bundy. It could have been an hour; it could have been a few minutes. I never saw the guard leave. I do know that, during the ten or fifteen minutes between the time I looked up and realized that the area was deserted and the time the guard ambled back to his position on the other side of the glass, I was a very good listener. I limited my responses to nods, friendly grunts, and the occasional monosyllable necessary to help the conversation along. Only one of Mr. Bundy's statements during that period of time remains with me: "The man sitting before you never killed anyone." During a previous interview with him, Theodore Bundy had described to me in detail several of the murders he had committed. I made a clinical decision: I chose not to point out the discrepancy between our two interviews. Alone in a room with a serial killer is neither the time nor the place to quibble about inconsistencies.

I used to be relatively fearless. I did not think twice about interviewing violent people all by myself. I figured, if I didn't threaten them, they would not hurt me. As I reflect on this patently idiotic assumption, I like to think that it is experience and not just middle age that has made me more cautious. I have learned a lot from the rogues gallery Jonathan and I have seen. Books can tell you how to interview, what kinds of questions to ask; supervisors and instructors can provide advice; but there's nothing quite like delinquents and criminals to teach you about talking with violent people. Timing matters.

I remember one of my first teachers. He was neither a serial murderer nor even an adult. He was a repeatedly assaultive adolescent boy who, because of his violent acts, was incarcerated in the secure unit of a juvenile correctional institution in Connecticut. The two of us were alone in a small room, just off the main corridor of the unit. There were no guards or picture windows. I don't recall exactly what we were discussing—whatever it was seemed to be making the boy increasingly agitated. Nothing I said made him comfortable, and long silences made things worse. When he could no longer sit still, he began to walk back and forth along the far wall of the room, opposite the door. My chair was nearest the exit. As his pace quickened, he mumbled to himself and began to punch his right hand into his left.

I rose from my chair and scooped up my papers. "I think we've talked enough for one day. Let's stop now and talk again tomorrow. Maybe next week." I tried to sound casual as I slowly inched my way toward the door. I turned the knob gently, opened the door, and slipped out. The boy followed me. I could feel him behind me. The next thing I knew, I heard a sharp crack behind me, like the sound of a thick branch splitting. I wheeled around in time to see another inmate, who had been walking down the corridor, minding his own business, and who happened to be passing our way, fall to the floor. I was dumbstruck. Had I not ended our meeting when I did, I surely would have been the one on the floor with a broken jaw. When I was able to speak, I asked simply, "Why did you do that?"

"He called me a motherfucker," came the instantaneous reply.

No one had said a word. Nevertheless, the boy was convinced he had been insulted. In this case (as subsequently with Theodore Bundy), I did not challenge his perception. With any luck, I would have time later on to explore what had happened and why. Jonathan and I have learned never to argue with paranoid misperceptions. It doesn't work. Paranoia—the unwarranted sense that one is being threatened, endangered, disrespected—is probably the most common symptom fueling recurrent acts of violence. Jonathan and I have found that this is as true of violent juvenile delinquents as it is of violent adult criminals. This does not mean that most violent people are schizophrenic. As Jonathan and I teach our trainees at Georgetown and Bellevue, paranoia is characteristic of almost any neuropsychiatric disorder: schizophrenia, mania, depression, brain damage, seizures, alcoholism, senility, and more. It can emerge whenever something goes awry in the brain. Paranoia must have strong survival value. Doctors who fail to appreciate this basic psychiatric truth get hurt; some wind up dead.

Fortunately, most prisons allow lawyers to sit in on diagnostic interviews with inmates. The presence of another person in the room, while not diminishing paranoia, helps keep rageful feelings and violent behaviors in check. There are other advantages than just safety to having a lawyer at interviews. Jonathan and I insist that the lawyers with whom we work observe what happens in our interviews: what we do, what we say, what we see, and what we hear. Some of the phenomena that come to light are so unusual, so bizarre, that they must be seen to be believed.

Prisons in Georgia, we have discovered, are different. In Georgia, defense lawyers are not allowed to be present during psychiatric evaluations of inmates. At least that has been our experience at the state penitentiary.

Once, when I came to Georgia to examine a young man on death row, although the lawyer was not allowed to join me, the prison offered to station a guard inside the room during the interview. This was obviously unacceptable. No inmate will tell you much about his feelings or symptoms, much less about a murder he may have committed, with a prison guard breathing down his neck. On that occasion I decided to ignore my own basic rule of safety, and I met alone in a locked cell with the condemned boy. The inmate had been a juvenile when he was tried and sentenced to death. His victim, as I recall, was a violent, abusive relative. Otherwise, compared to most of the death row inmates we have seen, the boy's record was pretty clean. People who do in family members tend, for the most part, not to be indiscriminately violent. In fact, it was hard to understand why this particular young man had been sentenced to death in the first place. I had seen far more dangerous delinquents at the correctional school in Connecticut. It would take me years to appreciate the fact that the trial lawyer has lots more to do with who gets The Chair than does the nature of the crime. Anyway, I felt pretty safe with the young inmate; therefore, with only mild trepidations, I met alone with him.

The interview went smoothly. In fact, as I recall, neither of us felt any uneasiness until I asked a question about discipline at home. Reluctantly, the young man revealed some of his stepfather's favorite punishments.

"He used to make us do the dead cockroach."

"The dead cockroach?"

"He made us lie on the floor on our backs with our bare feet in the air. We had to stay that way. It seemed like hours. If your feet started to go down, he would beat you on the soles with a switch."

Anyone facing execution can be expected to exaggerate, if not downright lie. I was skeptical. I needed proof. Therefore, I asked the young man to remove his shoes and socks. I looked: the soles of his feet were covered with scars.

In the course of the interview, I learned that the boy's father had also beaten him on the buttocks repeatedly and mercilessly. Sometimes he drew blood. Those kinds of punishments constitute possible mitigating circumstances. But in this boy's case, the issue of child abuse had never been raised, either during his trial or at the time of sentencing. It might not be too late to introduce this information on appeal, but I needed more objective evidence of it.

When a physical examination is necessary, an attorney can act as chaperone. But in Georgia, attorneys are banished from evaluations. The likelihood that anyone else would try to verify this history of abuse prior to the boy's execution was remote. On the other hand, I did not generally perform physical examinations on the backsides of murderers while locked up, alone with them, in dimly lit cells. I had to decide: safety and modesty versus documentation and mitigation. Then and there, in the dim light of the cell-cum-examining room of the Georgia State Penitentiary, the boy lowered his prison-issue drawers. I had no camera, but I did my best to draw a diagram of the shiny, faded, white scars that criss-crossed the flesh of his buttocks. Neither of us was embarrassed. On death row, modesty is a luxury no one can afford.

My next case in Georgia involved the psychiatric evaluation of a notorious serial murderer. Accounts I had read of his crimes indicated that I shared certain physical attributes with his victims. In that case, when the warden refused to allow the man's attorney (or anyone else except a guard) in the cell with me, I demurred. I was forced to examine him in a dark visitor's area, separated by a dense screen and unable to see or hear very much. I had broken a rule once before in Georgia; I had allowed myself to be locked in a room alone with the condemned boy with scars on his feet and buttocks. I had examined his bare behind and gotten away with it. In the case of this serial killer, I was not about to push my luck.

Over the past twenty years, Jonathan and I have come to realize that, if studying homicidal individuals is a science, communicating with them is an art. To do the former requires the latter. Anyone who would do research on murderers must, therefore, master the art of talking with them. The following are essentials: (1) the temperament to avoid locking horns; (2) the restraint at crucial moments to keep one's mouth shut; (3) the sensitivity to discern when to break a silence; and (4) the intuition to sense when to end an interview. The last is the most important. Failure to master it could cut short an otherwise promising career in the field of violence research.

I like to watch Jonathan interview a murderer. He conveys a quiet confidence. His body language says, "I won't hurt you. You won't hurt me. We have work to do together." Adopting this posture is hard for many men; in my experience it comes more naturally to women. I suspect that some of the same biological and societal factors that make men, as a group, about nine times as homicidal as women also explain the greater difficulty some male doctors have relating to violent men. Men are more confrontational. They don't like to have the wool pulled over their eyes. When faced with a violent criminal, they need to establish from the outset just who is boss. Unfortunately, many repeatedly violent inmates have had more than their share of difficulty with bosses. In fact, a fair proportion of their victims have either been bosses or have been perceived as such. One need look no further than recent newspaper accounts of the behaviors of disgruntled postal workers and fast-food chain employees for confirmation of this fact of life. A diagnostic interview with a murderer is just not the right setting in which to rekindle these kinds of unresolved conflicts. Besides, interviews are not contests and there can be no bosses. Good interviews are collaborative; the minute an inmate senses competition, the collaboration ends.

No psychiatrist, male or female, likes to be fooled. On the other hand, violent felons do not have a reputation for candor. Certainly no psychiatrist in his or her right mind believes everything a violent inmate says. Women are just as likely as men to recognize contradictions and confabulations. The difference is, men are more likely to confront them head-on. Women wait and listen. We don't forget; we simply hold off until the time is right to address them. Suppose, for example, that, as I sat alone with Theodore Bundy, I had confronted him with the discrepancies between his stories: "But, Mr. Bundy, last time I talked with you you told me you had killed . . ." Not a good idea. Based on the years I worked on his case, not a good idea at all.

There are excellent reasons other than just safety for mastering an inquisitive, not an inquisitorial, style. For one, not all inconsistencies reflect lying. In the case of murderers, there are usually numerous psychiatric and neurologic reasons why memory may fluctuate and stories may vary. If Jonathan and I always dismissed memory lapses and contradictions as lies, we would overlook valuable clues to the nature of many violent acts.

I would characterize my own style of interviewing murderers as matter-of-fact. To that extent, it differs little from my style with any other patient. I roll up my sleeves, literally and figuratively, and plunge into the task of trying to understand. I am in no hurry. It takes more than a couple of hours to understand another human being.

At the start of our interviews, both Jonathan and I try to stick to pretty ordinary, nonthreatening questions. Where were you born? Who raised you? What was school like for you? We ask in detail about medical problems, accidents, injuries, illnesses. They matter. There will be lots of time later to explore more charged topics like feelings, attitudes, temper, and, of course, inconsistencies. We usually leave the topic of murder for late in the interview. Violent offenders need lots of time to decide whether or not we can be trusted with this kind of information. We can wait.

After two decades of working together, our interviewing styles are remarkably similar. We have shared our knowledge and expertise so often that we can no longer be certain exactly which aspects of the interview each of us contributed. However, if our clinical approaches are similar, our philosophical positions are not.

My own way of perceiving myself vis-à-vis the rest of the world was clarified for me years ago, on a train from New York City to Cambridge, Massachusetts. I was returning to college, and my father had bought me a seat in a parlor car. There I found myself seated next to Paul Tillich, the theologian and Harvard professor. He was a friendly man (especially to Radcliffe students, I would learn years later from his *New York Times* obituary). We struck up a conversation. To my surprise, I discovered that his daughter, Miss Tillich, had been one of my English teachers. When I was in high school I had never heard of Paul Tillich. I learned it at Radcliffe, where everyone knew his name.

Paul Tillich and I talked nonstop from New York to Boston. We talked about the Ethical Culture Schools (where his daughter taught), about mysticism, about religion and philosophy. When we couldn't get a cab, we lugged our suitcases to the subway and took the MTA into Cambridge together. Along the way, we somehow got onto the subject of witches. Professor Tillich introduced the topic.

"When you read about witches being burned at the stake, do you identify with the witch or with the people looking on?" he asked.

"The witch," I replied instantly. I didn't tell him that in my mind I also walked into the gas chambers at Auschwitz and up to the gallows at Nuremberg. In seventh grade, when I read *A Tale of Two Cities*, Madame Defarge knitted and watched the guillotine come down on my neck.

"How about you?" I asked.

"The crowd, of course," came his response. I never found out why. Paul Tillich asked me to call him and we would go out to lunch together, but a week later, when I did, he had forgotten who I was. I did not forget him, nor did I forget his question.

Jonathan, I think, is more like Paul Tillich. He identifies with "the crowd," with society at large. He, like most people, is confident of his ability to control his own actions. I think he is even a bit critical, maybe suspicious, of anyone who can't. Hence we do not always see eye to eye.

Jonathan has few misgivings about the death penalty. I should amend that statement. When we started our work together on death row, he had no qualms whatsoever. Only after he evaluated a man on death row in Starke, Florida, who he was convinced was innocent, did he start having second thoughts. (I thought the man was guilty as hell.)

But by and large, Jonathan has always been concerned most for the public's safety. Jonathan does not worry that some day, in a fit of rage, or during a nightmare, he himself might kill someone. He trusts his central nervous system. He worries rather that some day his testimony on behalf of a brain-damaged murderer might loose upon society another Jack the Ripper. Suppose that person goes free and kills again? Then, Jonathan feels, the blood will be on his hands. Jonathan cannot live with that possibility.

I, on the other hand, am haunted by the prospect of condemning to death a person whose upbringing and brain function have made it hard, if not impossible, for him to control his acts. Granted, the person may be a menace. I have no problem locking him up forever in a humane place and throwing away the key. Until we know how to treat such individuals, the public must be protected.

Whenever Jonathan and I debate these issues, neither of us will budge. Our relationship reminds me of Peter Medowar's description of Reverend Smith and the Edinburgh housewives.* Reverend Smith, while perambulating the streets of Edinburgh, overheard a vehement argument between two housewives. When Smith looked up, he saw two women leaning out of their windows, shouting at each other across the narrow street that separated their buildings. Turning to his companion, Smith commented, "They can never agree, for they are arguing from different premises." That's us.

I am convinced that our different perspectives are in part biologically determined. Because of the inordinate length of time it takes me to finish a book, my tendency to spill coffee and bang into the corners of coffee tables, and my inability to perform well half the neurologic tests in Jonathan's repertoire, I find myself identifying with the poor miscreants whose damaged brains and traumatic upbringings have somehow landed them behind bars.

Recently, because of excruciating pain in my neck and arm, I consulted an orthopedic surgeon. He spent a long time studying my X rays. Finally he spoke. "I see an injury here in the first three cervical vertebrae. It looks like the kind of injury you see in divers who hit the bottom of a pool." He paused. "Were you ever dropped on your head?" he inquired. To the best of my knowledge I was not. But I empathize with those who have been.

Jonathan's allegiances, in contrast, are with "the crowd," the healthy, innocent victims on whom the criminals we evaluate prey. It is no wonder that he does not identify with our misbegotten inmates. First of all, Jonathan reads rapidly. His neck is in fine shape. He is bald, and the fine, rounded shape of his skull reveals that he could never have been dropped on it. And Jonathan can perform skillfully all

---

*Peter Medowar, *Pluto's Republic* (New York: Oxford University Press, 1982), p. 103.

of the neurologic tasks he requires of others. He can touch his finger to his nose with his eyes closed; balance for days on one foot; depress the lever of a tapping machine with his right and left index fingers dozens of times in ten seconds; he skips flawlessly. In fact, one of my only pleasures on a trip to death row is watching Jonathan try to teach a neurologically impaired murderer to skip. Guards in Texas and Florida gawk in wonder as they watch this six-foot-two professor prance gracefully around the examining room. Moreover, he has the sangfroid not to feel ridiculous doing it. We are very different from each other, Jonathan and I. That may be why we are a good team. I keep Jonathan in touch with the vulnerabilities of our violent patients; he keeps me in touch with the consequences of their acts.

CHAPTER 2

People ask me how I wound up on death row.

Once, in a maximum security prison, a guard approached me. "Ma'am, can I ask you a question?" Guards, especially in the South, can be very polite.

"Sure."

"Ma'am, how come you're . . ." he paused, looking from me to the large shackled figure, shuffling toward me. The death row inmate I was about to interview had decapitated one of his female victims, an act that had led to his own current precarious hold on life.

"How come . . . I mean, why do you come to talk with them?" He nodded in the direction of the hulking figure moving in my direction.

"You mean, what's a nice girl like me doing in a 'joint' like this?"

He didn't get it.

Another time I was lecturing about our research on violence at a scientific symposium. I was nervous. I am used to presenting our work at psychiatric meetings. I know what to expect: the audience and I speak the same language. But I had no idea what kinds of questions this group of basic researchers would throw at me. The moment I finished the talk, a hand went up toward the back of the room. I nodded in that direction. A man rose—an academic type, tweeds, beard, horn-rims. He strode toward the microphone in the center aisle.

"Doctor Lewis," he began. The voice was low and confident. When this man spoke, people listened.

"Doctor Lewis," he repeated, "I am a statistician by trade." My heart sank. I am a clinician. I waited to be told that the statistics of the study I had just presented were in error, that I had used too many variables for the number of subjects in the study, that I had conducted a multiple regression analysis when it obviously should have been a log linear analysis.

"Doctor Lewis." This academic seemed to enjoy repeating my name and watching me squirm. "How is it that a . . ." (he paused, seeking the proper words) "that a . . . petite woman like you, that a child psychiatrist, came to work with such violent individuals?"

My husband, an Englishman and a psychoanalyst, has put the question more pithily. On more than one occasion, as he has watched me trundle off to death row, briefcase slung over one shoulder, large black canvas bag weighing down the other, dragging a carry-on behind me, he has called out, "Dorothy, with two basic drives, how come you chose to study aggression?"

I have asked myself the same question. Certainly when I entered medical school, had anyone even suggested that I would someday spend a fair proportion of my waking hours behind bars, in the company of rapists and murderers, I would have thought the notion delusional.

I never intended to work with violent patients. I expected to become a psychoanalyst. As a premed student in college, I wrote my physics term paper on the influence of physics on Freud. I was flabbergasted when Professor LeCorbusier liked it. I'm sure he had never before had anyone turn in a paper quite like mine. My senior thesis was about Freud and the poet Valéry. It asked: who influenced whom?

Medical school was a lonely experience. French majors and biochem majors are rarely on the same wavelength, and I was surrounded by a forest of tall, blond biochem majors. One way I coped with my loneliness was to embark on my own psychoanalysis; that way I had at least one person who was willing to listen to me for an hour (actually fifty minutes) a day. Of course, I had to pay him.

Yale Medical School required a thesis on an original piece of research. The title of mine was: "The Development of an Abstract Design Test to Measure the Capacity for Intimacy." Freud had hypothesized two basic forces operating within human beings: sex and aggression, love and death. I would study the former. I set myself the task of devising a way to assess an individual's capacity to love. I had no inkling then that, twenty years hence, Jonathan Pincus and I would find ourselves periodically locked up on death row together, studying the causes and consequences of the capacity to hate.

Medical school was not my first taste of loneliness. In fact, as far back as I can remember I have always felt lonely. I remember lying in bed at night in the dark, wondering whether the world beyond the four walls of my bedroom was really there. Did it disappear when I turned off the light or closed my eyes? Maybe it materialized just for me each time I opened them. Sometimes I used to try to fool it, to catch the world "disappeared." I would keep my eyes closed and pretend to be asleep, then suddenly open them, expecting to see a void where the world as I knew it had been. Once or twice I am convinced I caught it "disappeared." That's pretty lonely.

I struggled throughout my analysis to understand the source of my loneliness. I know that when I was brought home from the hospital, I received an ambivalent reception. My mother (a former socialist), my father (a former dead-end kid from the Lower East Side of New York City), and my sister, a blonde, blue-eyed (former only child), all looked forward to the birth of a boy. My mother had twice miscarried sons. Not only was I a girl, but also I arrived prematurely and spent my first days of life imprisoned in an incubator. I was scrawny, with dark eyes and a shock of pitch-black hair. I was ugly. This is not false modesty; I have photographs. Try as my family might, they could not conceal their disappointment. My sister, just four and a half when I came on the scene, had an especially hard time.

If home was not a haven, school was no better. In fact it was worse. I was reasonably intelligent and I worked hard. But the good grades I received, though they pleased my parents, did not endear me to my classmates. They were merciless. One day, as I came in from gym, a girl in my class spat on me. At our twenty-fifth reunion, another girl apologized for saying some pretty awful things in fifth grade. I was grateful to her, but the words would have been more healing had they come four decades earlier.

I frequently admit to my young patients—children who are presently enduring the casual maliciousness of their classmates and siblings—that I would not be a child again for anything in the world. The pain is too intense and, as a child, one is helpless to do much about it. My patients look at me suspiciously. You mean you were picked last for the team? I nod yes. They feel better. I remember sitting on a concrete ledge in Central Park and whispering to myself, "Dear God, please let me be picked second to last, not last." I must have been something of a believer in those days. My identification with the underdog is no accident.

As a child, I yearned to get even, to destroy my tormenters. At the same time, I wondered what kept me from acting on those homicidal wishes and fantasies. How come some people punched out their enemies, even killed them, while others—like me—walked away, went home, and cried?

I grew up with Hitler. At least it felt that way—he seemed like a next-door neighbor. My mother worked for Youth Aliyah, an organization that rescued children from Hitler's gas chambers. She raised money to sneak them out of Germany and ship them to safety in

Palestine. My mother went to lectures by Goldie Myerson and Aubrey Eban (before they became Golda Meir and Abba Eban) and brought home the news. She knew (and hence I knew) what went on in the concentration camps of Germany years before the American government and decades before the German people. Remarkable.

Hitler was a source of fascination and fear. How, I wondered, could any human being do the things he did? I shrieked when I saw my uncle chop off the head of a chicken. When the bird appeared later on the dinner table, no one in the family would eat it. How, then, could Hitler torture and kill human beings? There had to be something wrong with him. He had to be crazy. I think I was the only one at school, if not on the face of the earth, who did not rejoice upon hearing of Hitler's suicide. Now I would never know what made him tick. What mysterious forces could turn a human being into a monster? I was convinced, even as a child, that Hitler could not have been born that way. No one could be born that way. I still believe that.

After the war, I listened to the radio and heard about the Nuremberg trials. What confused me most was the fate of the defendants: If it was not all right for the Nazis to kill people, how come it was O.K. to hang the Nazis?

I remember the Rosenbergs.

What really concerned me, of course, was my own fate. Sometimes I couldn't sleep. I would lie in bed, eyes wide open, worrying. How could I be sure that someday I would not do something violent? Then people would want to kill me. Already the kids at school were not too fond of me. From day one, it was clear that my sister would gladly have had me out of the way. She would lure me into her darkened room, then jump out of her lighted closet, shrieking, "The Green Witch will get you!" Once, when I was four or five and frustrated beyond endurance, I ran at her and bit her in the stomach, which was as high as I could reach. How could I be certain that one night, in my sleep, I would not wander into the kitchen, secure a cleaver, and wreak vengeance? Just last week I read an article about several people who actually did commit murder in their sleep. Lucky I did not know about that when I was small. That information would really have messed me up.

My father's favorite saying was, "There but for the grace of God go I." Well, didn't that mean me? I knew the intensity of my fury. What prevented me from killing someone and winding up dangling from a noose like Goebbels or Goering, or sizzling in the electric chair like the Rosenbergs? I suspect that my need to answer these kinds of questions explains at least in part how I eventually wound up on death row.

I did not expect to marry. My mother was convinced that the combination of my brains, my seriousness, and my predilection for tailored suits, Liberty of London cotton blouses, and black dresses would render me an old maid. When I did start going out on dates (we did that in those days), she would caution, "Do you have to let them know how smart you are?" Her other words of advice: "Shorten your skirts" and "Be a butterfly." I did not know how to sew (nor did she) and hadn't the foggiest idea what it meant to be a butterfly. I knew only, I was not one.

In spite of her misgivings about me, my mother and I were extremely close. In fact, she loved me passionately. I was her favorite, which no doubt sheds light on my relationship with my sister. At night, after my father had gone to sleep, my mother and I would stay up late, talking. Over and over again she would tell me how she had wanted to be a journalist, but she met my father and got married instead. In those days, if a man made a good living, his wife did not work. It did not look right. For her to have worked would have meant to her friends that my father could not support her. That's what she said. Occasionally, when we stayed up late talking, she cried. During one of those midnight conversations, when she was about the age I am now, she said, a certain determination in her voice, "Don't do what I did. Have a career."

I did not shorten my skirts. Nor did I molt. I could not and would not. But I did listen to this last piece of advice. I think her other admonitions were what she thought she was supposed to say. She must have figured that I would not be able to have both a career and a husband. Nobody did. Nobody in her world.

Meeting my husband during my senior year at medical school was not just a surprise, it was a miracle. Melvin Lewis—to my mind the brightest, handsomest, most desirable single male on the psychiatry faculty at Yale—wanted me; me with my long skirts and Liberty of London blouses. Two weeks after our first date we were engaged. When I told my family, they were so astounded and relieved that they failed even to ask if he was Jewish.

When news of my engagement filtered out to my classmates, they too were surprised. The other four women in my class had long since found partners. One of my classmates, a boy I had known since kindergarten at Ethical Culture, accosted me outside the hospital. "I hear you're engaged to Melvin Lewis. Is it true?" he demanded.

"Yes."

"Really?" My classmate sounded puzzled. "He's a great guy. What does he see in you?"

Instantly the old hurt and rage from grade school rose within me. I could have slaughtered him on the spot. Shortly after graduation I learned that he had died in Vietnam, shot down in a helicopter. I was shaken. Since childhood I had worried that my very thoughts could kill. Had I been right? Had my flash of anger at his cruel words done him in? Intellectually, of course, I knew that was not so. Nonetheless it reminded me of the old question that for years had flickered in my mind: Why could I feel homicidal and not kill while others acted on their impulses?

My marriage to Mel and the subsequent birth of our children convinced me that the world probably did exist, even when I closed my eyes. What is more, it was not half bad. Life clearly had improved with age. It does. I tell that to my adult patients who look with anxiety, even dread, upon forthcoming fortieth and fiftieth birthdays. The older we are, the more control we have of our lives, the less buffeted we are by the casual or deliberate maliciousness of those around us. I guess as we mature we also don't need to be loved by everybody—one or two people will do. Still, the question had been planted and remained: Why do some people when hurt or angry, just lose it while others don't?

Back in the lecture hall, as I stood before the scientific symposium, I was not about to share these intimacies with the tweedy statistician in the back of the room: they were none of his business. I smiled at him, then turned to another hand in the audience.

CHAPTER 3

My career path, like the paths of the killers Jonathan and I have come to know, was charted in childhood, long before I met Sidney. Hitler, and my curiosity about the differences between us, drew me toward the study of violence. But it was Sidney's defiant—one would have to say delinquent—act that catapulted me from a low, kiddie-size chair at the Yale Child Study Center's model nursery to the benches at the back of the juvenile court in New Haven.

Psychiatrists must understand normal child development. There-fore, during my training at the Yale Child Study Center, I was required to spend a morning a week—Mondays—in nursery school. There I observed normal preschoolers at normal play. It was a busman's holiday.

By the time I reached the nursery-school stage of my psychiatric training, I was already a wife and the mother of a four-year-old daugh-ter, Gillian, who, my husband and I liked to believe, was a relatively normal preschooler.

We were selfish parents, an appalling admission for a child psychia-trist. We worked hard all day, then came home and played with

Gillian. In order to accommodate our schedules, we modified hers. During the day, while in the care of her nanny, Gillian took long afternoon naps. Then, from six in the evening when we got home until eleven thirty at night when we flicked off the eleven o'clock news and went to bed, Gillian was forced to play with us.

Between the hours of six and eleven our house was a preschool. We finger painted; we sang nursery rhymes; we blew soap bubbles; we read *The Cat in the Hat*. Over and over, we read *The Cat in the Hat*. Watching the eleven o'clock news was the only concession to the adult world (except, of course, for her sleep pattern) that Gillian was required to make. Therefore, Monday mornings at the nursery school, watching other people's children do exactly what my daughter had done the night before, were a drag. Worse, the chairs in the nursery school were so low that just straightening up after a morning's observation was excruciating.

One Monday morning, as I sat on a Lilliputian chair, my knees almost touching my chin, I was propelled into the first stage of my career in violence. I witnessed a violent act. In retrospect it was an act of desperation, as are so many acts of violence. Furthermore, it was committed by a normal preschool boy, Sidney, thus demonstrating that violent acts can be perpetrated by normal individuals under sufficiently frustrating circumstances.

As bored with his soapsuds play as I was with watching it, Sidney informed the assistant teacher that he wanted to go to the costume corner, play soldier, and kill people. Three times he politely made his homicidal wishes known. Each time, in response, the large assistant teacher, smiled, ignored his request, and encouraged him to continue making beautiful bubbles. After several unsuccessful attempts to negotiate peacefully, Sidney felt obliged to resort to violence: he simply upended his large basin of beautiful bubbles. Not once looking backward, he slogged through the soapsuds toward the costume corner, creating in his wake, I noticed, an abstract design of puddles and foam. I smiled.

My pleasure was short-lived. "Mrs. Lewis, get the mop," bellowed the large assistant teacher. She could at least have said Doctor Lewis, I thought. That very afternoon I prevailed on the director of the Yale Child Study Center to accept my evenings at home—finger painting, reading Dr. Seuss, and mopping my own floors—as adequate training in normal early child development and to allow me to spend Monday mornings at the juvenile court instead of in nursery school. That I asked to spend my time at the court with angry, aggressive children, rather than at a school for the gifted, was obviously not accidental. The questions about rage, violence, self-control, and responsibility that since childhood had intruded on my thoughts were still alive and active. I did not realize it then, but when I set foot in the juvenile court I took my first step on the path that would eventually lead to death row.

As I have said, reading is slow-going for me. Furthermore, when I trained, most of the psychiatric literature was anecdotal and impressionistic. For both of these reasons, I read little of it. I compensated for my lack of written information by becoming a fairly astute observer of human behavior. I learned to rely on my own perceptions and believe my own eyes. However, I was not totally unprepared for juvenile court. I absorb information easily if I hear it. I was familiar with *Trial by Jury*, knew much of the *Mikado* by heart, and had almost perfect recall for the words of *West Side Story*. According to the familiar lyrics of the Broadway show, I could expect to encounter a bunch of engaging, pugnacious, streetwise kids.

I had also attended lectures in medical school, and had absorbed the prevailing psychoanalytic wisdom regarding delinquency. Children became delinquent because they acted out their parents' unconscious antisocial impulses. These children, I was taught, suffered from what were called *superego lacunae*. That is, as a result of parental moral failings, delinquent children had large holes in their consciences through which their sociopathic behaviors oozed.

Those professors who did not buy into the theory of the transmission of delinquent vibes from parent to child or the notion of leaky consciences stressed instead the consequences of social inequality. They taught that poor people who lacked legitimate ways to obtain the good things in life that people like me had were obliged to resort to illegal methods to acquire them. Sometimes this required violence. According to my professors, in impoverished "subcultures of violence" the use of knives and other weapons was no big deal. Criminality, they said, was just an alternative lifestyle. Once again, *West Side Story,* with its poverty, its gangs, its ethnic and racial tensions, its motto "We're depraved 'cause we're deprived," seemed to portray better than any textbook the forces that my professors at medical school were convinced bred violence. I knew the words and music backwards and forwards.

Every Monday morning for almost a year I sat in the back of the Juvenile Court of the Second District of Connecticut and watched as a parade of awkward, unkempt adolescents and befuddled parents made their way to the front of the courtroom and stood cowed before the bench. Where were those smart-ass teens whose exploits Bernstein and Sondheim had us all singing about? For that matter, where were those devious mothers and fathers with their subliminal antisocial messages my professors had described? The parents who actually made it to court for their children's hearings stood by helplessly as the judge pronounced sentence. Uncomprehending, inarticulate, most of them didn't even seem to understand what was going on. "What? You're sending my kid away?" The discrepancies between what I had been taught and what I actually saw were irreconcilable.

Judge Lindsey, the senior judge of the Juvenile Court, but for the absence of a wig, could have stepped out of a D'Oyly Carte production. Silvery white hair. Wire-rimmed glasses. Black robe with just a touch of white collar showing. He even had the voice. Sometimes it was hard to tell whether it was what he said or the tone in which he said it that froze children and parents in their tracks and rendered them mute.

Judge Lindsey had no children of his own. He had never finger painted on refrigerator doors or read Dr. Seuss. He knew nothing of Horton and his egg or *The Cat in the Hat*. No one had ever said, "Mr. Lindsey, get the mop." Nor had he sat on low chairs and observed other people's children at play. His view of children came strictly from on high, from the bench.

Judge Lindsey once took me to dinner at his club. There at the Quinnipiac Club, over a *copita* of sherry, he confided to me that he considered his childless state a decided advantage, at least in terms of his work.

"How is that?" I asked.

"It enables me to be completely unbiased," he explained, nibbling a cashew and washing it down with a sip of Amontillado. His ignorance of normal child development never fazed him. Justice was supposed to be blind.

Everyone at court had a favorite Judge Lindsey story. My favorite was the tale of Rodney, a thirteen-year-old black child who, after being flogged by his psychotic mother, set fire to a wastebasket in his kitchen. He immediately put out the fire, throwing the wastebasket into the kitchen sink and dousing it. Nevertheless, his mother called the police and Rodney was hauled off to court. In truth, Rodney had wanted to go to court. It was the only way he knew to get out of his home and away from his abusive, unpredictable, crazy mother. The fire was a flare in the night, an S.O.S., a signal that life with mother was intolerable. Rodney wanted out.

In Judge Lindsey's courtroom, justice was also deaf. Judge Lindsey listened to the probation officer's detailed account of Rodney's tortured relationship with his schizophrenic mother, but he heard nothing. After being told of Rodney's wish to get out of the home and away from the crazy lady, Judge Lindsey pointed a stern forefinger at the youth. In a voice that shook the chamber, Judge Lindsey intoned his inevitable, *"Don't you love your mother?"* Rodney, like the hundreds of children who had preceded him and the hundreds who would follow, was speechless.

My most uncomfortable moments before Judge Lindsey occurred on the stand. I had started to work at the court, evaluating children for the probation officers. Consequently, I had to testify about the mental condition of Donna, an adolescent girl whom I had examined.

Donna had killed her boyfriend; my assignment had been to figure out why. It seemed that Donna, who had been going out with Ramón for at least three weeks, and who considered him her "steady," discovered that Ramón had been keeping company with someone else as well. During an argument that took place in the kitchen (in New Haven, the kitchen is by far the most dangerous room in the house), Donna grabbed a carving knife, swung around with her arm outstretched, and slashed the faithless Ramón in the abdomen, knicking his aorta. She hadn't meant to kill him. "I just wanted to hurt him like he hurt me, Doctor Lewis," she explained. But when Donna's temper got going, it was best to steer clear.

Donna was retarded. Not severely retarded, but retarded nevertheless. She had been in special classes since first grade. To make matters worse, she was also brain damaged. I could never quite figure out whether her brain damage was caused by her premature birth, by an injury incurred at age four when her brother turned over a set of dresser drawers on her head, or by the dozens of blows to her head inflicted by her volatile, alcoholic father. Whatever the cause, Donna had the fiery temper, poor judgment, and impulsiveness of many brain-injured children who have been raised in violent homes. Her lethal act was similar to dozens of her previous violent outbursts. The only difference was that this time the knife she held was a little longer and the victim a few inches closer.

Since I had performed the psychiatric evaluation, it fell to me to explain to Judge Lindsey that Donna was retarded, brain damaged, and abused, and that these problems made her less able to control her rage than other fifteen-year-olds. When I entered the courtroom I found, to my dismay, that Donna and her alcoholic father were sitting in the first pew, directly in front of the witness stand. As I began my testimony, I was aware of Donna's presence as she stretched forward, struggling to take in every word that came out of my mouth.

During our interviews I had shown Donna a kind of courteous attention she was unused to receiving. She had learned to trust me. I could not betray her now. I could not destroy what little self-respect she had gained. I had to convey to the court the extent of her limitations without using the word *retarded*. What circumlocutions could I use to explain to Judge Lindsey the behavioral consequences of Donna's head injuries and avoid the words *brain damaged*?

I took a deep breath and began. "Your Honor, this child has an I.Q. of 67, which puts her reasoning capacity just a little below normal. She also has sustained injury to her cerebrum from trauma incurred at age four, when a set of drawers fell on her head and rendered her unconscious. What is more, she has also been the target of severe physical abuse. The combination of borderline cognitive functioning, severe head injury, and an upbringing in a violent household is often associated with poor judgment, impulsivity and . . ."

"Doctor," roared Judge Lindsey, "is she or is she not a Defective Delinquent?" At that moment I wished with all my heart that I had been succinct, to the point, dispensed with professional terms, and had settled for *retarded* and *brain damaged*.

Donna was no Maria, Ramón no Tony. In fact, even Leonard Bernstein would have been hard pressed to find anything to sing about in the lives of the hundreds of adolescents who traipsed through Judge

Lindsey's courtroom each year. But for me the seats at court were more comfortable than those at the nursery school; and, of course, the puzzles were infinitely more challenging. So I started a small clinic at the Juvenile Court of the Second District of Connecticut and stayed on, part time, as its director. It was the first and only court clinic in Connecticut. There I met Lee Anne.

CHAPTER 4

I can thank Sidney, the delinquent preschooler, for propelling me in the direction of the juvenile court. Rodney and Donna, and the rest of the bedraggled New Haven road company of *West Side Story* kept me there. But it was Lee Anne whose seemingly mindless homicidal act drew me once and for all into a career in violence. I must also thank Lee Anne for bringing Jonathan and me together. Had Lee Anne Jameson, a thirteen-year-old black child from the wrong side of the tracks of Waterbury, not asked the principal of her school for permission to leave early and walk home, and had the principal not denied her request, Jonathan and I would have gone our separate ways—he to the groves of academe, I into private practice. But shortly after the principal denied Lee Anne's request, a child lay dead on the school grounds and Lee Anne was nowhere to be found. The fatal consequences of the principal's refusal to allow Lee Anne to walk home early brought Jonathan and me together in our very first collaboration in violence.

———

Lee Anne had not felt right all day. From the moment she awakened she knew something was wrong. Her head ached and things around her looked blurry. They didn't seem quite real, and she wondered if she might still be dreaming.

As she made her way from the kitchen counter to the table by the window, she staggered slightly, and the checkered linoleum on the floor seemed to come up at her. She grabbed for the back of a chair and steadied herself. Maybe it was the smell in the kitchen. Something smelled rotten, dead. She looked under the sink to see if a rat had been stuck on the trap her uncle had set. She hated her uncle. She hated the way he lifted the little animals by the tail, then smashed them against the floor to kill them. The trap was empty.

"Are you crazy, girl? There's no smell here except the coffee. Now finish your doughnut and get going. You're gonna miss that bus," Lee Anne's mother looked up from her mug of coffee. "What's the matter with you, girl? Lately you've been looking funny. Something wrong?"

"No'm." Lee Anne took another bite of her doughnut. Suddenly a wave of nausea swept over her. She ran to the bathroom and emptied the contents of her stomach into the toilet bowl.

The nausea subsided. She stood leaning against the bathroom tiles, slowly breathing in and out. She began to sweat, and now a flood of anxiety washed over her. She didn't even know why she was scared. Sometimes these scary feelings just came for no reason.

It was going to be one of those days. Lee Anne could tell. Something bad was going to happen. She just knew it. Lee Anne's grandmother said that she had "the power," that she was just like her great grandmother who could tell the future. Lee Anne's brother said she was nuts. Lee Anne didn't care what her brother thought. Something bad was going to happen, and she'd better protect herself. She flushed the toilet, put some peppermint toothpaste on her finger, rubbed her teeth, then rinsed her mouth. That tasted better. The nausea passed, but the scared feeling stayed.

Danger. She sensed danger. She pulled her large navy wool coat with the wide sleeves from its peg and slipped it on. As she passed the kitchen counter, on her way to the door, Lee Anne spotted the knife. It was a small paring knife. Her mother must have used it to cut open the package of doughnuts. Lee Anne moved toward the door, leaving the knife on the counter. Surely she wouldn't need it today. Maybe no one would bother her today, and besides, school let out early. "Leave it there. Just leave it," the gentle voice in her head advised. She started to button her coat.

"Get going, girl!" Her mother was annoyed.

"Take it. Take it," hissed the deeper voice.

"Leave it," cautioned the gentle voice. She hated it when they disagreed. They made her feel crazy, and all that arguing inside her brain gave her a headache.

"Take it." It was the deeper voice again.

Swiftly, silently, Lee Anne slipped the paring knife, blade first, into the sleeve of her winter coat and bent her fingers around the end of its handle. Then she ran for the bus.

Usually, when these feelings came they lasted only a few minutes. Sometimes, when they lasted for hours she would come home and sleep them off. Sometimes she had nightmares and woke up shaking. Other times she fell into a deep, dreamless sleep, and when she awakened the feelings were gone. This particular morning the feeling seemed to hang about her like an evil spirit.

On days like this school made no sense. It was impossible to concentrate. She would see the teacher's mouth move, but could not hear or understand what the teacher was saying. Sometimes her spirit left her body. She could feel herself float to the ceiling. There she would stay, suspended, looking down on herself, seated in class. Sometimes she spaced out completely. She was somewhere else. Somewhere safe. People told her that her eyes were open, but Lee Anne saw nothing.

In first grade, this happened so often her teacher told her mother to take her to the doctor. Maybe she was having fits. The doctor said there was nothing wrong with her that a dose of mineral oil and a good spanking couldn't put right. Her uncle took care of that.

Lee Anne was forever complaining of aches and pains. First it was her stomach, then it was headaches. But the doctor never found anything wrong. After a while the doctor stopped listening. He figured she just didn't like school. He said she was a hypochondriac. Her brother said she was a goof-off.

"Lee Anne. Lee Anne!" At first her teacher's voice was so soft it seemed to be coming from miles away, then suddenly it was so loud it hurt her ears and made her jump. "Lee Anne, you're daydreaming again. Answer the question." Lee Anne could not answer the question. She had not heard it. "Lee Anne, pay attention for a change." Teachers were always getting mad at her.

Gym was the worst period. She hated the locker room. Lee Anne hated taking off her clothes. The shorts and cotton T-shirt made her feel exposed, unprotected. People could see the scars on her arms and legs. There were a few on her back. Her uncle had a temper when he drank. Sometimes the buckle of his belt made her bleed. Then it left a mark. Lee Anne couldn't remember where most of the scars had come from. When the other girls at school asked, she would make up something. "Oh, that's where my cat scratched me," or, "That must be where I burned myself on the stove." "That's where I fell off the sled."

Today gym was out of the question. There was no way Lee Anne was going to undress today, no way she would leave her coat in her locker. She needed her coat. It was thick and roomy. It had two big pockets. It had wide sleeves with a silky lining that gathered at her wrists. She could hide anything she needed in the sleeves. Wrapped in her winter coat, she was safe. This year she wore it late into spring, long after the other girls had cast aside their heavy coats in favor of sweaters or jean jackets.

Last month, in the locker room, when Lee Anne leaned over to tie her sneakers, she was sure that someone behind her had laughed and had called her a bad name. A week ago, she heard someone call her mother a whore. But when she turned to confront her tormentor, nobody was there. "Stop playin' tricks on me," she had yelled at the air. "I know you're hidin' behind them lockers." The next day, for the first time, Lee Anne brought a knife to school. She knew she would not use it. She would never use it—of that she was sure. It just made her feel safe to have it. After that, whenever Lee Anne woke up with those funny feelings, whenever she felt something bad coming on, she carried a knife.

Today was a knife day.

On knife days, of course, Lee Anne could not take gym. Her T-shirt was too flimsy, her shorts too tight to conceal a knife. And Lee Anne needed a knife. Not to use. Never to use. Just sort of like a good luck charm, she told herself. Today Lee Anne had to get out of gym.

At one-thirty, just before gym class was to start, Lee Anne made her way to the principal's office. Staring straight ahead, she moved past the secretary's desk, pushed through the frosted glass door, and, unannounced, entered the principal's office.

"Mr. Hamill, I have to go home." The principal looked up from the newspaper on his desk. He was obviously not surprised.

"Lee Anne, not you again? What's the matter with you this time? Now don't tell me you can't go to gym 'cause of your period. You said that last week." As it happened, today really was the first day of her period. Things got worse just before her period. But she couldn't use the same excuse she had used the week before. Besides, she wasn't even sure why she needed to leave school. She just knew that she did.

"Mr. Hamill," she blurted out, "something bad is going to happen."

"Darn right, something bad is going to happen! You're going to flunk gym if you keep this up. That means you're going to be left back."

"No, Mr. Hamill, I mean it. Something bad is going to happen. If I stay in school, something bad is going to happen. I have to go home." Lee Anne's fingertips played over the handle of the paring knife that she had transferred from her sleeve to the pocket of her coat, the coat that she had not taken off all day.

"Lee Anne, you have to go to. . . ." Mr. Hamill looked up from the half-finished crossword puzzle. Today's was a tough one. (He almost always finished the *Waterbury Republican* puzzle before the last bell.)

He stared at the frail adolescent standing before him, shivering in his overheated office, clutching her heavy coat to her skinny frame. Something that he couldn't quite put his finger on made him reconsider. Perhaps it was something about her eyes. She was facing him but looking through him. He put down his pencil and pushed the newspaper to the side of his desk.

In the weeks to come, when the police would force George Hamill to reflect back on that brief encounter in his office, to rethink his fateful decision, all he would be able to come up with was, "I guess maybe she looked a little out of it. . . . But there are rules."

No, he mustn't let her get out of gym. A principal can't keep making exceptions.

"Lee Anne, I've had it with you." The principal looked at his watch. "I don't have time to discuss this with you now. Go to . . ."

"I can't go to gym, Mr. Hamill. I know something bad will happen. Let me go home."

"What are you afraid will . . ." he started to ask what she was afraid of, but realized he didn't much care. There was just no reasoning with some adolescents. His tone became more authoritative. "Nothing will happen, Lee Anne. Now get into that gym."

"Mr. Hamill, let me go home."

Exasperated, unwilling to do further battle, the half-finished crossword puzzle beckoning, George Hamill relented. "Oh, forget it, Lee Anne. Flunk gym. Flunk school. Just go and wait on the front steps. The school bus will be here in an hour." Then, as an afterthought, "I want you to talk to your guidance counselor about this tomorrow."

"I need to go now, Mr. Hamill. I can't wait an hour. I'll walk."

"Take the bus, Lee Anne. We are responsible for you. Wait and take the bus." The least he could do was make sure that this spacey kid got home safely.

Weeks later, when Jonathan and I spoke with Lee Anne about the events of that day, she remembered the voices in her head that morning. She also recalled most of her meeting with the principal; she had no recollection, however, of leaving his office. Nor did she recall sitting on the school steps, waiting for the bus. People who saw her there said she just stared off into space. When the yellow bus finally pulled up in front of the school, her one girlfriend, Kesha, had to shake her before she realized that it had arrived.

Slowly, as if in a dream, Lee Anne moved toward the idling machine. She felt that everyone was staring at her. She hunched her shoulders and turned up the collar of her coat so that it covered half her face, and dug her hands into her pockets. The anxious feeling was back. She felt for the knife in her pocket and managed to maneuver it back up her sleeve. But this time she turned it around so that the blade was facing outward.

"Whatsa madda wit you? You out of it, Lee Anne?" The voice was more teasing than nasty. It was her friend, Kesha. She recognized the voice. Or did she? No, it wasn't her friend. Where had she heard those words before? Now she felt dizzy, the way she had felt in the kitchen that morning. She looked at the children moving toward the bus and wondered if they could tell what was happening to her. Their faces seemed to get closer, then to move away, then they got closer again. And the smell—that nauseating dead rat smell—rose from the pavement, gagged her, and made her want to throw up.

Someone stepped into her path and moved toward Lee Anne. It was Kesha. Was it really Kesha? The face looked different. Maybe it was someone pretending to be her friend. Everything was so confusing. Lee Anne grasped the handle of her knife.

"I asked you, whatsa madda wit you?" The face, which at first was far away, suddenly loomed large; it seemed to come right up into Lee Anne's face. And the voice, the teasing voice of her girlfriend, now sounded different, loud, menacing.

Lee Anne stood up straight, her shoulders square. Then her right arm flew upward, the blade of the paring knife catching the light of the afternoon sun. "It sparkled," one fourth-grader recalled. An instant later the arm, like the arm of a robot or a tin soldier, came downward, and the short blade penetrated the chest of the figure in front of Lee Anne.

It all happened so quickly that no one, including the victim, seemed to realize what had happened. Weeks later, when Jonathan and I asked Lee Anne why she had done it, why she had stabbed her best friend, all she could remember was the distorted face in front of her. And the young victim, whose heart had been pierced, stood dumbfounded for a good fifteen seconds before collapsing to the ground.

All attention now focused on the victim, who by now was coughing up blood. Lee Anne was forgotten as some teenagers who were gathered in front of the school rushed forward to help the dying girl. Only the younger children, who stood stock-still, afraid to move, would be able to describe Lee Anne's behavior to the police.

"She looked like a zombie," one of the more imaginative second-graders recounted.

"She just kept walking. That's what she did," another chimed in. "No, she never ran. She just walked away," a fifth-grader volunteered.

"She looked kind of like she was walking in her sleep."

"Yeh, that's right. She was like sleepwalking."

The last anyone saw of Lee Anne that afternoon, she was walking in the direction of a churchyard. To this day her whereabouts for the next several hours have remained a mystery. Neither she nor anyone else has been able to account for them.

Jonathan and I probably would have been able to discover what had transpired during those crucial hours, had we used hypnosis. But in those days the use of hypnosis was frowned upon. At the Yale University School of Medicine, neither of us was even taught how to do it. The Yale Department of Psychiatry was still heavily Freudian. Freud had abandoned hypnosis, therefore so had Yale. And for better or for worse, Jonathan and I were from Yale.

It was almost nightfall when Lee Anne finally came to her senses. She had walked miles from her school, and she found herself on the doorstep of complete strangers. They allowed her to use their telephone. She called her mother to come and pick her up. Instead, the police arrived, booked her, charged her with the murder of her best friend, then deposited her at the juvenile detention hall.

Having managed (with the help of the chief probation officer and the blessing, believe it or not, of Judge Lindsey) to squeeze enough money from the state of Connecticut to start a small child psychiatry clinic at the Juvenile Court, I found myself its one and only psychiatrist. Therefore, it fell to me to try to figure out the cause of Lee Anne's sudden violence. I had to make sense of a senseless murder.

There was a time back then when Jonathan and I, working together, thought we had an explanation. Now, looking back, I'm not so sure we were right.

Interviewing Lee Anne reminded me of the war movies I had seen as a child, of the Nazis interrogating American prisoners. Lee Anne volunteered nothing. She limited her responses to "Yes, ma'am" and "No, ma'am," making me feel that each of my questions was an assault on her inalienable right to privacy. Was she mocking me with her incessant "ma'am"? I couldn't be certain. Perhaps she was afraid of me. Whatever the explanation, Lee Anne had secrets and was not about to relinquish them to me.

No problem. It was the beginning of my work at the Juvenile Court Clinic. I was still green enough to think that Lee Anne's family would help me. It went without saying that Lee Anne's mother, Wanda, would share with me her insights into the forces at play on that fateful afternoon, when her daughter plunged a knife into her best friend's chest. Thank goodness, I thought, for one potential ally.

Sometimes I am embarrassed by my own naivete. I assumed that Lee Anne's family would trust me, take me into their confidence, and bare for my examination the secrets of their household. Over the quarter-century since then, I have learned that, when dealing with murder, nothing goes without saying. Nothing can be assumed.

Lee Anne's mother sat in my office, and that's just about all she did. Sat. If Lee Anne was withholding, her mother was almost mute. I could see immediately where Lee Anne had acquired her cryptic style. My questions were met with one syllable: no. No. No. No. No. I found that I got a bit further if I just sat silently. Once, during a silence, Mrs. Jameson volunteered that her daughter had always been a dreamer. She said that Lee Anne was also a loner. Lee Anne and her make-believe friends could play alone for hours. Mrs. Jameson could hear Lee Anne acting out the different roles—the sweet fairy godmother, the whimpering baby, the wicked villain. Lee Anne was a good actress; when she played the role of the villain she sounded just like a man. Once, during our interview, Mrs. Jameson mused, "You know, Doctor Lewis, my daughter lives in a fantasy world."

I nodded. Maybe now that Mrs. Jameson was a little more relaxed, she would answer my questions with more than one syllable. "So how do you explain what happened?" I ventured.

Mrs. Jameson paused. She began to shrug her shoulders, then seemed to reconsider. "Sometimes, Doctor Lewis," she looked down, self-conscious, "sometimes I think Lee Anne must have been possessed." The mother continued, "Sometimes I think she is possessed." So this was Mrs. Jameson's take on the murder. Some explanation! I, inexperienced, blind to the possible implications of this deceptively banal statement, let it pass. Today, twenty-five years later, it is hard for me to admit that I just let it pass. It was I, not Mrs. Jameson, who changed the subject.

"Does anyone in the family have a temper?" I asked.

Abruptly, the door to communication shut. No, nobody in the family had a temper. No, nobody had ever harmed or threatened Lee Anne. No, Lee Anne never got angry. Well, almost never. Maybe sometimes. But that wasn't like her. She was really a quiet child, a good girl. Everyone would tell you that; at least everyone in her family would. No, Wanda Jameson had no idea why Lee Anne had carried a knife to school. No, Lee Anne had never done that before. No. No. No. No. No. Wanda Jameson sounded to me exactly like those accounts in the *New York Post* of neighbors interviewed the day after a child has slaughtered his entire family. "Mrs. Jones, who lived next door, described the boy as a quiet lad, a good boy. He always took out the garbage for his mother."

I was frustrated and angry. Why wouldn't this woman help her own daughter? It just didn't make sense. Years would pass, and Jonathan and I would evaluate many more Lee Annes, before we would come to appreciate how much the families of children who murder have to hide. Only after Jonathan and I had evaluated a group of juveniles condemned to death, after we had tried to talk with their parents, their brothers and sisters, struggled in vain to reconstruct their pasts, would we understand that many of these families would rather see their children put to death than reveal what had happened behind the closed doors of childhood. What is more, we would find that many of the adolescents themselves preferred death to exposing their abusive parents. And even after having recognized this peculiar phenomenon, it would take us years to develop ways to penetrate or get around the ingenious barricades to communication that young murderers and their kin instinctively know how to erect.

I was not about to give up on Lee Anne's mother, not just yet. Perhaps if I took a less threatening tack things would move. I decided to strive for a medical rather than a psychiatric tone. Besides, it was important to learn whether any injuries to Lee Anne's central nervous system had diminished her ability to control herself. Brain injury can do that. Maybe a medical approach would enable Mrs. Jameson to relax and furnish a little useful information. I took a deep breath and pressed on.

"Now, Mrs. Jameson, I'd like to ask you some medical questions about Lee Anne. How was your pregnancy? Any problems?" I was pleased with the matter-of-fact tone I thought I had achieved. Wanda Jameson's lips began to form the inevitable "no," then she paused and thought for a moment. At last I was beginning to reach her. I listened attentively.

"It seems to me I may have had some problems."

"Problems?" I asked, balancing interest with nonchalance.

That did it. The conversation ended. Instead of facilitating communication, I had managed to terminate it. What had I done? I had simply repeated Wanda Jameson's last word, just as I had been taught to do. I had kept things wide open, left it to her to fill in the blanks. Big mistake. Wanda Jameson was no dope. She could smell a trap. She, like her daughter, was not about to discuss "problems," at least not with me. I was still years away from achieving the kind of straightforward give and take that makes an interview flow. I had not yet got out from under my nondirective, Freudian training. I blew it.

"No. Now that I think about it, it must have been with my other pregnancy, with her brother."

Right. Where to go from here? "How about illnesses?" I ventured. "What sorts of illnesses has she had?" I would avoid yes-no answers.

"She was a healthy child."

Right. "Accidents?"

"No."

"Injuries?"

"No."

I couldn't believe it. The very first time I saw Lee Anne it was impossible to overlook the scar on her forehead. Then there were the dark stripes on her back and the keloids on her upper arms. Where had these scars come from? When I asked Lee Anne, she had shrugged and said she did not know. How, in the face of this evidence, could her mother say that Lee Anne had never had any accidents or injuries? Mendacity. I, like Big Daddy in *Cat on a Hot Tin Roof*, smelled mendacity. Then how come your little girl has all those marks all over her? I wanted to scream at the woman. How could a mother stonewall this way when her child's future was at stake? I could not understand it. In those days there was a lot I could not understand. I had much to learn, not just about murderers but also about their families. I did not yet have the skills to make mothers either comfortable enough or guilty enough to spill the beans.

If the Jameson family would not talk to me, perhaps there were other ways to learn about Lee Anne. Surely some record of those injuries must exist. Some of them had to have been treated somewhere.

Reluctantly, Mrs. Jameson signed permission for me to obtain her daughter's hospital records. I could pick up photocopies of them on Friday. I would set aside an hour or two on Sunday to review them. To my surprise, when I went to retrieve the records, I was handed two thick volumes. How, I wondered, had such an allegedly healthy young girl managed to create such a mound of medical paperwork?

Sunday morning at nine o'clock, fortified with a mug of coffee and half a toasted bagel with cream cheese, I sat down with pad and pencil and opened volume one. For the next seven hours I barely moved. At four that afternoon I turned over the last page of volume two and walked to the phone. I had managed to fill the pages of an entire lined pad of paper with notes. My fingers ached from clutching the pen. I took a deep breath, stretched, and smiled. I had something to run with.

Lee Anne's medical records started off with a bang. The very first entry revealed more relevant information than all of the hours put together that I had spent with Lee Anne and her mother. I discovered that before Lee Anne was born, during her mother's pregnancy, her mother had been treated for syphilis—syphilis, that ancient scourge that attacks in utero the organs of growing babies. What is more, Mrs. Jameson had also been hypothyroid. This condition had not been recognized until she was well into her second trimester. Here was a medical problem bound to put a lid on any child's intelligence. Lee Anne's was not an auspicious start in life.

Adding injury to insult, neither labor nor delivery was uncomplicated. By the time she was wrenched by forceps from her mother's narrow pelvis, one clavicle had been fractured and the soft bones of Lee Anne's cranium had been squeezed together. Interns attending the birth, trained to recognize potential problems in bonding between mothers and critically ill newborns, kept encouraging Lee Anne's mother to pick a name for the struggling infant. Two years after our daughter Gillian's birth, Mel and I were encouraged by a pediatric resident to name our struggling, ten-weeks premature, three-and-a-half-pound son. It made for bonding, he said. We named him David. Twenty-four hours later, David died. Wanda Jameson, unlike Mel and me, was determined to wait a day or two before naming her daughter. It was nip and tuck whether the infant would survive, and she did not want to become too attached.

Compared with that opener, the subsequent entries in the medical record paled. At least that's how it seemed to me. There had been accidents and injuries, but two-year-olds are notoriously clumsy creatures. It takes a watchful eye and a quick reflex to protect a toddler from himself. Why nature bestows gross motor skills on children before bestowing judgment is to me an evolutionary riddle.

Nowadays I read a medical chart the way I read a detective story. Clues to behavior hide behind every scrawl. But twenty years ago a medical chart was just one more tedious obstacle to get through on the way to what seemed to me to be the real work: interviewing the patient and family. I look back and my ignorance appalls me.

Bored, almost resentful, I forced myself to scribble down the date and the nature of each bump and bruise, every cut and burn. Often I couldn't even figure out just what brought Lee Anne to the hospital. For example, when she was four, Lee Anne arrived at the emergency room with a large bump on her forehead and two black eyes. She told the doctors she had fallen off a swing; her mother told the nurse that Lee Anne had fallen down a flight of stairs. Whatever the cause, I figured that it accounted for the hitherto enigmatic scar on Lee Anne's forehead. Then, six months later, Lee Anne was treated for a burn. Lee Anne told the doctors that she had burned herself on the stove; her uncle, who brought her to the hospital, said she had been playing with a hot iron. None of the doctors ever noticed the discrepancies, not even I when I first reviewed the charts.

Only now, as I review my own notes, now, after having evaluated dozens of similarly violent children, do these inconsistencies spring up at me and have meaning. I look back, embarrassed at the many times, as an intern and resident, I accepted a parent's implausible explanation for a particular injury. It was a car accident. It was a terrible fall. Today it seems obvious that so many of the wounds I dismissed as accidental were the consequences of deliberate batterings, sometimes torture. But in those days I was starting my own family. I had young children, and I suppose I could not see what I could not bear to see.

As Lee Anne approached puberty, the nature of her hospital contacts changed. She began showing up at the clinics and at the emergency room for what were dismissed by the doctors as inconsequential symptoms. Her stomach hurt. Her head hurt. She felt dizzy. She felt like throwing up. After a while all of the entries began to sound alike. Over and over, I read the dry, emotionless accounts of Lee Anne's visits to the hospital.

"This nine-year-old female presents with the chief complaint of abdominal pain."

"This nine-and-a-half-year-year-old child presents with the chief complaint of nausea and stomach pains."

"This ten-year-old girl comes to the emergency room with a chief complaint of headaches and stomach pains."

This child. This girl. This female. Where was Lee Anne? Each event was treated as though it stood alone. It seemed that no one ever paused to review the whole chart. Had they just weighed it, the mass would have raised suspicions. Hospitals are busy places. Doctors are busy people.

After more than a dozen visits for ostensibly imaginary problems, a frustrated pediatrician concluded that Lee Anne's problems had to be psychological. He called in a child psychiatrist. The brevity of the consultation note (eight lines) suggested to me that the psychiatrist was bored, was in a hurry, or was annoyed. I imagine Lee Anne had been as forthcoming with him as she was with me. One interview convinced the psychiatrist that Lee Anne was "manipulative" and "attention seeking." He advised the pediatricians to play down her complaints. As he put it, "Try to avoid secondary gain." Psychiatrists love terms like *secondary gain*.

My eyelids grew heavy as I, too, struggled to pay attention to the endless list of hospital visits for vague, elusive aches and pains. My coffee mug had long since been drained, and I found myself nodding off. The importance of the early accidents and injuries, the later somatic complaints, completely eluded me.

Then a short note toward the very end of volume two awakened me. The handwriting was different; it was legible. Could this be the communication of a physician? I looked for the signature. Just as I thought: it was written by a medical student and countersigned by an M.D. The note read as follows: "Lee Anne Jameson, a twelve-year-old black female with a long history of vague complaints, came to the pediatric clinic today with a chief complaint of headaches and dizziness. During this visit she stared off into space and could not be aroused for several seconds." A similar entry, dated two weeks later and written in the same hand, reported: "Today again Lee Anne lost consciousness for no apparent reason, and she fell to the ground. Blood pressure normal. R/O (rule out) a seizure disorder. Plan: Get EEG." The student actually used her name. Lee Anne was a person to him, not a case. I flipped through the remainder of volume two, seeking the result of the encephalogram. None was to be found. In fact, there was no indication that the pediatrician who countersigned the chart note paid any attention to the medical student's observations. An electroencephalogram had never been performed. Now I was wide awake.

Suppose, I thought, the medical student was onto something. Just suppose that he, unblinded by preconceived notions about manipulative patients and secondary gain, had seen something no one else had been able to see. Suppose that Lee Anne did have something wrong with her brain. Could that have had anything to do with her violent act?

One year before Lee Anne Jameson plunged a knife into her classmate's chest, two doctors up at Harvard—a neurosurgeon and a psychiatrist—had reported finding abnormal electrical activity in the brains of some of their episodically violent patients. Vernon Mark, the neurosurgeon, and Frank Ervin, the psychiatrist, had inserted electrodes deep into the brains of these aggressive individuals. They found that these patients had episodes of violence that coincided with abnormal electrical discharges, localized in the most ancient structures of their brains. We humans share these brain structures with alligators and other primitive, unfriendly creatures. At the onset of these episodes, patients experienced auras—that is, weird feelings. Some complained of odd perceptions and sensations. Others described being assailed by vile odors. In other patients, the sweet smell of perfume presaged an episode. Some patients saw blinding light. Others experienced nausea and vague abdominal pains. Some felt dizzy. And some patients reported feeling as though they were reliving past events. Was it possible that Lee Anne's premonitions of danger, that her complaints about foul odors and dead rats, her episodes of dizziness and her history of vague stomach pains, were auras heralding a seizure?

I sat for several minutes, pondering the medical student's neat, legible script. Then I rose from the couch, walked to the phone, and dialed Jonathan's number.

CHAPTER 5

I knew about Jonathan Pincus long before he knew of my existence. Everyone in my class knew of him. While I was still struggling through anatomy, Jonathan was applying for a neurology residency at Yale. By the time I finished my study of the capacity for intimacy, completed my pediatric internship, and began my psychiatry residency, Jonathan was a junior faculty member of the Yale Medical School.

As an assistant professor, Jonathan cut a rather dashing figure at the hospital, at least in my eyes. I remember watching him stride confidently down the corridors, white coat open, coattails flying, trailing what looked like contingents of admiring neurology residents and medical students, who walked double-time to keep pace with him.

Everyone who has worked with Jonathan knows his laugh. When Jonathan laughs, patients sit up in bed, medical students grin, and floor nurses mutter, "Shhhhh!" The best thing about Jonathan is that he can laugh at himself (an uncommon trait in a Yale professor). Thus, though Jonathan frequently laughs at me, at my idealism, at my peculiar ability to get us involved with unsavory characters, he is just as likely to laugh at his own foibles.

Psychiatry Board Examinations are not easy. Psychiatrists must pass tests in neurology as well as psychiatry. Today the tests are different, and the neurology section is all written. But in my day, psychiatrists had to see live neurology patients; psychiatrists had to examine them, actually touch them. (Psychiatrists rarely touch patients. In psychoanalysis, doctors and patients don't even look each other in the eye.) Then the psychiatrists were quizzed by neurologists. The prospect was intimidating; therefore, psychiatry residents spent months before the boards examining neurology patients.

Word had it that whoever studied for boards with Jonathan Pincus passed with flying colors. Thus, my first encounter with Jonathan, like just about all of my subsequent encounters with him, was as a supplicant. Would he tutor me for the neurology part of the board exams? He agreed. This was the first and, I believe, only time that Jonathan had no misgivings about granting a request of mine.

Jonathan was a patient teacher. Week after week I followed him on rounds and watched as he took histories and performed neurologic examinations on patients who suffered from all sorts of exotic neurologic diseases. (Jonathan taught me to say neurologic, not neurological.) After several weeks observing Jonathan, my turn came. Jonathan sat back and watched as I examined the patient. Afterwards he quizzed me. What symptoms had I noted? What signs had I elicited? What had I overlooked?

Often I found myself at a loss. What was Jonathan getting at?

"The eyegrounds, Dorothy. What about the discs?"

"The discs?"

"Yes, the discs. What did they look like?"

"They were blurred. I couldn't make them out. I think my ophthalmoscope needs new batteries."

With that, the famous Pincus laugh burst forth.

"Shhhh," a private-duty nurse stuck her head into the corridor and frowned.

"Of course, you couldn't make them out," Jonathan whispered. "The edges were blurred because the discs were swollen. Why were they swollen?"

"Increased intracranial pressure?"

"Right. Now why does this unfortunate fellow have increased intracranial pressure?"

"Easy. He was admitted for a brain tumor." I breathed a sigh of relief. Home free. But Jonathan was not finished.

"Good. What else can cause increased pressure?"

Pause. "A subdural hematoma."

"Good. What else?"

"Infection. Encephalitis."

"And what else?"

Longer pause. "Ideopathic hydrocephalus."

"And what else?"

On and on, Jonathan would pursue the questioning until I had exhausted all of the possibilities I knew. Invariably there were several I had overlooked. Then Jonathan would abandon the role of board examiner and teach me what I did not know. Which was plenty.

On the day that I passed the boards, I snuck into Jonathan's office and deposited a bottle of my favorite wine, Château Margaux, on his desk. The note beside it read, simply, "Thank you." My days of examining patients with Jonathan Pincus were over—or so it seemed. And indeed such would have been the case were it not for Lee Anne Jameson's puzzling act of violence. Now, instead of bestowing gifts on him, I found myself in his office, arguing with him.

"Dorothy, suppose this kid you're telling me about is brain damaged. Suppose she does have seizures. If I testify, and because of me she's found not guilty, what's to say she won't go out and do it again?" Jonathan had a point. Besides, we both knew that violent acts rarely occur during actual seizures. Just before? Sometimes. Afterwards? Maybe. In between? Occasionally. During? Almost never. Still I would not let him off the hook so easily. I had to figure out why Lee Anne was a murderer and I was not. To do this I needed Jonathan. If, ultimately, Jonathan refused to see Lee Anne, at least I would have instilled a little guilt in him.

"Jonathan, she's made thirty-two visits to the hospital. Something must be wrong."

"So?"

"Jonathan, you're the only neurologist I know who can figure her out. I mean, you wrote the book."

If reason, ethics, and guilt would not prevail, flattery might. Jonathan had co-authored the classic *Behavioral Neurology*. He was and is one of the few neurologists who is comfortable dealing with the fact that the mind and the brain are inextricably connected. When the brain is out of whack, thinking goes awry; when thinking goes awry, feeling goes awry; when thinking and feeling go awry, behavior goes awry. That's the way it is. Something was wrong with the way Lee Anne Jameson perceived and reacted to the world. Jonathan had to help me figure out what that was.

As Jonathan tells it, "Dorothy pleaded. She cajoled. She charmed." I would not argue with his description. I did what I had to in order to convince Jonathan to see Lee Anne. I needed his help and, by hook or by crook, would get it. After thirty minutes of unabashed flattery, Jonathan surrendered.

"O.K., Dorothy. O.K., I'll see her." I did not even suspect that my obsequious plea would prove but a practice session for much bigger requests to come.

Jonathan sat behind a desk in a tiny room at the detention center, awaiting the murderess. When she tiptoed in, accompanied by a matron who left her at the door, Jonathan was convinced they had brought him the wrong girl. He described her in his report as, "a slender, frail, sliver of a prepubertal girl, about five feet tall and weighing no more than ninety pounds." Throughout the examination, their eyes never met. In response to Jonathan's questions, she emitted the same monosyllables she had produced for me.

Jonathan is one of the few neurologists I know who spends more time talking with his patients than tapping their knees and testing their muscle strength. It's easy to talk with Jonathan. His relaxed, laid-back attitude and easy laugh instill trust.

Well, Lee Anne wasn't buying it. She sat, tight lipped, on a metal chair, hands in her lap, looking down. Jonathan moved from behind the desk and took a seat to the side of it. Sitting across a desk from her was too much like a courtroom. But no matter what position he took or what tone he adopted, Jonathan could not make the anxious child comfortable. Maybe her suspiciousness was normal. Maybe anyone in her shoes would keep her mouth shut, he thought. For the past twenty-five years, Jonathan and I have struggled to distinguish between paranoia and good healthy suspiciousness. When in doubt we interpret silence as adaptive.

Jonathan did not give up. He slid low in his metal chair, trying to diminish the difference in height between him and his young patient. Then, in the softest of tones, he asked, "How about that day? The day of the stabbing? What was going on in your life that day?"

No answer. Lee Anne looked upward. Her eyes darted from side to side. Her lips moved, but no sound emerged. Jonathan waited.

"So what was happening that day?"

Lee Anne was startled, as if she had just been tugged back into the real world. She blinked a couple of times, then responded.

"Nuthin'."

"How about the knife? Do you always carry a knife?" Maybe it was a usual practice where she lived. Maybe all the kids in her neighborhood carried knives. These were years of increasing awareness, a time when doctors were being trained to recognize ethnic and cultural differences. Unfortunately, some of us were so well trained, or so we thought, that we often dismissed the pathological hallucinations and delusions of many sick African-American and Hispanic children as normal religious experiences or cultural beliefs and we failed to treat them. White children, on the other hand, with the very same symptoms, we referred posthaste to child guidance clinics. So much for cultural awareness.

"Nope," came the response to Jonathan's question.

"Whom do you know who carries a knife?" Jonathan would not give up. The stabbing occurred years before teenagers came to school armed—decades before students were screened for weapons by walking through metal detectors.

"No one. . . . My uncle. He cut someone."

Jonathan tried to appear calm as Lee Anne provided the first clue to her family's violence and, possibly, to her own.

"Whom did he cut?"

"Someone."

"When?"

"I dunno. He's in jail."

"Who's in jail?"

"My uncle."

At last a hint that tranquillity did not always reign in the Jameson household.

"How about those marks on your arm? On your back? Where did they come from?"

That was it. Jonathan had pushed his luck too far. The door closed and he found himself again on the outside.

They sat in silence, Jonathan looking at Lee Anne, Lee Anne staring down at her hands.

"Do you remember what happened that day?"

Lee Anne shook her head, no.

"How about just before it happened?"

"Sick. Dizzy." Jonathan could barely hear her.

"How about afterward?"

She shrugged her shoulders.

"What happened afterward?"

Lee Anne's eyes rolled upward as if she were seeking answers from heaven. Her lips moved silently.

"I called my mother."

"And then?"

"The police came and got me and took me here."

The three hours between the murder and the time she called her mother were a blank.

Detectives determined that Lee Anne had walked clear across town, had even waded through a shallow pond. Lee Anne recalled nothing.

Jonathan opened his medical bag and withdrew his elegant Queens Square neurologic hammer, a tape measure, four coins, a safety pin, and the other paraphernalia that neurologists carry around.

Lee Anne cringed and pulled back when he took her arm to tap her biceps tendon. He put down his equipment and, before making another move, explained each test to the frightened child; each step of the way he paused to prepare her. "Now, Lee Anne, I'm going to place a coin in your hand. I want you to feel it and tell me what it is. A quarter? A dime? A nickel?" "Now I'm going to test your sense of pin prick. It won't hurt. I promise. Tell me if you feel anything."

The findings from the physical part of the neurologic examination were, as neurologists like to say, fairly unremarkable. For a child who had been wrenched from her mother's womb and apparently batted around ever since, she had amazingly little to show for it. She was a bit clumsy. Jonathan could skip better than she, but then again, Jonathan had had lots of practice. And unlike Jonathan, when Lee Anne stretched out her arms and spread her fingers, she could not keep them from moving jerkily up and down. "Choreiform movements," Jonathan noted in his report. But compared with my performance on some of Jonathan's exercises, Lee Anne wasn't half bad. Jonathan found what neurologists call "soft signs"—that is, nonlocalized evidence of some sort of brain damage or dysfunction. Many neurologists disdain these kinds of signs. As one contemptuous Yale neurologist put it, "Soft signs are for soft neurologists."

Had Jonathan not been trained as a child neurologist, trained to measure the circumference of infant skulls, he would have missed one of his most important findings—his only "hard sign." His tape measure revealed that Lee Anne was microcephalic. Her head, and therefore her brain, were significantly smaller than they should have been. When I studied for boards with Jonathan, he taught me that 95 percent of the time diminished head circumference and diminished intellect go together.

"And what can cause microcephaly?" he demanded during one of our practice sessions.

"Maternal alcoholism. Drug abuse."

"Good. What else?"

"Birth injury."

"What else?"

"Cranial synostosis." I was reaching.

"Good. What else?"

"I don't know. You tell me."

"How about maternal infection? That's a little more common than cranial synostosis, Dorothy, wouldn't you say?" I had to agree. But I never forgot that lesson. The things I get right the first time often sail right out of my head. I have an unforgiving memory for just about all of my mistakes.

In the end, Jonathan's neurologic findings proved to be as equivocal as my psychiatric findings had been. The evidence for seizures was slim, but Jonathan ordered an EEG (a brain wave test) anyway. The results were normal.

In our teaching sessions, Jonathan had stressed that a normal EEG did not necessarily mean that a person did not have seizures. In between seizures, even people with grand mal epilepsy might have a normal EEG. If you get three or four EEGs, you stand a better chance of picking up a seizure disorder. But for the most part, psychomotor or temporal lobe epilepsy (now called complex partial seizures), the kind we suspected Lee Anne suffered from, is a clinical diagnosis. Before this diagnosis can be made, the doctor must talk to the patient at length, ask dozens of questions about the patient's sensations before, during, and after suspected seizures. How much does the patient recall of what happened? Even then, you can't always be sure.

Lee Anne had many signs and symptoms of a seizure disorder. She had auras, funny feelings in her stomach, peculiar smells no one else perceived, unexplained waves of anxiety. Sometimes she seemed to be in a trance. In fact, that is the way she looked to the kids in front of the school who saw the stabbing and watched her walk slowly into the distance. She also could not remember the time period between the murder and finding herself on a stranger's doorstep. Amnesia is another classic symptom of epilepsy. But Lee Anne's EEG was normal and Jonathan and I doubted that Judge Lindsey would be up for a course on the fine points of epilepsy and encephalography. Besides, neither of us was positive that Lee Anne had epilepsy. Years later we would look back at our records and the possibility of a very different sort of picture would emerge—that of a dissociative disorder. This was our first likely diagnostic error. It would not be our last.

A week before Lee Anne's trial, Jonathan and I collected our notes and whatever records we could get our hands on and sat down in my kitchen to ponder Lee Anne's condition. What could we say about her to Judge Lindsey to convince him that she should not be sent to a reformatory? Nothing was clear diagnostically. Nothing was definite.

Was Lee Anne brain damaged? Maybe. Her medical history and her neurologic examination convinced Jonathan that she had some central nervous system dysfunction; but, were Jonathan asked exactly where the damage was, he would have been hard pressed to localize it. What we could say was that children with Lee Anne's kind of medical history and neurologic picture tend to be irritable, impulsive, emotionally labile. They tend to fly off the handle. But, we had to admit, they usually do not kill people.

"How about psychomotor seizures, Jonathan? Do you think she has seizures?" I asked.

"Maybe."

"Maybe? What do you mean, maybe? She has auras. She doesn't remember what happened. She fell to the ground unconscious a couple of times. The medical student saw it. That sure sounds like seizures." At least it sounded that way to me then. Since then, I have seen several dissociative children with the very same symptoms who do not have epilepsy. But twenty-five years ago I had seen fewer patients and I knew less. "Does she have seizures?" I demanded, as though the forcefulness of my question would clinch the answer.

"Maybe. Let me put it this way, Dorothy. I'm 51 percent sure she has psychomotor seizures." Jonathan paused, and laughed. "Then again, when I'm 100 percent sure, I'm only right 80 percent of the time."

"Very funny, Jonathan. That will really go over big with Judge Lindsey next week."

Now it was Jonathan's turn to challenge me.

"How about you? Can you say she's psychotic? Can you say she was insane at the time of the murder?"

"She's paranoid. We both agree on that. That's why she carried the knife," I equivocated.

"But is she crazy?" Jonathan demanded.

I could not answer that. Now that the tables were turned, Jonathan enjoyed putting me on the spot. "Is she insane?" he persisted.

I could not answer directly. Rather, I began to think aloud, "She hears voices. The voices talk to each other. They tell her what to do. All the books say that makes her schizophrenic." Psychiatrists were taught then (as many are now) that auditory hallucinations of voices talking to each other, especially if they tell the patient what to do, probably indicate schizophrenia. If, in addition, the patient feels controlled by outside forces, the diagnosis is clinched. As it happens, it is not true that these symptoms always indicate schizophrenia. Over the years Jonathan and I have learned that this constellation of symptoms is even more common in dissociative disorders. But twenty years ago, to have suggested that command hallucinations, voices talking to each other, and the sense of being controlled by external forces was anything other than schizophrenia would have been heresy. Even today that idea does not sit well with many of our colleagues.

The older I get, the easier it is for me to understand and almost forgive Freud for renouncing some of his most important discoveries. For example, he took back his assertion that many of his sickest female patients were sexually abused by their fathers. I see now why he decided that these women must have imagined it. Colleagues can be intimidating adversaries when you question the prevailing wisdom. They certainly made Freud's life miserable. It is a lot easier to recant than be burned at the stake. Jonathan and I have had the fortune or misfortune to stumble into several controversial areas. Colleagues have said some pretty nasty things about us. One of Jonathan's colleagues called us a "traveling road show"—in print!

"Is she schizophrenic?" Jonathan demanded. We both knew that the answer to that was no. No matter what the books said, it was clear to us both that, whatever caused Lee Anne's symptoms, she was not schizophrenic. She bore no resemblance to the chronically psychotic patients we had seen in the back wards of state hospitals. Nor did she look like the acutely psychotic, so-called paranoid schizophrenic patients who episodically heard voices, thought people were out to get them, entered the hospital, swallowed their Thorazine, and emerged, temporarily hallucination- and delusion-free.

"So what are *you* going to tell His Honor?" Jonathan challenged.

"I'll tell him what her mother told me. She lives in a fantasy world with her imaginary friends. She hears voices."

"And that's why she's violent, Dorothy?"

"No. I'll explain to him that sometimes she's paranoid. She misunderstands signals. She feels threatened. Then her voices tell her to defend herself. When that happens, she lashes out." I stopped. As I listened to myself, I had to admit that I was making a pretty weak psychiatric case. I doubted that Jonathan felt much more confident.

I sat straight up, glowered at Jonathan, and, in my best Judge Lindsey voice, intoned, "Tell me, Professor, you're a neurologist. Is she or isn't she a Defective Delinquent?"

Jonathan smiled, recalling the story of my appearance before Judge Lindsey on behalf of Donna. Then Jonathan's face became serious. He rose and looked directly at me.

"Your Honor," he began, "there is no single, simple diagnosis that explains what this child did. Yes, Lee Anne Jameson has signs of brain damage. Her head is small and she does badly on I.Q. tests. She is not very smart. There are also indications that she may have a seizure disorder. To that extent, I guess, you might call her a Defective Delinquent. (Jonathan does not mince words.) But most brain-damaged people, most epileptic people, most retarded people, don't murder. So why did Lee Anne?" Dramatic pause.

"Dr. Lewis, over there near the toaster," Jonathan nodded in my direction, "has told you that Lee Anne is paranoid. She hallucinates. She hears voices. Sometimes she does what they tell her. Did they tell her to stab her friend? I don't know and Lee Anne doesn't remember. What we do know is that she was not in touch with reality that day on the bus when she stabbed her friend. She was not herself." At that moment, neither Jonathan nor I appreciated the significance of those four words: *she was not herself.*

Jonathan stopped and thought. He continued. "But you know and I know that most crazy people don't commit murder. So what was it about Lee Anne's condition, about her situation, that caused her to lose control and kill her best friend? What secrets could she not tell us? What secrets would her mother not tell us? What secrets, too terrible for words, account for this inexplicable murder?" Jonathan was now interrogator as well as witness, judge, and jury.

Jonathan walked over to my kitchen table where the two volumes of medical records rested and lifted them. "Here they are. Here are the secrets. Thirty-two of them. Thirty-two times Lee Anne came to the hospital. Thirty-two times she tried to tell a doctor what was happening under her roof. But no one would listen. No one could hear.

"Lee Anne Jameson was abused; she was maltreated from the time of conception until the day of the murder. The record of her mother's syphilis. The burns on her arms. The scars on her back, all bear witness to this abuse." Jonathan was not finished. "But lots of kids are abused, and they don't kill anyone. So how come Lee Anne did it?" Jonathan paused.

I stood up and, in a clear, confident voice, picked up the argument. "Maybe, Your Honor, just maybe Lee Anne's violent household, maybe, just maybe Lee Anne's brain damage, maybe, just maybe Lee Anne's paranoia, maybe, just maybe Lee Anne's voices telling her, urging her to pick up the knife, to protect herself, maybe, just maybe all of her impairments and all of her abusive experiences came together and made it impossible for her to control her behavior that day." We both sat down. We were drained. But we were great witnesses, especially while testifying in my kitchen.

And that is what we told Judge Lindsey. Of course, we were not nearly so articulate. Courtrooms are scarier than kitchens. In court nothing comes out as smoothly and logically as it should. But somehow, together, without a hard-and-fast diagnosis, we made our point. We managed to convey to Judge Lindsey the way neuropsychiatric vulnerabilities and external events can come together in a child's life, interact with each other, and cause an explosion of terror and rage. What is more, we were able to convince His Honor that Lee Anne Jameson needed treatment. She should not be sent to a reformatory.

In what seemed to be a compromise of sorts, Judge Lindsey found Lee Anne guilty of what, in an adult court, would have been labeled manslaughter, not murder. Best of all, as a result of our testimony, rather than dispatch her to Long Lane, the correctional school, Lee Anne was permitted to remain at the detention center while her probation officer tried to get her into a residential treatment center.

On the down side, it took the probation officer twelve months and about a dozen applications to find a treatment center willing to take Lee Anne. No place was eager to add a murderess to its population, even a small, skinny one. Eventually a fancy facility, out of state, accepted her. Ironically, Lee Anne was the only one among all of the children who came through the court that year who obtained such a therapeutic (and expensive) disposition.

Jonathan and I celebrated the news of Lee Anne's acceptance at the treatment center by going out to dinner. "You know, Jonathan," I thought aloud over dessert, "these days you've just got to kill to get good treatment."

After dinner Jonathan and I parted, each convinced that we would not be working together in the foreseeable future or, for that matter, ever again. Jonathan would never again allow me to pull him into a murder case. As for me, I knew I would never again have the nerve to ask. But, of course, I did.

CHAPTER 6

Not long after Lee Anne Jameson stabbed her girlfriend in the school-yard in Waterbury, another murderous act by a juvenile took place, this time on the streets of New Haven. Lee Anne's violence—the murder of one black child by another—went relatively unnoticed by the public. This second homicide did not. This time, a white Yaley was killed by a black teenager. Public reaction to this murder was swift and intense. The citizens of New Haven were furious that the culprit would be treated by the courts as a child. He would be sentenced at most to a few years in a juvenile reformatory and then released. People felt helpless.

In response to this homicide, Connecticut changed its laws. Instead of handling all offenses of minors within the juvenile justice system, the state legislature made it possible for Judge Lindsey to transfer violent juveniles to the Superior Court. Now children as young as thirteen years old could be tried and sentenced as adults in Connecticut. Connecticut would no longer coddle its violent young. After all, at that time, in other states like Indiana, children as young as thirteen years of age could be tried and sentenced to death. Maybe the prospect of a life sentence would make Connecticut's delinquents pause and think twice before pulling the trigger or reaching for a knife.

Of course, this change in the law had no such effect. The Donnas and Lee Annes and disadvantaged kids in tough sections of Connecticut's inner cities did not read the newspapers, much less keep up with the finer points of the law as it applied to juveniles. Besides, even if they had, their violent acts, like those of most violent people, were impulsive, of the moment, and totally unreflective. Over the years it has become increasingly clear to Jonathan and me that most sentences intended to deter violent crimes ignore the state of mind most perpetrators are in at the time of their violent acts. In theory punishment as a deterrent makes sense; in reality it is often irrelevant. As Jonathan once observed, "The death penalty doesn't have any deterrent effect on the murderers we see. Now if it were imposed in New York City for double parking, then we just might have fewer traffic jams in the garment district."

From the outset, the new tough stance toward juveniles posed problems for Connecticut. If violent kids were to receive long sentences, where on earth was the state to put them? When they reached majority they could go to adult prisons, but what could be done with them in the meantime, between ages thirteen and eighteen? Hard-hearted folks had no qualms about locking them up with adult criminals, but more benevolent citizens were reluctant to subject children to the dangers inherent in such an arrangement. Besides, the federal government prohibited the practice. If Connecticut chose to place its violent young in adult jails and prisons, the state would lose federal dollars.

The alternative was to send these juvenile adults or adult juveniles (it was hard to know just how to think of them) to the reformatory, Long Lane. But the reformatory had an open campus. What was to prevent the violent delinquents from escaping and again menacing the public? The solution was to build a secure unit for them on the Long Lane campus in Middletown.

Middletown is where the people of Connecticut sequester their more problematic young citizens. There, about thirty miles from New

Haven and a good forty or fifty miles from fancier towns like Westport and Greenwich, stands Connecticut's one and only institution for juvenile delinquents.

Whether by chance or intention, Long Lane is only minutes from one of Connecticut's largest state psychiatric hospitals. This proximity is convenient, since from time to time the more troubled Long Lane inmates require transfer to the hospital. Reciprocally, many of the more obstreperous young patients at the hospital tax that institution beyond endurance and wind up at Long Lane. In fact, in those days, a good third of the Long Lane children had previously been residents of psychiatric institutions of one sort or another.

Psychiatry is a funny discipline. Size often dictates diagnosis, and, of course, diagnosis dictates treatment. Mentally ill children have a tiny repertoire with which to make known their pain. Even the smartest are not articulate when it comes to expressing feelings. Children do things; they don't say things. Sometimes they do pretty awful things.

When sick children are small, no matter how aggressive they are, we doctors and other grown-ups are willing to talk with them, play with them, try to discover what's eating them. When we can't quite figure out the source of the trouble, we usually give them the benefit of the doubt and make a relatively harmless diagnosis such as ADHD (Attention Deficit–Hyperactivity Disorder). We diagnose a condition with treatment implications. If the child is really off the wall (say, he hears voices or is paranoid), we may diagnose schizophrenia or some sort of psychosis. Whatever the diagnosis and whatever the behaviors, if the child is small enough, even if he or she has set his mother's hair on fire or thrown a puppy out the window or taken a knife to his sister, we send that child to a hospital for treatment. At Bellevue we see such children.

But something seems to happen to these children, or to their doctors, when the children reach about five foot, two inches in height. The very same children that the doctors saw as hyperactive, or brain damaged, or borderline psychotic when they were, say, four foot, nine inches, now look different. Diagnoses change. Schizophrenia, ADHD, and organic dysfunction of one sort or another turn into conduct disorder. (The term *conduct disorder* is relatively new. Years ago, when Jonathan and I trained, the term for the same set of behaviors was *unsocialize aggressive reaction*; such is progress.) A look at the children's charts will reveal in an instant that their symptoms or behaviors have not changed, just their size. They still hallucinate occasionally, or can't sit still, or feel persecuted. In fact, just about every psychiatric disorder of childhood can manifest itself as a behavior problem. No matter. That is why so many children who arrive at Long Lane with the diagnosis of conduct disorder once suffered from other potentially treatable disorders. Unfortunately, there is no specific treatment for conduct disorder.

As time goes on, the diagnostic metamorphosis continues. Adolescence progresses and the children get even bigger. Now age dictates diagnosis. Eighteen is the magic number that transforms the diagnosis of conduct disorder into *antisocial personality disorder*, or what used to be called *sociopathic personality*. Once again, nothing much about the patients has changed—just their ages. At eighteen or twenty they are bigger and older, but they still have the same symptoms and do the same scary kinds of things that they did when they were six, or ten, or twelve, or even sixteen. They also still experience the same kinds of symptoms that they did as small children: paranoid misperceptions, threatening hallucinations, irritable depression, manic rageful feelings. But at age eighteen, these underlying symptoms seem to get lost once and for all.

As I write these paragraphs, the reason for the diagnostic metamorphoses I have described becomes clearer. Doctors are taught to base their diagnoses on patients' symptoms and signs. *Symptoms* are the subjective discomfort patients experience and can talk about. *Signs* are what doctors see for themselves. Doctors don't mind spending time with small patients or even with big, docile ones. We listen to them. If these patients have trouble talking, we eagerly help them express their thoughts and feelings, describe their pain. Contrariwise, we don't much care for large, violent patients. That's understandable. They scare us, especially patients who have already been designated delinquent or criminal. Hence, we don't spend a whole lot of time helping those patients relax enough to confide their symptoms. The problem with symptoms is that, unlike signs, you can't see them. Symptoms must be verbalized. Even then, doctors have to be close enough to hear. Because we doctors tend to keep our distance from big, violent patients and minimize the time we spend in their company, their diagnoses often rest on signs, not symptoms.

There are books—diagnostic manuals—that tell doctors how to diagnose. Some psychiatric diagnoses reflect symptoms. Take schizophrenia. To make that diagnosis, the patient tells his doctor that he hears voices, feels persecuted, believes he is controlled by outside forces. Or consider depression. To diagnose depression, doctor and patient must talk with each other at length. The patient tells his doctor he feels sad, doesn't want to eat or have sex; he says he sleeps badly and sometimes feels the urge to kill himself. We listen carefully. These symptoms, elicited over time, add up to a diagnosis of depression.

Then there are diagnoses based on signs—just signs. They reflect what the patient does, not what he thinks, feels, or experiences in his mind. Conduct disorder is such a diagnosis. To make that diagnosis, a child must manifest three or four undesirable behaviors from a list of over a dozen. Thus the child who steals, lies, runs away, or the child who fights, smokes pot, and tortures cats, has a conduct disorder. One hardly needs a diagnostic manual to come to that conclusion. One doesn't even need to be a doctor. When that child grows up and is on his own, if he still fights and steals, if he can't quite stick with his family and provide for them, if he keeps getting in trouble with the law, then he qualifies for the diagnosis of antisocial personality disorder. He is a sociopath. Forget about what this person thinks or feels or experiences. It's what he does that counts diagnostically. In this way the wide variety of subjective experiences behind violent acts, the forces motivating them, get lost. To diagnose conduct disorder or antisocial personality disorder, the doctor barely needs to see the patient, much less talk with him. The person's actions speak for themselves. Unfortunately, the fact that a variety of potentially treatable social, psychiatric, and neurologic vulnerabilities can underlie violent acts that on the surface appear similar to each other is overlooked or, worse, ignored. That's how the American Psychiatric Association's *Diagnostic and Statistical Manual of Mental Disorders* works when it comes to conduct disorder and antisocial personality disorder. As I said, I have trouble with psychiatry books.

While the state was busily constructing the secure unit at Long Lane, I was working at the Juvenile Court Clinic, examining delinquents. Lee Anne, I discovered, was not unique. Most of the delinquents who crossed the threshold of my office had similarly horrendous backgrounds: car accidents, falls, burns, meningitis, even carbon monoxide poisoning. These were the kinds of catastrophes to be found in their medical records. Years later it became clear to Jonathan and me that a good number of the injuries that parents attributed to accidents or bad luck were not caused by reckless drivers, broken tree branches, or overturned coffeepots. They were caused by parents. But when I was at the Juvenile Court Clinic I did not see that.

Many of the delinquent children, like Lee Anne, had psychotic symptoms: they heard voices and felt persecuted. Their aggressive acts, like Lee Anne's, were often responses to imagined insults and hallucinated threats. It looked to me as though the most violent delinquents were the most impaired, psychiatrically and neurologically. But the books said otherwise. The books said that most delinquents suffered from conduct disorder.

The books said that the parents of delinquents were sociopaths: alcoholic, addicted, and antisocial. They were described as irresponsible and unable to provide discipline. That's why their children were in trouble. To the extent that many of the parents of the delinquents I saw were in trouble with the law, I guess they could be called sociopaths, or antisocial personalities. Many drank heavily. Some took drugs. They could be called alcoholics and addicts. They, like their children, did not need to be interviewed to be diagnosed—at least not with those diagnoses.

But when I sat down and actually spent time talking with them, a different picture emerged. The parents of children coming through the court had a host of psychiatric and medical problems similar to those of their children. In fact, these very problems often led to their addictions, messed up their thinking, loosened their controls, and in short, made them unable to function as parents. If discipline was a problem for them, as the books said, it was not an issue of too little but rather of too much and the wrong kind. They were harsh. These parents were too enthusiastic about meting out punishments. And again, the most aggressive delinquents I saw tended to have been the most severely disciplined.

Gradually, during my years at the Juvenile Court Clinic, a constellation was beginning to emerge of the different vulnerabilities and experiences that, interacting with each other, created violent children. I was gathering clues; I was discovering why one person cried in pain while another lashed out in response to it. But the Juvenile Court was not really the best place to study violence: most of the delinquents coming through had committed minor offenses. If I wanted to understand what made people kill each other, I would have to look elsewhere. After three years as its clinical director, I left the Juvenile Court Clinic and returned to private practice.

The questions in my head about Hitler and me and what made us different from each other did not go away. I knew that everyone at one time or another had homicidal fantasies. What thwarted adolescent has not pictured a parent smashed to smithereens in a car accident? What small child has not yelled at his mother or father, or sibling or friend, "I wish you were dead!" But most of us don't kill anyone. The Donnas and Lee Annes and the people behind bars whom Jonathan and I have examined do. Why?

I could not let go of this question, and so, in my spare time, I conducted a study of the medical histories of delinquents and nondelinquents. I found that what I saw at the Juvenile Court Clinic—the extraordinary numbers of accidents and illnesses—were not peculiar to the delinquents referred to me. Delinquents as a group had horrendous medical histories compared to nondelinquents. Black delinquents were the most injured and sickliest of all. They had the worst medical histories from conception onward. Again, my findings contradicted the books. The books said that delinquents were healthy, muscular—stronger, in fact, than most other kids. The books called them "mesomorphs."

During my years at the clinic and afterwards, if I discovered something new or different (such as the fact that delinquents were not all that healthy), if I came upon something that contradicted or conflicted with conventional wisdom, I wrote it up and sent it to a psychiatric journal. I hoped it would make my colleagues take a second look at the so-called conduct-disordered children and adolescents who crossed their paths.

Someone in the Connecticut state bureaucracy—someone concerned with delinquents—must have been reading the psychiatric literature. Somehow, she knew about the findings that were emerging from the Juvenile Court Clinic. One day, as I sat in my private office, waiting for an adolescent patient to arrive (she made it a point to come twenty minutes late for each session), the phone rang. A woman whose name I do not know but to whom I shall always be grateful was calling to invite me to design a study of Connecticut's violent juveniles. It seems that along with funds for a secure unit for violent delinquents had come funds to try to learn what they were really like. Would I be interested in studying these dangerous adolescents? Here, out of the blue, was an opportunity to tackle the question that had gnawed at me since childhood.

When, years before, I had planned the Juvenile Court Clinic, I had no idea that delinquents might have medical or neurologic problems. Now I was wiser. I knew that any study of violent juveniles had to include an examination of their neurologic status. I needed Jonathan. I figured that, in light of his previous reluctance to see Lee Anne, I'd better not rely on the telephone. I would make an appointment to see him in person.

I stood in Jonathan's minuscule, book-encrusted office at Yale, and I begged. Jonathan was adamant. "You're not going to find anything, Dorothy. You're just not. There's nothing wrong with them neurologically or, for that matter, psychiatrically. They're just like everybody else." With the self-confidence that only a six-foot-two, recently tenured associate professor of neurology at Yale could muster, Jonathan plucked a small black book, *Criminality and Psychiatric Disorder* by Samuel Guze, from the top shelf of his bookcase. The trouble with Jonathan was that he was a good reader.

My mother was like Jonathan, an excellent reader; she was an omnivorous reader. The difference between her and Jonathan was that she almost never believed what she read. If my father's motto was, "There but for the grace of God go I," my mother's was some combination of "The Emperor has no clothes" and "I'm from Missouri. Show me." She had to see something with her own eyes to believe it. What was more, she didn't much care whether others saw things the same way. Although I did not inherit my mother's superb reading skills, I did absorb much of her philosophy. I have to see for myself. I certainly do not put my faith in books, especially not psychiatry books. Anything that changes as often as the diagnostic manuals cannot be entirely trusted.

I am not implying that Jonathan believes everything that he reads. Not by a long shot. He is, in fact, extremely critical. He does, however, have great respect for systematic research. He also has more respect for authority and for the wisdom of his elders than do I. His mother obviously did not repeatedly whisper in his ear, "The Emperor has no clothes." Guze was our elder, and an esteemed elder at that. When he spoke (or wrote), people listened. Guze's book in hand, Jonathan proceeded to riffle through its index. He found the reference he was seeking. Turning to page 124, he began to read. "Sociopathy, alcoholism, and drug dependence are the psychiatric disorders associated with serious crime. Schizophrenia, primary affective disorders, anxiety neurosis, obsessional neurosis, phobic neurosis, and [he paused meaningfully] *brain syndromes are not.*" Book closed. Case closed.

Guze, Emperor, chairman of one of the country's most distinguished departments of psychiatry, the Department of Psychiatry at Washington University in St. Louis, had spoken. What is more, he had based his statements on research, on statistics. While psychiatrists like me were merely sponging up clinical impressions, trying to make sense of what our patients were telling us and showing us, Guze was counting. He was ahead of his time. Guze had data. A lot of data. Guze had used interviewers who talked with hundreds of criminals. How could I presume to argue with that?

On the other hand, I knew what I had seen with my own eyes at the Juvenile Court Clinic. If the delinquents I had examined were anything like the criminals that Guze was writing about, then at least on this issue Guze was wrong. But go prove that to Jonathan! How was I to convince Jonathan to travel thirty miles each way once a week to perform neurologic evaluations on violent delinquents who Guze and the rest of the world insisted were perfectly healthy? They were not sick. They were bad. Their characters were warped.

I knew that Jonathan and I would never be able to examine the number of criminals, violent or otherwise, that Guze had studied. Not in our lifetimes. Jonathan and I are slow. It takes us hours to examine just one individual. Worse, paradoxically, the more experienced we are, the longer it takes us. It isn't age—at least I hope not. With each new case, we learn more; we become aware of issues we have failed to explore previously. We learn what we have missed. Awareness lengthens evaluations.

"You won't find anything," Jonathan repeated, tapping Guze's book.

"Fine, Jonathan. Fine." I hated the way I sounded. To my ear, I sounded like my daughter when I asked her to clean up her room. "Fine, Mom. Fine." Clearly I was not going to convince Jonathan that violent delinquents might have something wrong with their brains. Who was I compared to Guze?

I cajoled; I flattered; I appealed first to ego, then to intellect. When that did not work, I fell back on my Ethical Culture training. I argued morality and philosophy. I got nowhere. Jonathan was getting bored. In the end I stooped to bribery. I took a deep breath and said, "Jonathan, there's $10,000 in that state grant for a neurologist. That's about a hundred bucks a kid." Now I had his full attention. Academic careers can be intellectually rewarding. They are not financially rewarding, especially at Yale. Jonathan had three sons to put through college—it was as simple as that. We were a team. Years later Jonathan inscribed the Second Edition of his book, *Behavioral Neurology*, as follows: "To Dorothy, who taught me that crime can pay."

Jonathan worked at Yale all week long. Saturdays were out because he is Orthodox. That left Sunday. Therefore, almost every Sunday morning for a year, Jonathan drove out to Middletown and examined violent delinquents at the correctional school. The children's records were locked up. Jonathan was on his own. He knew nothing of what I had found.

One Sunday evening, three or four months into the project, I got a phone call. It was Jonathan. By then he had examined a couple of dozen delinquents.

"Dorothy?"

"Yes."

"I just wanted to let you know, you were right. I've never seen anything like it before. I've never seen so many neurologically impaired kids together in one place at one time." Jonathan was hooked. Getting him from Long Lane to death row would be easy.

CHAPTER 7

The funds at Long Lane were fast drying up, and my collaboration with Jonathan on the study of violence was coming to a close. I found myself pondering ways to spend the extra daytime hours I would have when our project ended. By now Mel and I had two children, Gillian and Eric. Perhaps I would work half-time, spend afternoons with the children, and even permit them to go to bed before the eleven o'clock news came on the air.

Then one morning our lives changed. As Mel walked Eric up the slight incline leading to Eric's first-grade classroom, Mel felt a twinge in his chest. He paused and the pain subsided. He continued and the pain returned. Mel, barely fifty years old, had angina. Mel had suffered diphtheria as a child in England. He went into heart failure twice and spent months in the hospital; he nearly died. The experience left him with an extraordinary appreciation for what he calls "children in hospital" and a vulnerable cardiac muscle. I no longer had the luxury of looking upon my research as an avocation, a hobby, dependent on my ability to acquire funds here and there. Nor was it realistic to work half-time and play with our children the other half. The possibility loomed that someday soon I might have to become the major, possibly the sole, breadwinner of a young family. I needed an honest job.

I wanted to work in New Haven, and Yale was the obvious place to begin my job search. I was already a clinical professor at Yale, but that title was an honor bestowed in lieu of a salary. I applied for a real job at Yale—never, of course, letting on the reason for my request. Yale was not interested. Yale had never in its history given a tenured faculty position in psychiatry to a woman psychiatrist; maybe once to a pediatrician, once to an epidemiologist; never to a woman psychiatrist. Yale was not about to break with tradition for me. I, in turn, was not about to beg. Begging Jonathan to work with me was a challenge. Begging Yale would be a humiliation. Neither Mel nor I was willing to use his angina to get me a job.

However, the tendrils of the academic grapevine reached from New Haven to New York, and thanks to my research on violence, once I let it be known I wanted an honest, full-time job I received offers from medical schools in New York City. Columbia seemed brisk, stimulating, almost aggressively academic; Cornell was gracious, intelligent, and elegant. But New York University, especially Bellevue Hospital, felt like home. At Cornell I was served a lunch of quiche lorraine and white wine in the faculty dining room. I was tempted—I love French food. At Bellevue it was lox and bagels in the cafeteria. But Columbia and Cornell were reluctant to have violent adolescents on their wards. Bellevue, on the other hand, could not help itself; it was a city hospital and had to accept these teenagers. What is more, Bellevue had a prison ward, an ideal setting in which to study adult violence. I joined the N.Y.U. faculty and spent the first year of my academic career warring with families of cockroaches and a nest of mice that had set up housekeeping in my radiator.

I like to think of myself as a world-class commuter. After eighteen years of traveling for two hours each way on Metro North between New Haven and New York, I have seriously considered writing a

Michelin-type commuter guide. I know the best cars (the ones that still have "no smoking" stenciled on the outside, have no bathrooms, and smell better). I know which seats have the most privacy (the singles without windows). I also know what to carry with me at all times: a Snickers bar, a novel, lined pads; three ballpoints (one to lend, one to run out of ink, and a spare); at least one newspaper with a fresh crossword puzzle. Nowadays a cellular phone comes in handy, even a computer. But if you have to choose, carry a Snickers. You never know when a trip will take five hours instead of two, and you can't eat a laptop. I also like to think of myself as a New Yorker. In my soul, I am one; thirty years in New Haven has not changed that. And Bellevue feels like home.

Shortly after joining the N.Y.U. faculty, I managed to get a small Ford Foundation grant to study the prisoners on the Bellevue forensic wards. To my delight, I discovered that Jonathan felt the same way about New York and Bellevue that I did. Dragging Jonathan to New York to continue our work together at Bellevue took no wheedling at all. Jonathan was raised in Brooklyn and went to medical school at Columbia. He even had done some of his medical school clerkships at Bellevue. Jonathan was fond of the old Bellevue Hospital with its marble floors, elegant staircases, and its enormous chandelier.

On Bellevue's famous forensic service, Jonathan and I examined some of New York's most notorious murderers. Evenings on the train, returning to New Haven, I would pick up the *Post* (someone else's, of course) and often see on the front pages pictures of the murderer I could expect to encounter the next day on the forensic psychiatry ward. At Bellevue, Jonathan and I examined Mark David Chapman, the man who shot John Lennon. We also saw a less famous but more flamboyant inmate who cut off his father's head and penis and chucked both out the window. It was a colorful period in our collaboration. Patients in New Haven do not do these sorts of things, at least not the ones I met.

At Bellevue, extraordinary violence is not limited to inmates on the forensic service. A study of the patients on our children's psychiatric ward revealed that, of fifty-five children admitted one year, twenty-one had been homicidal. For example, one child was admitted after trying to strangle her sister; another took a knife to a homemaker; another set fire to the couch on which his mother slept; another stood over his sleeping mother with a raised hammer; and the youngest in our study, a four-year-old, held a knife to his mother's throat. What distinguished these homicidal young children from their less aggressive peers on the ward were signs of neurologic impairment, such as histories of seizures, and households filled with abuse and family violence. I wrote up these findings. When they were published in the *American Journal of Psychiatry*, they caught the eye not only of colleagues but also of Diane Sawyer. Were it not for her, Jonathan and I might never have set foot on death row.

Diane Sawyer invited me to be interviewed on the "CBS Morning News" and discuss my study of homicidal children; not at length, mind you—for no less than sixty nor more than ninety seconds. I would have to talk fast. Little time for little children, I figured. Whatever the explanation, if I became long-winded and spoke for ninety-five seconds, I would be cut off promptly by a commercial. There would be a brief warning in the form of tinkling bells.

To ensure that I made the best use of my ninety seconds, a program assistant rehearsed the questions with me in advance. She even let me suggest what I wished to be asked. She assured me that there would be no surprises, no questions like whether a mother could tell if her toddler son would grow up to be a serial rapist.

"Mom, were the cue cards on the ceiling?" my daughter inquired afterwards.

"What do you mean?"

"Well, every time Diane Sawyer asked you a question, you looked at the ceiling."

Although most of the interview remains a blur, I do recall the gist of the very first question. It went something like this: "Dr. Lewis, can the mother of a two-year-old with behavior problems predict if her child will become a murderer?" I felt like screaming, "But you promised not to ask that!" So much for the word of program assistants. I suspect that the first time I looked skyward I was seeking help from the Almighty. After that it must have been a mannerism or a spasm. Somehow, during what became an interminable ninety seconds, I managed to convey the fact that children were not born assassins, and that even in the case of young children, neurologic and psychiatric problems coupled with a violent, abusive upbringing often bred violence. At some point—I think when I was assuring Diane Sawyer that most epileptic children were not homicidal—the tinkling notes of the CBS theme cut me off, and I was promptly replaced on the screen by a steaming cup of freeze-dried coffee. I was insulted when that happened to me, but I have subsequently witnessed the same thing happen to Henry Kissinger.

While on the show, I did not realize that my minute and a half in the limelight was being transmitted around the nation. That morning a public defender in West Palm Beach was sipping his own freeze-dried coffee and watching the "CBS Morning News." My description of homicidal children rang a bell: they sounded very much like a couple of his homicidal clients—inmates awaiting execution in Starke, Florida.

The next day my phone rang at Bellevue. The voice on the other end was soft, male, and mellow; the accent was hard to place, but some of the words revealed a faint trace of the South.

"This is Dick Burr. I'm a public defender in Florida. A lawyer in my office saw you on the news yesterday. He said that your description of homicidal children sounded a lot like some of our death row clients. I wonder if you would be willing to evaluate one or two of them. They haven't had psychiatric or neurological evaluations before. After hearing what you had to say, we thought that we just might be missing something."

And that is how Jonathan Pincus and I wound up on death row together.

CHAPTER 8

Starke. The name says it all. Starke, Florida. A geographical oxymoron. A scattering of trailerlike one-story houses blossoms on the otherwise barren landscape. Along the highway into town, in ever increasing numbers, signs beseech the motorist to visit Reptile Land, Starke's second most popular tourist attraction. Nobody does.

Starke can be cold even in late spring. Once, in April, when Jonathan and I came to death row to examine some adult inmates, it snowed. We watched as a few lazy snowflakes floated to the ground and melted on the concrete, surrounding the empty swimming pool in the center of our Econo Lodge. The first time I stayed there, this rectangle of cubicles was a Ramada Inn. But by the time we came to see the younger inmates, the condemned juveniles, the management and name had been changed to reflect an increasing austerity.

And yet Starke survives, its economy fed by a steady trickle of visitors all year long. No one comes to Starke for the fun of it, nor did we. Neither weather nor scenery accounts for its desultory stream of transients. It is the prison, the Florida State Penitentiary, that draws folks to Starke.

Prisoners are, in fact, the town's main industry; without them there would probably be no Starke at all. The penitentiary is its major employer, and the continuous movement of friends, families, and public defenders in and out of Starke provides a modest income for the motels and cheap restaurants that line the main drag.

Every so often something happens to break the monotony of the otherwise routine flow of people to and from the prison. The pace of life quickens, and for a few days, sometimes even a week or two, the economy picks up. Just when it looks as though its going to be a dead season, just when it seems that another motel or a couple of dives will fold, the governor signs a death warrant and Starke gets a new lease on life.

The chance that Starke's first and foremost tourist attraction, Old Sparky, will be put to use generates the kind of nervous excitement needed to attract dozens, occasionally hundreds, of reporters and cameramen. The windfall from such an event, like a good apple harvest in New England or a bountiful wheat crop in the Middle West, can sustain the town for four or five, maybe six dormant months.

Old Sparky is the fond name given by the townsfolk to Starke's antiquated but refurbished and, over the past few years, exceptionally active electric chair. Occasionally Old Sparky shows his age; he can't quite generate the voltage needed to dispatch the customer in the chair. Like an aging geezer with a young broad on his lap, Old Sparky just can't get up the energy to perform the act. They say that in 1979, when the death penalty was reinstated, it took two or three jolts to shock the life out of John Spenkalink, Sparky's first customer in over a decade. When this sort of thing happens, the presses roll. The local newspapers cluck their disapproval on a back page, while providing a minute-by-minute account of the miscreant's lingering death on pages one through five. Old Sparky sells more papers when he's impotent than when he scores. I suspect that this is why Florida has never chosen to amend its form of execution: lethal injections are boring. It is easy to see why, in Starke, Reptile Land comes in a poor second.

Ted Bundy's four or five execution dates alone kept several greasy spoons from bankruptcy. Periodically his impending death breathed life into the moribund town. In fact, when Bundy's final appeal failed, and he was executed, many of the townsfolk were secretly sorry to see him go. Bundy put bread on their table.

Our first visit together to Starke coincided with one of Bundy's several scheduled execution dates. Brightly colored signs outside motels, service stations, and restaurants sang out the sentiments of the people within, and gave the usually drab community a festival air. The diner down the highway from our motel, an establishment destined to sustain us during that stay and our many future visits, registered its enthusiasm with a large sign out front, "BURN, BUNDY, BURN!"

Jonathan and I paused to consider the message.

"Is he one of ours?" Jonathan asked. I pulled out the paper Dick Burr, the public defender, had given me and scanned the list. It contained the names of ten condemned men we were scheduled to evaluate over the next four days. The name Bundy did not appear. We would not be seeing him—nor would we ever, if the authors of the billboard's message had anything to say about it.

"Nope. He's not one of ours."

"Fine, let's eat."

I could count on Jonathan to be decisive. I was the idealist on the team; Jonathan, the realist. We needed food. The politics of the chef were irrelevant. Besides, in those days Jonathan had no problem with the death penalty. We ate.

Just as inmates in prison learn survival skills—how to make booze, how to make a shiv out of a toothbrush, how to wangle a conjugal visit with a woman one has never met before (readers will recall that Ted Bundy fathered a child while awaiting execution)—so doctors who evaluate prison inmates (like Metro North commuters) develop their own survival tactics. Food, safe, good food is hard to come by for inmates and doctors alike. I have met death row inmates who would not dream of putting into their mouths a forkful of the food served to them by the prison. They survive, as do I, on Snickers bars, but they get theirs from machines in the prison commissary. One of Dick Burr's clients, James Adams, (may he rest in peace), destroyed his esophagus with a couple of bites of beef stew laced with lye—someone in the kitchen did not like James. It cost the state of Florida a pretty penny to reconstruct his gastrointestinal tract. They saved his life so that he could have the distinction of being the first black man put to death in Florida in twenty years.

Because food, safe, good food is so hard to come by in the prison, and because getting in and out of the prison is so time-consuming, breakfast is an important meal for anyone planning to spend a day behind bars. It has to keep you going for eight hours or more—unless, of course, you're up for Snickers and packaged enchiladas.

Orthodox Judaism and Starke cuisine do not go together. It was, therefore, almost impossible for Jonathan to find sustenance at the greasy spoon with the Bundy message out front. Jonathan marveled at the number of dishes that could be made from pig. My own brand of Judaism permitted me to eat whatever I found on the menu that seemed safe, which I took to be anything heated above 180 degrees for five minutes. I passed on the chicken fried steak and selected the one fried meat that could also be found up north—chicken. Jonathan settled for an enormous salad.

The next morning, before leaving for prison, Jonathan was delighted to discover that our Econo Lodge breakfast provided him with skim milk, cornflakes, sugar, coffee, and fresh orange juice. Back in New Haven, he described this meal as "hidden culinary treasures in a barnyard of fried eggs and ham, fried eggs and sausage, fried eggs and bacon, and biscuits made with lard and covered with butter." The biscuits could also be served covered with sausage gravy, a Southern treat composed of fried bits of pork sausage, flour, and heavy cream.

We eyed each other's breakfast trays critically. I was certain that Jonathan's bowl of cornflakes would never sustain him through the examination of four murderers. He surveyed my collection of plates and was aghast. "I can't believe you're eating that stuff." My breakfast included two fried eggs, several sausages, a rasher of bacon, a heap of grits with some melted butter on top, and two biscuits, one with butter and jam, the other smothered in sausage gravy.

"I can't help it, Jonathan. If I don't eat fat, by eleven o'clock I get hypoglycemic and I can't think straight. My stomach starts to make terrible sounds." Jonathan could not conceal his disgust, but I was not intimidated. "You'll be sorry you only ate cornflakes," I warned. After several excursions to death row in the South, I learned that Jonathan would choose starvation over biscuits and sausage gravy.

Breakfast over, we were off to prison, driven by a public defender who was supposed to smooth the way once we got there. Shortly before entering the prison grounds, I spotted a lonely, all-night convenience store of the variety many of Starke's inmates had seen fit to relieve of cash. It was our last chance to buy a packaged sandwich and secure calories for the long day ahead. When I broached this idea to the attorney, he assured me that the chance of smuggling in a tuna sandwich was slightly less than the chance of smuggling out Ted Bundy.

As we approached the prison, the scenery improved, the flat, trailer-pocked land giving way to expanses of cultivated fields. We had entered a farm. Hundreds of acres surrounded the prison walls, providing food for the prison tables. Here and there we glimpsed the light blue uniforms of prisoners working the land. In the distance grazed a herd of black and white cows, the prison's source of fresh milk and meat, so we were told.

This bucolic scene soon gave way to a grimmer picture: a mass of high, rectangular, pale green structures connected by occasional towers and surrounded by a high metal fence. "See that block there," the public defender pointed to the first visible building complex. "That's the death house. That's where they keep the condemned prisoners."

Then, as if to enhance the macabre scene, he added, "That's where they keep Old Sparky."

Over the years, attorneys have provided Jonathan and me not only with fascinating information about the legal system and how it works, or fails to, but also with information that once imparted has remained forever with us. Burdened by knowledge regarding the fate of their clients, from time to time attorneys have used Jonathan and me as receptacles for secrets too terrible to bring home to their wives and children.

On this, our first morning together on death row, as we drove from our motel along the main drag, through the flat countryside and onto the prison grounds, the public defender saw fit to describe to us the week-long ceremony leading up to an execution at Starke.

Several days before a scheduled execution, the prisoner is moved from his death row cell to a small holding cell close to the death chamber. There a light burns day and night so that the prisoner can be watched closely and prevented from taking his own life. The condemned is visited there by a tailor, who takes careful measurements for the suit that the inmate will wear in his coffin. The prisoner, we were told, also has the option of being comforted and counseled spiritually by the prison chaplain. Given the common knowledge that this man of the cloth is an outspoken partisan for the death penalty, few if any prisoners avail themselves of his services.

The prisoner is also allowed a last meal of his choice, the parameters of which were not spelled out to us. Julia Child recently published an account of her own preferred last meal. If I recall it correctly, it began with fois gras, oysters, and caviar, followed by pan-seared duck and topped off with crème brûlée. She asked that each course be served with an appropriate wine. If my memory serves me, dessert was accompanied by a 1976 Château d'Yquem. I somehow doubt that a request like Julia Child's would or even could be honored at Starke. I do know that according to our public defender-informant, wine and beer are forbidden even at this final meal. Château D'Yquem is out.

An inkling of the tastes of the condemned can be obtained from postexecution newspaper accounts. From these, my impression is that fried chicken ranks high. (My choice, as well, when in Starke.) But, unlike me, their choice is not influenced by safety. Not long ago, a man in Oklahoma was reported to have requested a couple of Big Macs or Whoppers—I don't recall which. Then there was the unfortunate retardate in Arkansas, a man who had shot himself in the head shortly after committing the murder for which he was nevertheless condemned to death. Like James Adams in Florida, doctors saved his life so that he could eventually be executed. His final meal proved to be a textbook example of how damage to certain parts of the frontal lobes affects planning. According to our public defender sources, this man set aside his dessert—pecan pie—so that he could have a midnight snack after his execution. In theory, prisoners cannot be executed if they do not understand what is happening to them or why. So much for theory.

During a prisoner's final days on earth, visitors are severely restricted, though lawyers have access to their clients. At Starke, however, prisoners are usually permitted a final "contact visit" with a loved one. This contrasts with most visits during the final days leading up to execution, which occur behind glass. The prisoner is separated physically from his friends and family. However, for a brief period of time on the evening prior to execution, the prisoner can see his nearest and dearest without the glass barrier and embrace them for the last time. Occasionally this privilege is denied.

An example of such a denial occurred in the case of Ted Bundy. I had known Mr. Bundy over a period of several years, and he had come to trust me. Therefore I was only mildly surprised to receive a call from his lawyer, Polly Nelson, on the Saturday before his scheduled execution, which was to take place the following Tuesday. He had asked to talk with me before he died. I, of course, agreed to come. I had hoped to arrive in Starke on Sunday evening, but a combination of engine trouble, schedule changes, and an unexpected layover in Atlanta delayed my arrival. Monday morning Polly Nelson picked me up at the airport, and we raced to the prison.

There, in one of the little glass-walled cubicles not far from the one in which years before we had been locked in together, we sat and talked—Polly Nelson, Ted Bundy, and I. No glass separated us from each other. His wrists and ankles were shackled. For approximately four and a half hours the three of us talked. Early in the afternoon, a secretary or prison administrator entered, carrying a steno pad and pencil. With the air of a personal secretary, she asked Mr. Bundy exactly what his desires were for that evening; with whom did he wish to spend his final hours? Prison rules dictated that he could speak with friends or family for an hour or two, but that these visitors would be separated from him by a glass barrier. A time would be reserved, however, for a contact visit with a loved one. It was evident to me that these arrangements had already been discussed. The only change in Mr. Bundy's request, as I understood it, was that I be added to the list of visitors to be seen behind glass. The arrangement for a final contact visit alone with his most recent conquest, a female attorney who bore a slight resemblance to several of his victims, would remain as planned. The secretary's gracious demeanor, combined with her obvious efficiency, reminded me of a Delta Airlines stewardess in, say, business class. Polly Nelson had similar associations. I recall her turning to me on our way out of the prison and chirping, "And what else would you care for with your execution, Mr. Bundy?"

As things turned out, Mr. Bundy neither saw all of the visitors he had selected nor gave his lady love a final embrace. When we returned to the prison that evening, our car was stopped at an entry gate and I was told that not only could I not visit with Mr. Bundy, but I could not even enter the prison grounds. Warden's orders. Apparently the warden was fearful that I would suddenly take it into my head to declare Mr. Bundy incompetent to be executed. In order to be incompetent for execution, a prisoner must not understand what is happening or why. With Mr. Bundy, that was hardly the case. Nonetheless, one of the local newspapers had already published an article stating that I had been called to the prison and had declared Mr. Bundy incompetent. I had not. But the warden was taking no chances. In fact, rumor had it that three psychiatrists were called to Starke and were at the ready to declare him sane and competent should I be so foolish as to suggest otherwise. Eventually Polly prevailed on the prison to allow me to enter and sit in a hallway while she and the other selected visitors met behind glass with Mr. Bundy.

The female attorney, dark hair parted down the center and flowing to her shoulders, was denied a final embrace. The warden had had second thoughts about her as well and deemed such a visit too risky. I guess he was afraid that she might slip Mr. Bundy a cyanide pill. This particular change in plan—the warden's prohibition of a contact visit between Ted Bundy and his lady love—left me, to the best of my knowledge, the last woman to kiss Ted Bundy before he died. I had certainly not planned it that way. In fact, I had no intention of ever kissing Ted Bundy. I worked for him and his lawyers. It was my job to determine whether any psychiatric problems had been overlooked that were relevant to his case. This was my job—no more, no less. He, in turn, permitted me to study him on the chance or in the hope that I would discover the forces within him and around him that had made him so extraordinarily violent. When I began our final interview, I asked him why he had wanted to talk with me. His response: "Because everyone else I've talked with these past days only wants to know what I did. You are the only one who wants to know why I did it." We are still studying the data from the Bundy case and hope some day to report what we find in a scientific journal.

Whatever his motives for asking me to come to Starke, and mine for coming, our four and a half hours together on the day before his execution were riveting. In fact, until the secretary interrupted, I had quite lost track of the time. When I realized how much time had gone by, I felt a bit guilty. There must be others waiting to say their good-byes. There was so much more to learn, but since these might be Theodore Bundy's last hours on earth, I felt obliged to leave. An appeal to the Supreme Court was still pending, so I decided to end the interview by shaking Mr. Bundy's shackled hands and wishing him luck on the appeal; we would not hear the Supreme Court's verdict until almost midnight. We both stood up to leave. Then, as I took his hand in mine to shake it, he bent down and kissed me on the cheek. With that, I put my arms around his neck and kissed him on the cheek, exactly as he had kissed me. And that is how I came to be the last woman to kiss Ted Bundy.

I flew home on Tuesday evening. My husband opened the door for me and I placed my bags on the kitchen floor. Trying to sound light about what had obviously been a harrowing experience, I said, "You are looking at the last woman to kiss Ted Bundy." Mel's comment: "And live."

According to the attorney driving us to the penitentiary, the final hours of the condemned are the most grotesque and humiliating. A prison barber comes and shaves the prisoner's head and the skin around one ankle, ensuring a proper flow of electricity from the machine through the body. The final degradation occurs toward the very end. The prisoner showers, then before donning fresh prison garb, he is restrained while guards shove large wads of cotton into his rectum. This is done to ensure that Old Sparky is not fouled by the feces that would otherwise be expelled involuntarily when the switch is thrown and the prisoner convulses. More than one public defender has seen fit to share these details with Jonathan and me. They must figure that if they have to live with them, so should we.

As we neared the entrance and turned into the parking lot in front of the prison, we saw that what from a distance appeared simply to be a wire mesh fence encircling the prison was in reality a double row of fences running parallel to each other, separated by about fifteen or twenty feet. Between these fences, coils of razor-sharp barbed wire gleamed in the Florida sun. This was not ordinary barbed wire. Obviously it was manufactured especially for prisons, each barb sharp enough to carve a roast and long enough to skewer a turkey. Anyone attempting to escape over or through this lethal network of wires and blades would be sliced to ribbons.

In front of the electronically controlled entrance gates stood an old-fashioned guard tower, the kind that lends atmosphere to prison movies, especially when filmed at night. At its base a telephone enabled visitors to identify themselves to an invisible guard stationed at the top of the tower. The attorney did just this, explaining who we were and clarifying our mission. Our visit to the prison had been cleared days before and our names were on a list. All that was left was proof of our identities.

Then an amazing thing occurred. The guard, as if to mock the otherwise high-tech security system, proceeded to lower a plastic bucket on a string. We thereupon deposited our photo I.D.'s in the bucket, which the guard then slowly raised to his perch atop the tower. Eventually, having confirmed to his satisfaction that we were who we purported to be, he slowly lowered the bucket and returned our I.D.'s. I realize now that there was absolutely no way that the guard, so high above, could possibly match the tiny photographs in his hand with the faces of the people below seeking entry. Nevertheless, each time we have visited Starke, we have participated in this ritual.

Having passed this first test, we moved toward the entrance and passed through an electronically operated wire-mesh gate that closed behind us. As we waited for a second gate to open, we looked back and watched the empty plastic bucket slowly ascend the tower and disappear into the turret. With the first gate solidly closed behind us, the second not yet open, and coils of razor-sharp wire on either side, Jonathan and I had a taste of what it was like to be a prisoner in the South.

CHAPTER 9

It was a far cry from Yale and a stone's throw from the death chamber. Jonathan and I found ourselves inside the prison, trapped together in a steel cage through which all visitors to the Florida State Penitentiary must pass. It was nip and tuck whether we would ever get in to examine the inmates, much less out again. Behind us an electronically controlled set of sliding steel bars had already slammed shut, separating us from the entrance area through which we had come. A few feet in front of us a second row of steel bars came between us and the corridor leading to the inmates. Crowding us on our right loomed a temperamental metal detector. On our left stood a table upon which, at the moment, rested an assortment of Jonathan's worldly goods: his watch, two sets of keys, and a Cross pen. Underneath the table sat his medical bag.

For some inexplicable reason, in spite of my metal earrings and watch, I had sailed soundlessly through the metal detector. But Jonathan had beeped twice. He seemed unable to make peace with the suspicious machine. An hour had elapsed since we first set foot on state property. It was 10 A.M. and we had not yet examined a single prisoner. In fact, we had not even seen an inmate save a lone trusty who moved methodically up and down the corridor beyond our cage, slowly pushing a floor polisher back and forth over the already glistening white linoleum. We marveled at the cleanliness of this passage; its hygiene would have been the envy of Yale–New Haven Hospital, not to mention Bellevue.

"Why do you think they keep the floor so clean?" I whispered to Jonathan.

"Wouldn't want anyone to catch a cold on the way to the chair," he muttered back. Jonathan dug his hands in his trouser pockets and came up with a small luggage key and an errant paper clip, overlooked during his first two bouts with the machine. He had already removed his jacket and shoes, and he appeared a bit forlorn standing in his stocking feet. Shoes, the guard explained, have metal in the instep. Blazers have buttons. Jonathan tried again. Still he beeped.

"Trah yore belt," coached the guard. Jonathan fumbled with its small metal buckle and slid it out through the loops of the waistband.

"This could get embarrassing," I hissed. Jonathan was not amused. Later that evening one of the public defenders informed us that the guard controlling this aspect of our clearance into the prison could set the machine at whatever sensitivity suited his fancy.

"If they don't like you," he explained, "they can make the fillings in your teeth beep." Clearly, this guard did not like us. We have never been very popular at Starke. We are interlopers, interrupters of rhythms and routines. Worse, we are there to "get off" dangerous criminals who deserve to die. That is how most of the guards see us. They are not about to make things easy for us. Only if we are willing to humble ourselves and remove whatever article of clothing they designate are we allowed to enter.

On his fourth try, Jonathan and the metal detector made peace with each other, and he was allowed to pass. Even the guard, whose function it was to escort us to the examining rooms, looked relieved.

Jonathan slipped into his shoes, slid his belt through the loops of his trousers, buckled it, and put on his jacket. I picked up my yellow lined pads and roller ball pens from the table top, and Jonathan reached under the table and retrieved his medical bag. "We're off!" exclaimed Jonathan, his usual good humor having returned.

"Not so fast, Doctor. What's this?" demanded the guard, scowling at the medical bag in Jonathan's hand. He acted as though he had never seen an object like it before in his life.

"This? It's just my medical bag. I carry my instruments in it." Psychiatrists have it easy when it comes to entering prisons. A few pads and something to write with are all we usually need to do our job. But neurologists are different. They need all sorts of instruments to do theirs: reflex hammers, tuning forks, ophthalmoscopes, stethoscopes, blood pressure cuffs, flashlights, ergometers for measuring muscle strength, and a variety of objects such as cotton swabs and safety pins for testing sensory modalities.

"Can I take a look-see, Doctor." This was not a question.

During the next half hour we stood back silently as the guard scrutinized, palpated, squeezed, shook, and whenever possible, pulled apart each of the instruments in Jonathan's bag. Things seemed to be going well.

Suddenly the atmosphere changed. "Hello. What have we heah, Doctor?" The guard stared at Jonathan as though he had just discovered a semiautomatic masquerading as an ophthalmoscope. Jonathan peered at the offending item.

"It's a safety pin."

The guard studied the object, turning it over and over between his thumb and index finger, opening and closing it. He looked stumped.

"It's for testing one of the senses; you know, pain—pin prick. It's part of the neurologic examination," Jonathan explained.

The guard thought long and hard. His speech slowed, and his Southern accent became increasingly pronounced, one syllable words stretching into two. "Well now, Doctor," he drawled, "we cay-ent have something lahk thay-et come into the prison, now, cay-en we?" He spoke to Jonathan as though he were addressing a slightly dim-witted seven-year-old. He obviously relished locking horns with the big-city professor from up north. "Someone maht get hurt."

Jonathan is not accustomed to being thwarted. He needed that pin to perform a thorough neurologic examination. He would reason with the guard. Jonathan does not give up; unfortunately, neither did the guard, who stood silently, arms now crossed in front of his chest.

"Forget it, Jonathan," I whispered, "or we'll never get into the prison to test anything."

We began to catch on that our tedious progression into the prison did not reflect a laid-back Southern way of life, nor were we experiencing justifiable caution on the part of prison personnel. We were being harassed. Jonathan relinquished the safety pin. "We ca-yen return it to you later, Doctor, if you'd lahk," the guard reassured him.

Having tasted victory, the guard now threw himself into the rest of his task with gusto. The leisurely pace of his initial search had ended; fingers moved deftly through the pockets and compartments of the medical bag, exploring every hollow and crevice.

Once more, a look of discovery. "Hello. What have we here, Doctor?"

Jonathan and I looked at each other. I raised my eyebrows. Jonathan shrugged. What could possibly have caused such concern? The guard's expression remained serious as he continued to forage. Finally, a smile as he carefully maneuvered the incriminating evidence up the side of the bag and into his palm. One by one, he placed the offending objects on the table: a penny, a nickel, a dime, and a quarter. We stared, first at the coins, then at the guard, then at each other. We were baffled.

"Money, Doctor. Money. You know the rules for visitors. You cannot bring money into the prison. It's a rule."

Now Jonathan smiled, an endearing, self-deprecating smile. He was no longer angry. This was obviously just a small misunderstanding. He could explain.

I watched in disbelief as Jonathan attempted to teach the guard about the phenomenon of stereognosis. He explained: These innocent discs of differing shapes and sizes—coins with raised pictures of historical figures and patriotic mottos—were not brought into the prison to function as legal tender. They simply enabled the neurologist to assess a person's ability to distinguish one item from another through touch. How sensitive were the person's fingertips? For example, patients with peripheral nerve damage from, say, alcoholism, cannot feel subtle differences in shape and size. Similarly, patients with diseases like syphilis, which damage the posterior columns of the spinal cord, have difficulty with this task. The guard waited. Jonathan continued: Assuming these sensory pathways were intact, and the tactile message reaches the brain, can the patient then process the information? Can he then communicate verbally what he has perceived? Patients with dementia and certain kinds of strokes cannot do this. By the time Jonathan concluded the lesson, it was clear, at least to me, that the entire examination of the central and peripheral nervous systems hinged on the use of these four coins.

"Sorry, Doc. No money."

Poker-faced, the guard handed the coins to Jonathan. "Whah don't you take these here coins and that there safety pin back to your car and lahk them in the trunk," he suggested. The implicit message was, "Then just try to get back in here before closing time."

The guard had won. Without a word, Jonathan placed the forty-one cents next to the safety pin on the table. At last the bars of our cage slid open, admitting us to the glistening white corridor. It was almost eleven o'clock.

The clinical evaluation of a violent person is complex. It is time-consuming and requires the expertise of disciplines other than just psychiatry and neurology. (It also requires more than small change.) Certain neuropsychological tests and educational assessments can identify qualities of impairment that psychiatric and neurologic evaluations do not tap. Jonathan and I needed additional talent to do a thorough job. I turned for help to an old friend, Barbara Bard. Barbara, an expert in special education and a colleague from Long Lane days, readily agreed to join us and do the learning disabilities assessments. She threw in some hearing tests as well. We had no funds for a licensed psychologist, however a psychology graduate student, Marilyn Feldman, took time off from her studies to come to Starke and do basic psychological testing. Neither Barbara nor Marilyn required much coaxing. Death row had a certain cachet. Of note, neither of them had any difficulty getting through the metal detector. They, their pencils, booklets, and forms appeared harmless to guards and metal detectors.

We found Barbara and Marilyn awaiting us in the large dining room that, we discovered, was to be our communal examining room for the week. It did not matter that Barbara's and Marilyn's evaluations required silence, that mine required confidentiality, or that Jonathan's required privacy. These were the accommodations that the warden had furnished. We considered discussing our needs with the guards, but realized we would only waste more time. The dining room, its tables and seats riveted to the floor, was the only area that the prison was willing to provide us at this time. (A year or two later, when we returned to study condemned juveniles, the warden was more accommodating and turned over the entire infirmary to our team of clinicians.) But, for the duration of this trip, the dining room was it. Take it or leave it. We took it. Now that we were all together, a guard who had been awaiting our arrival slowly lifted the receiver of a phone on the wall and called the cell blocks to summon the prisoners. It would be another twenty minutes before the first inmate arrived. Each of us used this time to set up shop as far away from each other as possible, to carve out for ourselves a small area of relative privacy and quiet.

As each inmate arrived, a guard removed the shackles chaining his ankles to one another and unlocked the handcuffs that linked his

wrists behind his back. The inmate then docilely placed his wrists together in front of him, whereupon they were recuffed to each other.
Some of the inmates used the moments between shacklings to rub
their reddened wrists where handcuffs had been fastened too tightly.
Over time we learned that the degree of tightness of handcuffs varied
according to the guard and his relationship with the inmate. You learn
a lot of things in prison.

The guards at Starke were a pretty rigid crew, nothing like the laid-
back Texas guards with whom we would share lunch in Huntsville a
year or two later. The Huntsville guards were unfailingly gracious.
When one considers the fact that these facilities—death rows, that
is—are created to serve the same purpose (i.e., housing and dispatching the condemned), they are remarkably different, one from another.
At Huntsville, you get the feeling from the top down that they are not
too keen about what they are doing—the execution aspects of their
jobs. One of the deputy wardens even said so. He was a former New
Yorker, a black man who had worked in prisons back east before New
York State reinstated capital punishment. In fact, he seemed almost
apologetic about his job in Texas. In Texas, he explained, they used
lethal injection. This, he asserted, was far more humane than electrocution, the method of dispatching prisoners in Florida. Jonathan liked
him so much that, on our second trip to Texas, he brought him a
dozen New York bagels.

At Starke, on the other hand, the deputy warden and the guards
seemed to have no qualms about their work, at least none that
showed. On my very first visit, the guard escorting the prisoner I was
about to see growled in the inmate's ear, "I'll see you fry." Granted, this
remark was in response to a rather obscene comment by the inmate
regarding the tightness of his handcuffs.

On one of my expeditions to Starke, I joined a small group of visitors on a conducted tour of death row. Until then, all of my contacts

with inmates had taken place in the dining room, the infirmary, or the administrative area, and I was curious to see the conditions of death row itself. I also had an ulterior motive. One of the men that Jonathan and I had examined on our first visit was refusing to come out of his cell and speak with his lawyers. He had some extremely good issues for appeal, but he had fallen into a deep depression and had lost all hope. He also refused to come out to talk with me. I hoped that my tour would pass his cell and enable me to coax him to come out and resume his appeals. It did (pass his cell); I did (coax him); and he did (come out and resume his appeals).

But three quarters of the way into the tour, to my dismay I realized that it would include a visit to the death chamber. There was no turning back. Gates had already locked behind me, and the only way to return to the infirmary where we were all stationed on that visit was to follow the tour through to its completion. That is how I came to find myself face to face with Old Sparky.

I was shaken. The leader of our tour was the deputy warden of the prison. It would have been hard to imagine a person more different from his Huntsville counterpart. This prison official, a white man, obviously enjoyed his work; indeed, he seemed to throw himself into it. For example, it was not enough to show his already tremulous audience The Chair. He made an extra effort to ensure that we would not forget our tour. Opening a door to the side of a large glass window from which witnesses view electrocutions, he bade us enter the death chamber itself. There, in front of us, within arm's reach, stood Old Sparky. Ushering us into a small, semienclosed area to the left of the chair, he pointed out a panel of dials and switches. Patiently he described how the executioner first sets the desired voltage and timing. Then, he explained, the executioner signals an officer standing directly behind the chair. This officer, in turn, reaches for a large, metal, leverlike switch attached to the wall and throws it. As he spoke, the officer alongside pulled the lever. The clang, to my ears, was thunderous. It was also cruel, because, as we learned, it was not that loud switch that turned on the electricity. It sounded like it, but it wasn't. Only after the switch was thrown did the executioner silently push the lethal button. Thus, whoever had the misfortune of being seated in the chair heard the clang and believed that the machine had malfunctioned: he was saved. Only a couple of seconds later did the surprise come.

The deputy warden continued; he explained that the "juice" was administered twice for several seconds each time. But I was not fully listening. I was the one sitting in that chair. I was the one teased into thinking I was saved. And I was the one who suddenly realized I was about to die. It was the stake and the guillotine all over again, only this time there was no Paul Tillich or Madame Defarge watching.

The ordeal was not yet over. I came back to my senses to see the deputy warden seat himself in the chair. "Glenn, show our guests how you fasten the inmates' wrists to the arms of the chair. Show them how you fasten the ankles with the leather straps." Glenn did as he was told.

As we left the death chamber and made our way back to the administrative area, the deputy warden took the opportunity to describe the way in which an executioner is selected. The selection process highlights the peculiarities of the role—the honor and the ignominy. According to the deputy warden, Floridians vie for the job. The warden keeps a list of volunteers, and there is fierce competition to get one's name on it. When an execution is about to take place, the lucky person chosen is alerted. At this time, the state takes elaborate measures to ensure anonymity. According to the deputy warden, only the warden knows the identity of the executioner.

Throughout history, the position of executioner has been a dubious distinction. It would be interesting to study executioners.

CHAPTER 10

I watched from my enclave at the back of the dining hall as a guard and his lumbering captive moved haltingly in my direction. The prisoner's ankles were still shackled, as were his hands, and he was obviously having trouble maintaining his balance. This large inmate, like a clunky, unbalanced freighter, listed toward port.

When the pair reached my table, they stopped. The guard bent down, unlocked and removed the chains connecting the captive's ankles, then rose and unlocked the handcuffs securing his arms behind his back. Docilely, the inmate placed his wrists side by side in front of him, and the guard refastened the cuffs. As he did this, the guard bent away from his prisoner and whispered in my ear, "This one's not wrapped too tight." As Jonathan and I would learn shortly, this guard was not a bad clinician.

Before we talk with most inmates, we already know a fair amount about them. Their attorneys have provided us with descriptions of offenses and with previous clinical reports, if they exist. But Lucky Larson's attorney did not trust us. He feared that knowledge of his client's bloody acts would influence our findings. How could we perform un-biased assessments if we knew that Lucky Larson had hacked not one but two victims to death? The attorney made a big mistake.

The nature of a person's offenses provides a window into his pa-thology. For example, overkill—the infliction of multiple gratuitous wounds on an already dead or dying victim—which characterized Lucky's crimes, tells much about the attacker. These assailants just can't seem to stop. Psychotic murderers sometimes do this; their fury can reach extraordinary heights. Sometimes they respond to imagined threats to their own safety. Sometimes their "voices" tell them to keep going, to further mutilate the victim or violate the body. Sometimes they mistake their victims for other individuals in their lives—incestuous mothers, violent fathers, or taunting siblings. Manic states, too, have been associated with extremes of violence. And damage to certain parts of the brain can lead to paranoid misperceptions, impul-siveness, and extremes of emotion, especially rage. Once started on a course of action, brain-damaged killers sometimes cannot stop. Alco-hol can loosen controls and may, in some people, trigger or exacerbate psychotic states. Substances such as cocaine, LSD, and PCP have been reported to distort reality at times, increase paranoia, and pre-cipitate extraordinary violence. Jonathan and I have found that, in in-stances of overkill, the offender usually was psychotic, manic, or schizophrenic; had some type of brain dysfunction; was under the in-fluence of alcohol or drugs; or suffered from some combination of the above. Criminals just out to make a fast buck don't go on rampages.

But Lucky Larson's lawyer was taking no chances. He kept valuable information to himself and instructed Lucky to do likewise. As a result, it took Jonathan and me weeks to piece together the facts of the case.

Eventually we learned the following: When Lucky Larson was in his early twenties, in response to a dare, he tried to rob a convenience store. (Just about all of our inmates' careers in serious crime began in convenience stores. *Convenience* means different things to dif-ferent people.) Lucky's career did not progress much beyond the convenience store stage, and it was a short career at that. On this first venture he entered the store armed only with a knife. To his surprise, he was an instant success; the teenaged clerk immediately handed over the few bills and change in the till. Suddenly it occurred to Lucky that he had taken no precautions to disguise himself. The clerk would be able to identify him. (Lucky, as will become clear, had a few unmistakable physical characteristics.)

As a result of some of Lucky's neuropsychiatric problems, whatever he thought was on the tip of his tongue and usually spilled out of his mouth; he could not resist sharing this insight into his predicament with the clerk. The clerk, cleverer by half at least than Lucky— which does not say much—assured the oafish robber that he would never disclose his identity. He supported this vow by pointing out that the store did not belong to him; he cared little what happened to the money. Besides, the clerk had no love for the police. He too, he claimed, had experienced his share of run-ins with the law. Thus reassured, Lucky made off with the meager loot, whereupon the clerk called the police and Lucky was apprehended. So much for trusting strangers. Lucky was tried, convicted, and incarcerated.

Five years later, free and again short of money, Lucky entered another convenience store. He seemed to look upon convenience stores pretty much as bankcard holders regard ATMs—a ready source of immediate cash in a pinch. But Lucky had learned a thing or two from his previous encounter. This time there would be no witnesses. As the clerk turned around to reach for a carton of cigarettes to add to the take, Lucky pulled out a knife and plunged it into his back. According to the autopsy, the first blow was fatal. Then Lucky just lost it. Once Lucky got started, there was no stopping him. No longer in danger of being identified, Lucky nevertheless continued to stab the body fifty-three more times. Then, for good measure, he cut the clerk's throat.

Lucky Larson's violence did not end with the murder at the convenience store. He was on a roll; some might call it a rampage. Seventy-two hours later an elderly used car dealer lay dead, his throat slashed and seventeen stab wounds on his arms and torso. The cash register was open and empty. Lucky had needed wheels and was again short of cash. We never learned exactly how this simple transaction between Lucky and the used car dealer escalated into a lethal confrontation. According to court records, the entire take from these two fatal encounters was no more than one hundred dollars and a carton of cigarettes.

Lucky Larson was apprehended and put in jail to await trial.

If his brain damage (later well documented) contributed to Lucky's homicidal rages, his deficient reading skills contributed to his self-incrimination. Following his arrest, Lucky could not resist making a slew of phone calls on a jailhouse phone that was clearly marked "monitored." Among his calls was one to an uncle, to whom he confessed the murders. Lucky must have heard a note of criticism in his uncle's voice. Lucky, no dope he, detected this implicit lack of enthusiasm and got scared. Maybe his uncle would turn on him in court and testify against him. In a flash the solution came to him. No sooner had he hung up than he picked up the receiver again and called a pal, whose help he tried to enlist to bump off his uncle. All of these transactions, of course, were recorded by the sheriff's department and used in court to convict Lucky. And the uncle, apprised of the abortive plot on his life, also testified against his nephew. Lucky was found guilty and sentenced to death.

Ever since the Supreme Court of the United States reinstated the death penalty, all capital trials have consisted of two phases. In the first phase, the jury determines the guilt or innocence of the defendant. If the defendant is found guilty, a sentencing phase follows. During this second phase of the trial, the prosecution presents what are called aggravating circumstances—all the reasons why the defendant's crimes should be considered especially heinous and why he deserves to die. In contrast, the defense is supposed to take this opportunity to present to the jury all of the mitigating factors that can be mustered to enlist the jury's compassion. Now is the time for the defense to invoke the culprit's miserable childhood, his psychiatric problems, his intellectual deficiencies.

In Lucky Larson's case, the prosecution had no difficulty bringing home to the jury the brutality of the crimes. One look at the photographs of the victims was sufficient. On the other hand, Lucky's trial attorney felt hard pressed to come up with a single mitigating factor. A lone psychiatrist whom he had recruited prior to trial, after a brief meeting with Lucky, had dismissed him as a sociopath. A neuropsychologist who usually worked for the state tested Lucky and found "no neurological impairment at all." She concurred with the psychiatrist. Lucky, she said, was a sociopath. As for a history of child abuse, the defendant could remember none. Lucky Larson was unlucky indeed.

I stood, smiled at the figure standing in front of me, reached for his shackled right hand, and shook it. He smiled back. Only half of his face moved. I stared at him. Then, before I could stop myself, I blurted out, "Mr. Larson, would you please smile again." He obliged by once more crinkling up the left side of his face into what became a lopsided grimace; the right side remained flabby and immobile. I did not need Jonathan to tell me that there was something very wrong with this man neurologically. At Long Lane, the children's neurologic signs tended to be subtle, not obvious. They had so-called soft signs. Here, before me, was definite paralysis; it was what Jonathan would call a good "hard" sign.

It seems fair to assume that a death sentence would dampen the spirits of any man. Impending execution, especially electrocution, must be a sobering event to contemplate. It would be to me. We expected to encounter in the inmates at Starke a combination of terror and depression. Such, we would learn over time, was not always the case. In fact, a few years later, just prior to one of Ted Bundy's numerous execution dates, he waved good-bye, and in response to my look of concern, called out gaily, "Don't worry, Dr. Lewis. It's not going to happen!" That episode occurred during one of his manic states; he came within six hours of execution during that go-round.

Lucky Larson, like Ted Bundy, in spite of what seemed to me to be his precarious tenure on life in this world, was remarkably sanguine, even jovial. When I commented on his apparent good cheer in the face of death, Lucky Larson responded, "Fear is not one of my words. There is nothing to be afraid of in this world, especially dying."

I know that he said this because, as he started to speak, I found myself struggling to take down everything he said verbatim. I sometimes settle for abbreviated notes; I try not to disrupt the flow of an interview with the scratching of my pen. Only when I encounter a "nobody will believe this when I tell them" situation do I strive to record exactly what is said. We were having a "nobody will believe this" exchange.

It was not just what Lucky said but the way he said it, the very atmosphere he created, that gave our meeting a surreal quality. Words tumbled out of his mouth and flew in all directions, confusing me and making it impossible to get everything down on paper. Lucky's answers to my questions rarely targeted the topic at hand. Instead he latched on to a syllable, a word, a phrase and took off with it. Whatever came out of my mouth or his became an irresistible invitation to digress, a springboard for free association. Innocuous comments and piercing questions met with the same kinds of responses. No matter the stimulus, it invariably evoked a string of disconnected thoughts.

Sometimes even Lucky got snarled in the threads of his disorganized thought. Suddenly he would interrupt himself and ask, "Where'd I go? What was the question?" Once, in a moment of uncharacteristic insight, he volunteered, "I just get carried off into something else."

There was no way for me to obtain a logical, sequential history from Lucky. The most I would come away with that day was a sense of his irrepressible mood and his tangled thought processes. His high spirits were not like Ted Bundy's. Bundy's thinking was more organized. Lucky's garrulousness and infinite capacity to be sidetracked reminded me of the happy ramblings of a lobotomized patient I had once examined on the back ward of a state hospital during my board examinations. Then again, at times, the jocular prisoner in the handcuffs and prison garb seemed distinctly manic.

Eventually the time allotted me to examine Lucky Larson came to an end. He had exhausted me. I, in contrast, had not even slowed him down. In fact, when we parted he was more ebullient than when we began. With a certain sense of relief, I escorted the loquacious Lucky to the other side of the dining hall and deposited him in the care of Jonathan. Perhaps Jonathan would have greater success examining Lucky than I had. I decided to give myself a rest, sit back, and watch Jonathan do his thing.

Watching Jonathan Pincus try to teach Lucky Larson to skip was worth the trip to Starke. "First you hop on one foot, then on the other. While you do this you move forward," Jonathan illustrated the task.

"O.K., now you try it."

It took Lucky a little while to grasp the concept. Now it was the exercise itself that defeated him, an exercise any normal seven-year-old masters with ease. He could hop just fine on his right leg; it was when he tried to move forward and transfer to his left that things got rocky. His left leg gave way; it simply could not bear the weight of his entire body.

Lucky was unruffled by this defeat. Had Jonathan not terminated that task and moved on to another, Lucky would have kept trying indefinitely. He was no quitter. Failure did not dampen his spirits; rather, throughout the exercise, a steady stream of happy verbiage poured from his lips.

Eventually Jonathan and Lucky sat down to rest. "You know," Jonathan remarked, "you have an unusually optimistic outlook on life." No response. Perhaps Lucky did not understand him. Jonathan rephrased his comment. "As I see it, you are a pretty happy fellow for someone facing the chair."

Now Lucky caught on. Lucky grinned his lopsided grin and proclaimed in tones audible to the rest of us in the dining hall, "I am one of those guys that doesn't fear anybody because I can handle the situation. The car accident changed my personality. I learned that death is that simple," and he awkwardly tried to snap the fingers of his right hand to illustrate his point. "I started living every day to its fullest. Yesterday's done and I won't get it again. It's a carefree type of life," he concluded.

Accident? I pricked up my ears, as did Jonathan. My earlier questions about his health, about whether he had ever been in any serious accidents, about cars and bikes and falls, had elicited little. Now, spontaneously, Lucky spoke of a car accident that had changed his life. Gently, trying not to distract him, Jonathan asked, "What car accident?" Jonathan had turned on the right tap and in response a torrent of relevant information spewed forth.

"When I was sixteen, maybe seventeen, I crashed my car. They told me I cut a nerve on the right side of my face. That's why it doesn't move." Here was the explanation for Lucky's skewed smile. Lucky continued.

"I broke my jaw in a couple of places. But at least I'm alive. You know I was in a coma for a few weeks. They thought I was going to die." According to Lucky, shortly after obtaining his driver's license, while speeding along a country road, he crashed headlong into an oncoming car. What happened to its occupants was never clear. Lucky's head crashed into the windshield, shattering it and putting Lucky into a coma that lasted for weeks. The right side of his head took the brunt of the impact. The consequent trauma to the right side of his brain probably accounted for his left-sided weakness and the overall list toward port that I had noticed. The shattered glass had transected his facial nerve, making it impossible for him ever again to move the right side of his face. Medical records that we subsequently acquired indicated that the doctors who saved Lucky's life required two hundred stitches just to patch up what remained of his face. His left foot and right collarbone had also been shattered.

Jonathan is a good detective. Amid the scarred flesh and underlying shattered bone of the right side of Lucky's face, he noticed another abnormality. Lucky's right eye, which was sunken in its socket, was smaller than his left. It was also blind. Therefore, Jonathan deduced, the car accident was not the first trauma to the right side of Lucky's brain. This small, blind eye had to reflect a much earlier trauma. The eye, Jonathan explained to me later, is an extension of the brain. An injury severely impeding the growth of one eye would have to have occurred very early in development. Lucky's left eye was of normal size; it had grown at a normal rate along with the left side of his brain. The right, in contrast, must have been injured in utero, at birth, or in very early infancy. The medical records would prove Jonathan's deduction correct. Lucky Larson had been the product of a traumatic forceps delivery. According to Jonathan, Lucky's left-sided weakness probably did result from the car accident that injured the right side of his brain when he was sixteen years old. His left limbs were normal in size and were in proportion to the rest of his body. They were not withered, as they would have been had their nerve supply been compromised at birth. They were just weaker than normal.

Jonathan is thorough. His careful examination revealed that the left side of Lucky Larson's brain, as well as the right, had not been totally spared. Although Lucky was right-handed, wrote with it, caught with it, stabbed with it, Jonathan discovered that his coordination on the right was poorer than on the left. Each side of the brain controls the musculature of the opposite side of the body. Therefore, difficulty manipulating the right hand can result from left-brain lesions.

Lucky Larson's abnormal reflexes confirmed Jonathan's suspicion of damage to both sides of his brain. Jonathan ran a tongue depressor along the outside of the sole of Lucky's left foot. His toes, instead of curling under in a normal response, extended upward and splayed out, like a fan. Jonathan next ran the wooden stick along the outside of Lucky's right sole. As on the left, his big toe rose while the remaining four fanned upward and outward. Jonathan repeated the examination twice more on each side, each time recreating a fan of toes. "Bilateral Babinski signs," he jotted in his notes. This abnormal reflex reflected injury to both right and left cortico-spinal tracts—nerve pathways that extend from the cerebral cortex, through the middle and lower sections of the brain where they cross, and down each side of the spinal cord. Jonathan had elicited another hard sign of central nervous system damage.

In spite of the attorney's failure to trust us and share with us essential information, and in spite of Lucky Larson's inability to string two coherent sentences together, Jonathan and I had managed to glean important insights into some of the reasons why Lucky Larson had killed, indeed overkilled, the hapless young clerk and the unsuspecting car dealer. His illogical thought processes, his poor contact with reality, his manic exuberance, and most of all, his demonstrable brain damage were all relevant to issues of mitigation. All had been present at the time of his initial trial, but for some reason, nobody had noticed them. Now, thanks to our evaluations, the attorney had something to run with. He could put the findings before a judge and try to convince the judge to give Lucky a new trial. And that is exactly what the lawyer did.

Lucky's attorney did not win a new trial for his client. He did manage to convince the judge that Lucky was deserving of a new sentencing hearing. Not only did the judge, an intelligent, fair-minded gentleman, agree to a new sentencing hearing, but he also gave the attorney the wherewithal to document further Lucky's abnormalities. He acceded to Jonathan's request that an EEG (electroencephalogram) and an MRI (magnetic resonance imaging) of Lucky's brain be obtained and, at my request, ordered a battery of sophisticated neuropsychological tests. Most important, Lucky's attorney also came away with adequate funds for an investigator to help him find and interview family members and search records. Thus, if Lucky could not provide a history, perhaps a combination of family informants and records could.

The first results to come in were from the EEG lab. Lucky's brain waves were "diffusely abnormal." This was not big news. Lots of normally functioning individuals have diffusely abnormal brain waves. Still, it was a step in the right direction. When the MRI results came in, showing distinct scarring in both frontal lobes, we had hard, visible evidence of severe brain injury. Lucky's car accident had resulted in the equivalent of bilateral frontal lobotomies.

The investigator, too, struck gold. He managed to track down one of Lucky's brothers, Frank, who until recently had been living a thousand miles from Starke with his wife and children. As fate would have it, shortly before the investigator made contact with Frank, his children had been removed from his home by court order. It seems that Frank had been sexually molesting them and teaching them to molest each other. The question was, where had Frank learned these practices?

The investigator, a real pro when it came to digging up dirt people did not want you to uncover, somehow managed to get hold of the social service records of Frank's case. (Investigators have ways of gleaning confidential information that would make any citizen of this country uneasy. Jonathan and I have learned when not to ask where or how certain information has been obtained. "Don't ask, don't tell" seems to be the motto not only of the army but also of the best investigators in the field.) Frank's records provided our first glimpse into the secrets of Lucky's childhood. A picture of life in the Larson household emerged.

Lucky was the oldest of four children and was his mother's favorite. So favored was he, in fact, that when he was six years old she taught him to pleasure her. Lucky is no doubt one of the youngest boys ever to master the art of cunnilingus. Frank could describe this to his social service worker because he often watched. Sometimes, however, Frank and the younger children were locked out of the house in order to give Lucky and his mother privacy. When Lucky's mother tired of his attentions to her, she would force Lucky, Frank, and the other children in the house to perform sexual acts on each other. Now we knew the origin of Frank's predilection for sex games with young children.

Although Lucky was his mother's favorite, he paid for this exalted position by becoming the focus of his stepfather's wrath. Lucky's mother had always insisted that this man, who fiercely beat Lucky, was Lucky's biological father, but Lucky always suspected he was not; the stepfather knew for sure that he was not. Once, Frank recalled, when Lucky was being chased by his stepfather, Lucky scrambled up a tree to escape. Thereupon the stepfather chopped down the tree with an axe and captured the terrified child. Without this information from Frank and from his social service records, we would never have known of the extraordinary abuse, sexual and physical, that Lucky had endured at the hands of his mother and stepfather. Lucky just did not remember. Frank and his records had provided the missing pieces to the puzzle of Lucky's extraordinary violence. I often think back to this case, and to dozens like it, when I read articles asserting that there is no such thing as a repressed memory. When we evaluated Lucky Larson, though we were aware of the concept of repression, Jonathan and I had no idea of the extent to which memories like these could be submerged, hidden from conscious awareness, and still influence behavior.

I was pleased with the results of our evaluation. There was a strong case to be made for mitigation, and I was prepared to help Lucky's attorney make it. Jonathan, on the other hand, had qualms. His eldest son, against Jonathan's wishes, had worked the "graveyard shift" at a convenience store in New Haven and had twice been robbed by drunken, gun-wielding thugs. The night before testifying, as Jonathan studied the photographs of Lucky's crimes, tears welled up at the sight of the clerk's corpse, lying facedown on the floor of the convenience store. To Jonathan, he looked so young and innocent, his obviously stacked shoes betraying his adolescent efforts to appear taller and older. As in Lee Anne's case, Jonathan worried. Suppose his testimony helped release Lucky into the population; suppose Lucky killed again. The blood would be on Jonathan's hands.

The attorney quickly reassured us both that nothing we said would ever cause Lucky Larson to be returned to society. The most the attorney would ask or could hope for was that Lucky's life be spared, that he be permitted to live out his remaining years in the prison at Starke. His highest possible aspiration could be to become a trusty and be allowed to polish the white linoleum corridors of the prison. He would never again be on the outside.

Sensing Jonathan's continued reluctance to testify, the attorney turned to him and said simply, "Tell me now if you cannot, not tomorrow in court." Jonathan took a deep breath and resolved then and there to go ahead, take the stand, and tell the truth, the whole truth, and nothing but the truth.

The next day, I took the stand first. Psychiatry, as every prosecutor who has ever cross-examined me has never hesitated to point out, is a "soft" discipline compared with the "harder" medical discipline of, say, neurology. The difference between neurology and psychiatry is analogous in some ways to the difference between hard neurologic signs and soft neurologic signs. Hard neurologic signs can be demonstrated easily and often point to localized brain damage. The patient cannot move a limb; he lacks sensation in a particular area of his body; the MRI shows an abnormal mass in the brain; the EEG shows localized spike and wave complexes. In other words, evidence of brain damage is clear. Soft signs, demonstrated by certain abnormal reflexes, by peculiar hand movements, by coordination problems, can also be indicative of severe impairment. People with soft signs can actually have tiny hemorrhages scattered throughout their brains. The lesions may severely impair functioning; they just can't be localized. Similarly, a person with psychiatric problems can experience a myriad of symptoms, including hallucinations, delusions, and strange feelings of being possessed. These are found in the most severe psychotic disorders. However, these symptoms, like soft signs, cannot be localized in the brain or documented biochemically through laboratory tests. They are subjective, their existence revealed only in the course of a sensitive interview. The psychiatrist cannot prove their existence.

Judges and juries are not the only skeptics when it comes to psychiatric findings. Other doctors also have trouble accepting their existence. For example, the pediatrician at Long Lane had trouble with them. When Jonathan and I worked at Long Lane, we encountered a number of adolescents who hallucinated. Several had visual hallucinations, saw things that were not there; others heard voices that frightened them or told them how to act; a few experienced both auditory and visual hallucinations.

Jonathan and I were reluctant to make use of antipsychotic medications. There are a host of reasons why one must be especially careful with these kinds of drugs. However, from time to time they were required and we prescribed them. This put us at odds with the institution's pediatrician, Dr. Delbert.

I recall Jonathan's account of locking horns with Dr. Delbert, who had precipitously discontinued the medication we had prescribed for a psychotic child. As Jonathan recounted his telephone conversation with Dr. Delbert, it went something like this:

"Doctor Pincus, I am discontinuing the Mellaril you prescribed for Andrew."

"Why are you doing that, Doctor Delbert?"

"I see nothing that leads me to think he has visual hallucinations. I hear nothing from him indicating he suffers from auditory hallucinations. I am, therefore, stopping the medication."

"But, Doctor Delbert, it is the patient, not the doctor, who sees things that are not there. It is the patient, not the doctor, who hears the voices."

As I recall, we lost that round. Dr. Delbert discontinued the antipsychotic drug and Andrew reentered his world of threatening hallucinations. Shortly thereafter he bit the thumb of a shift supervisor.

I accepted the fact that my account of Lucky's rambling, illogical thought processes and inordinate exuberance in the teeth of death would probably not impress the resentencing jury. Too soft. Too subjective a set of observations. But surely the tales of brutality and incest could not help but move them. The very fact that Lucky had never invoked them, that he had actually forgotten or repressed them, could be expected to carry some weight. After all, were it not for Frank and for his social service records, the abuse that Lucky had endured throughout childhood would have remained hidden. No one could accuse Lucky of fabricating an abusive past in order to manipulate the jury.

The attorney saved his best ammunition for last: Jonathan. Jonathan is an impressive witness. He exudes a confidence that springs from having a six-foot-two frame, a tenured professorship (then at Yale, now at Georgetown), and expertise in an area that, at least in the field of medicine, could pass as a relatively hard discipline. The running joke has always been that neurologists are superb at identifying what is wrong with a patient; they just can't do much about it. In Lucky's case, Jonathan could show the jury exactly where the lesions were that paralyzed the right side of his face and weakened the left side of his body. Using a slide of the MRI of Lucky's brain, Jonathan could even point out where his frontal lobes lost contact with the rest of his brain, preventing Lucky from exercising control over his aggressive feelings. Jonathan described for the jury how Lucky's devil-may-care attitude, so inappropriate to his current situation, reflected these neuroanatomical discontinuities. The lesions between the cortex of the frontal lobes and the rest of the central nervous system, between the self-reflective portions and the more instinctual portions of the brain, also contributed to Lucky's episodic violence. In some ways, his actions were like those of a decorticate cat. When the cortex of a cat is separated surgically from the rest of the brain, leaving only the lower centers of the brain intact, the cat may at first glance appear normal. In fact, it will purr and respond positively to affection. However, its responses to stimuli that ordinarily would cause expressions of mild discomfort or annoyance are no longer moderated by the frontal cortex. The decorticate animal, when stimulated, becomes ferocious, directing its attack at anything it perceives as threatening or uncomfortable. The fifty-four knife wounds that Lucky inflicted on the store clerk were the expression of a limbic system (that part of the brain we have in common with the denizens of Reptile Land) released from higher cortical control. Human beings, like other animals, require the modulating influences of their frontal lobes if they are to function in a civilized way. Lucky, Jonathan argued, could not and should not be held completely accountable for behaviors beyond his control.

The evidence of Lucky's neurologic damage was strong. Any judge, any juror could recognize his impairment even at a distance. They could see his contorted smile, his sunken, atrophied right eye, his awkward, lumbering gait. The physical and sexual abuse he had endured was also convincing, especially because Lucky had never tried to use it in his own defense. He never even remembered it. Never before (or since) have Jonathan and I testified in a case in which there was clearer evidence of injury to the brain and of its behavioral consequences. Never have we had better objective evidence of extreme physical and sexual abuse. If ever there were a case in which mitigating factors existed and could be demonstrated, this was it. We left the courthouse pleased with our work.

We were astounded. In spite of Lucky's lobotomized brain, his paralyzed face, and his brutal and incestuous upbringing, the jury saw fit once more to sentence him to death. As we reflected on the situation, the only comfort we could find was in our knowledge that the very lesions that separated Lucky's frontal lobes from the rest of his brain and caused him to act ferociously also protected him from appreciating the reality of his situation and kept him in perpetual good spirits.

CHAPTER 11

As I said, the route to death row for some murderers is straight and swift. In fact, for some it's a veritable speedway. Several of the murderers Jonathan and I have seen were advised by their ill-paid, ill-motivated attorneys, "Plead guilty and throw yourself on the mercy of the court." Big mistake. Courts in the South are not noted for their mercy.

Over the past twenty-five years, Jonathan and I have evaluated dozens of murderers, some on death row, some off. From a psychiatric or neurologic perspective, we can't tell the difference. I have pondered why it is that one man commits a grotesque homicide and is electrocuted, and another, who commits an equally grizzly murder, is not. Studies show that black people who kill white people are in big trouble. Even white people who kill white people have their problems. But that doesn't seem to explain it all—not by a long shot. I think a lot more has to do with lawyers.

I have a theory. With a little help from that tweedy statistician in the back row of the scientific symposium, I could probably find a mathematical formula to prove it. Forget about motive—that doesn't always seem to matter. I am also pretty sure that the mental health of the perpetrator does not make a difference. Most of the time nobody even thinks about that, certainly not the murderers. The killers Jonathan and I have met usually would rather be thought bad than nuts. It pretty much boils down to the lawyers.

The mathematical formula for who does and doesn't get sentenced to death would go something like this: Multiply the number of hours spent by the defense lawyer preparing for trial by the number of previous capital cases he or she has tried and won. Take that product and multiply it by the number of other people, such as investigators, helping out in the case. These calculations will undoubtedly lead to the finding of a statistically significant difference between murderers on death row and murderers who spend their remaining days tilling the fields or working in the shops of the very same penitentiaries in which their less fortunate peers are executed. If, in some cases, you throw into the equation some measure of the difference in motivation between the trial attorney and the prosecutor, you will wind up with p values (i.e., significance values) that would knock the socks off any statistician.

I am not talking about public defenders. They are dedicated; they certainly don't work for the money. But many—probably most—of the murderers Jonathan and I have seen were not represented at trial by public defenders. Their representation tended to be local, private attorneys. Granted, there exist a few talented, motivated, experienced, successful private defense attorneys willing to give their all, pro bono, to the representation of an indigent client here and there. But more often, impoverished defendants must settle for the skills of very junior attorneys who are just getting started or for older attorneys whose practices are not flourishing and who are looking to augment their unstable incomes with the paltry fees paid by the court. In a couple of our cases, the court-appointed lawyers themselves were under indictment for felonies. It can't be easy to give your attention to the problems of an indigent murderer when your own future to practice law is up for grabs. In one of our cases, the trial attorney was disbarred shortly after his client was sentenced to death. That lawyer could not assist himself, much less his client.

In short, few of the private attorneys who take on the representation of indigent murderers are William Kunstlers or Alan Dershowitzes or Gerry Spencers. From time to time you come across one—they are exceptions. Most of the private attorneys initially assigned to our death row cases accepted the $25 to $40 an hour offered by the court because they were having a little trouble attracting a paying clientele. Think of it this way: The Gottis of this world, not to mention the Von Bulows and Simpsons, do not select their lawyers by twirling the judge's Rolodex. As I reconsider my formula, it is obvious that it is much too complicated. Its predictive value probably would be just as accurate if years of experience, success rates, and hours and numbers of assistants devoted to the preparation of a case were simply converted to dollars.

Now for the exceptions, and there are many. Jonathan and I have had the pleasure of working with some amazingly skillful and devoted court-appointed attorneys. They were smart, well trained, experienced, and willing to put in the necessary hours. In these cases, everything I have said about time and motivation did not apply; these factors could be thrown out of the death row equation entirely. The money factor could not. These fine court-appointed attorneys had to scrounge for every dollar they needed to prepare an adequate defense. They had to beg for funds for investigators and medical experts. They were obliged to fight for every EEG, X ray, CAT scan, or MRI they got. Travel funds to seek out and interview relatives in other states were usually nonexistent.

I remember one case I worked on in Seattle in which funds played an interesting role. I was evaluating a man, Roger, who had hacked to death a woman, her small child, and their sheepdog. He did not deny the murders—he just didn't remember them. He also did not remember where, when, or how he had acquired the elaborate crisscross of long scars that covered his back. In truth, he recalled almost nothing about his childhood. If I wanted to learn anything about Roger's past, I would have to talk with his brothers.

After some pretty elaborate detective work, Roger's devoted court-appointed attorney managed to locate all three of his brothers. She also squeezed enough money from the court to transport them to meet with me at a motel near the prison where Roger was incarcerated. The plan, as I recall, was to interview the three brothers in the morning, then that afternoon have a meeting at the prison together with Roger. They would return home that evening. Perhaps when we all met together, the brothers would be able to provide clues to the origin of Roger's scarred flesh. Their presence might also jog Roger's memory. But as is often the case in this work, my meeting with the brothers got started late. Meetings with relatives of murderers are notoriously unpredictable. (Once, in West Virginia, I had to wait until midnight to start an interview with the mother of a teenaged murderer. The exhausted mother and I sat opposite each other on two queen-size beds in my $16-a-night motel room and talked until neither of us could keep our eyes open any longer.)

Last year Jonathan and I found ourselves in Louisiana, at the home of an adolescent accused of murder. We began interviewing parents, siblings, aunts, uncles, cousins, and grandparents at about ten at night and did not leave until two or three in the morning. The boy's lawyer had managed to capture this memory bank and get everyone in one place at one time; we were damned if we would push any interviews into the next day and risk losing a single cousin. I had learned about disappearing relatives the hard way. Roger's brothers taught me the risks of postponements.

I hear a lot of pretty awful stuff—it's part of the work. Sometimes, when my students are upset by information that does not faze me, I worry that I have become hardened. Stories that a decade ago would have shaken me today seem commonplace. I am unmoved. But, in the course of my interview with Roger's three brothers, during a break in the interview, a break that I requested, I went into the bathroom and wept. I have never done this before or since.

They were a motley crew, Roger's three brothers. All had histories of alcoholism, but two—David and Wesley—thanks to A.A., considered themselves recovered. The third—Albert—admitted that he still had a pretty serious problem. The three brothers, the attorney, and I sat around a small conference table in a meeting room at the motel where I was staying. I think it was a Holiday Inn. It was definitely a step up from Starke's Econo Lodge and two steps up from my $16 digs in West Virginia. I came to the point quickly: I had found dozens of long, ugly scars on Roger's back. Could any of the brothers tell me how they had got there?

Blank stares. I waited.

The first to speak was Wesley, the one I thought of as the "Preppy." He was the youngest, the best looking; he wore a shirt, striped tie, gray slacks, and a blazer (my husband's uniform). He boasted of being free of drugs and alcohol for years, and he held a responsible white-collar job in a medium-size business. In response to my question, he shook his head from side to side. "No, I don't remember any abuse, if that's what you're getting at."

I fixed my gaze on Albert, the brother who admitted he was still an alcoholic. His hands trembled. What did he remember of his childhood? Not very much. "But I don't remember much of anything," he admitted.

I turned now to David, the eldest. He was breathing with difficulty and had an oxygen tank at his side. He had been a heavy smoker and was being treated for lung disease. I tried, therefore, not to read too much into the difficulty he was experiencing catching his breath. We all stared at him—the lawyer, the other two brothers, and I—and we waited. The room was silent but for his labored breathing. Then, to my amazement, I watched as a tear filled the lower lid of his right eye, splashed over, and trickled down his cheek.

"Don't you remember?" David asked. The others looked blank. Whatever had moved the eldest brother to tears was a mystery to the younger two.

"Don't you remember Hyram?" Albert, the alcoholic, seemed to be struggling to remember. His brows furrowed. Preppy stiffened and buttoned the top button of his blazer. Now tears were running down both of David's cheeks as he fixed his gaze on his buttoned-up younger sibling. "Hyram. You must remember him . . . what he did to us, especially to you." Preppy showed no sign of recognition; he looked nonplussed. But a squint, a twist of the mouth, a grimace indicated that Albert was beginning to remember. Finally Albert spoke. His voice was low and a bit hoarse.

"I remember Hyram."

Hyram, I learned, was a sadistic older foster brother. Because of their own parents' cruelty and neglect, all four brothers had been taken out of their home. A well-meaning social worker had placed them on a farm in the country, in the care of a foster mother, Mother Carry, and her twenty-year-old son, Hyram. There, in what looked like a wholesome atmosphere, the social worker assumed the four brothers would be safe and happy. Appearances were deceiving. Mother Carry turned out to have rigid religious convictions and a temper to match. She was determined to follow her Bible and refrain from sparing the rod. Roger and Preppy got the worst of it. When the spirit moved her, Mother Carry would tie them to a fencepost and wallop them unmercifully with a leather strap. I had heard this kind of story many times before and was neither surprised nor, I regret to say, moved by it. Tales of beatings are a dime a dozen in the histories of murderers. They make me sad, but they do not make me weep.

The story was not over. David struggled to take in enough oxygen to continue. "You two remember what Hyram made us do?"

Preppy as usual looked blank, but Albert was showing a flicker of recognition. Something in David's voice fired up a long-dormant set of dendrites, triggered a memory. Albert spoke. "I remember the cattle prod." He turned toward David, who was now silently weeping and wheezing. A picture was slowly forming in Albert's brain. "It was electric. I remember how he would shove it up the ass of the calves in the barn, then turn it on and watch them jump. I remember how he made us shove it up their ass." I cringed and tightened my own buttocks.

David had not finished the story. "Do you remember what he did to us?" wheezed the eldest. A slow duet of pain commenced as the two brothers, David and Albert, took turns describing the episodes of repeated sodomy that all four brothers had endured during the years when their safekeeping was entrusted to Hyram and Mother Carry. Never before had anyone spoken of the farm and its terrible secrets. Hyram had enforced silence, threatening to do to the brothers what he did to the calves if they told. Afterwards it seemed better to forget. This was the first time during an interview I wished that the reminiscences would end; I had heard enough. But the reservoir had been tapped and there was no stopping it. The grotesque events on the farm bubbled forth, David jostling Albert's memory while Preppy looked on in a trance.

"Remember the sheep?" wheezed David.

"Yes, I remember."

Then, as Preppy stared into the distance and tuned out, his siblings recalled the castration of the sheep. David described the way Hyram, carrying the electric prod, would herd all four brothers to the field. As they stood and watched, Hyram would grab a young lamb, secure its limbs, and bite off its testicles. Then he made each of them do it.

Preppy could stand it no longer. He interrupted, "That may have happened to you. It never happened to me. I never had to do things like that." The eldest turned to his blazered brother. The tears on his cheeks had dried. With contempt, not pity, he spat out the words, "Sure you didn't. You couldn't stand doing it. When Hyram brought you out there, when you watched him, when you watched us, you threw up. That's what you did. You couldn't do it." Then from a well of pain, compassion, and contempt came the words "I did it for you." Silence. David continued. "When Hyram wasn't looking I—yes I—bit off the testicles. Then I wiped the blood on your face; I wiped it on your chin, around your lips, so Hyram would think that you had done it. I did that for you."

Silence.

"Let's take a break now, and meet in half an hour," I suggested.

I rose, left the room, and walked down the motel corridor to the ladies room. The next thing I knew I was sobbing, sobbing uncontrollably, and retching over the sink. Ten minutes later, I rinsed my mouth, touched up the makeup around my eyes, powdered my nose, stuck half a stick of sugarless gum in my mouth, and returned to the conference room for round two.

I remember little of our second session. I was still processing the images of the first. However, I do recall spending some time examining the limbs and backs of all three brothers. When Preppy's turn came, he balked at taking off his blazer and pulling up his shirt. He assured me that I would find nothing. When he finally acquiesced, a crosshatching of lines—worse than those on his brothers' backs— attested to the fact that he had been the major victim of his foster mother's wrath. The amazing thing was that he had no idea that these scars existed.

The memory of these events came to me in the context of the funding problems of court-appointed defense attorneys. My interview with the brothers took far longer than expected. As I mentioned, the more knowledgeable Jonathan and I become, the longer it takes us to complete an evaluation. There was simply no time left to go to the prison and see Roger that day. If we were to meet with Roger as a group, the brothers would have to stay over at the motel that night. This posed a problem. The court had provided travel funds for two of the brothers.

The third, Preppy, had driven there in his own Chevrolet. But our meeting was supposed to take only one day, and the court had allotted no money for motel rooms. What is more, it was a weekend and there was no way to seek emergency funds. The brothers, unwilling to foot their own bills, decided to leave.

This made no sense to me. I had traveled three thousand miles to see Roger and his brothers together. We now had three of them in one place. The next day, at the prison, we would have all four. Such a convocation might never happen again.

"If you three are willing to stay overnight, I'll pay for a room here," I offered. The brothers agreed reluctantly, and only if I agreed to pay for two separate rooms so that David's wheezing would not disturb the sleep of the other two. It was a deal.

I took out my credit card and handed it to the motel clerk. He made an imprint and handed back a charge slip for my signature. I was about to sign it when it occurred to me that writing my name on that slip was like signing a blank check. I handed it back and had the desk clerk imprint the cost of two rooms, $75 each. (Seattle, I discovered, costs lots more than West Virginia.) But it was worth $150 to me not to have to travel back and forth from New York to meet with them again. Now we could all get together at the prison the next morning. Roger's attorney arranged to have another lawyer pick me up at the motel and get me there. Wesley would drive his brothers to the prison.

Some prisons are especially unfriendly. Roger's prison opened early and evicted you at 2:30 in the afternoon, no matter who you were or how far you may have traveled to interview an inmate. Therefore, we would all have to get up early and take advantage of every minute allowed us.

The next morning, in preparation for what promised to be a long day without food, I ate my usual pre–death row breakfast. The assigned lawyer picked me up and we drove together to the prison. I wondered what Roger's reaction to his three brothers and their grotesque memories would be. Would he be like his alcoholic brother and allow himself to remember? Or would he be like Preppy and deny everything?

As we pulled into the prison parking lot I saw Roger's lawyer. She did not look happy; she looked tired and pale. I figured she must have worked late, preparing the agenda for today's meeting. She was alone. The brothers must have been delayed; or perhaps they had gone into the prison first to have a few private moments with Roger.

Neither was the case. There would be no family meeting. That morning only Albert, the avowedly alcoholic brother, appeared at the prison. If the reminiscences of the previous day had reduced me to tears, they had caused major relapses in Albert's two other allegedly recovered brothers. In fact, the memories had nearly killed the eldest, or so he thought. In the middle of the night, David complained of chest pains and was rushed by ambulance to a nearby hospital, where he now occupied a bed in the intensive care unit.

Preppy, for his part, after six years of sobriety, had anesthetized himself with Valium, washed down with generous amounts of bourbon and soda. Early that morning he dropped off Albert at the prison parking lot—his Chevrolet was last seen headed east, out of town. Albert, who could hold his liquor, having never given up the addiction, was the only family member able to keep our appointment. He met briefly with Roger, then relaxed with a six-pack in the back seat of the court-provided limo that drove him home.

As for us, the two lawyers and I met with Roger and Albert, then returned to the motel to pack up our belongings and leave. There, Roger's attorney was confronted by the management with the brothers' hefty bill for food and refreshments—mostly refreshments. Three hundred dollars of alcoholic refreshments. I was lucky. I got off easy with a bill for just $150 dollars, the cost of two rooms for one night.

Driving to the airport, I tried to console the attorney. Wasn't it better to find out now what these brothers were like? Suppose later on she had depended on them to testify in court. Suppose they didn't show up or showed up drunk. She was not consoled. Years later, out of the blue, I received a check from the state of Washington for $150, reimbursing me for my unforeseen expenses. I had totally forgotten about them. The defense lawyer obviously had not. I wonder how many hours of her time it took, filling out state forms, to get back this money. I wonder whether she ever got back her $300. I wonder if the state of Washington pays for bourbon and soda. I wonder whether Roger ever saw his three brothers again. I wonder if any of them is still alive.

CHAPTER 12

The terrain where murder, multiple personality, and the law intersect is murky and treacherous. Psychiatrists and neurologists, brave or foolhardy enough to venture there, do so at considerable risk. I certainly never intended to wade into that swamp, nor did I plan to drag Jonathan in after me. For years I had managed to steer clear of it. Only after Marie Moore's attorney pulled me into it in the summer of 1984 did I discover that it was a place, like the death chamber in Starke, from which there was no turning back.

In November 1981, almost three years before I was asked to evaluate Marie Moore, and over a year before the murder of Belinda Weeks, a twelve-year-old girl named Amanda made her way to the Elmwood Park Police Station in New Jersey. She was battered, bruised, and terrified. She claimed that she had somehow managed to escape from an apartment where she had been held captive and tortured by two people, a woman and a teenaged boy. She pointed to her raw, painful wrists and mumbled something about being handcuffed to a steam pipe.

The story sounded preposterous to the police. Her tale was dismissed as the ramblings of a crazy adolescent. The officers arranged for Amanda to be admitted to a psychiatric facility for observation. Years later a district attorney would explain to an outraged public, "They didn't believe her. . . . They sent her to a diagnostic center because they didn't believe her story."

Since the police did not believe Amanda, they did not bother to investigate her claims. The events had not happened, and you can't investigate events that have not happened.

The following spring, the New Jersey Division of Youth and Family Services received a call from School Number Sixteen. The nurse had noticed what looked like cigarette burns on a student's back, and she was required by law to report this evidence of apparent physical abuse. The student's name was Belinda Weeks. In this instance, the police decided to investigate the situation.

Why the police looked into this case and dismissed Amanda's injuries and her claim of maltreatment as fantasy has never made sense. Probably the report by an adult, especially by a nurse, called for more action than the claims of a distraught child like Amanda. In both cases, the physical evidence was there. At the clinic I now run at Bellevue for severely abused, dissociative children, we also find that the claims of children are rarely heeded. Even judges, not to mention police officers, often dismiss what children say. When I ask children with lash marks and burns on their backs and limbs, children with torn hymens and stretched, scarred vaginal openings, children with anal tags and incompetent sphincters, why they told no one of the abuse they endured, their responses are often, "They wouldn't believe me," or "I tried, but they didn't believe me." Clearly Belinda Weeks's school nurse had more clout than Amanda.

When the police investigated the nurse's report, they discovered that Belinda Weeks was the ward of her grandmother; her mother had long since abandoned her. The grandmother, though ostensibly well meaning, was past her prime and well past her ability to meet the needs of a teenager. As a result, Belinda had found a surrogate family at the apartment of a girlfriend, Debbie, and her mother. The address was 989 Madison Avenue. This apartment, the police learned, functioned as a halfway house for an assortment of wayward children and dysfunctional adults. In addition to Belinda, the household counted among its transients Juan, an adolescent Hispanic boy; Amanda, the child whose plea for help from the police had been ignored; Anna Giusseppi, a fifty-two-year-old woman; and Tony Rogers, a boy in his early teens. Debbie's mom was a sort of den mother to this motley crew.

The police concluded that the peculiar establishment at 989 Madison Avenue was not a wholesome environment for Belinda. They advised her grandmother to keep a more watchful eye on her ward and make sure she no longer visited there. It was good advice, but hardly a rule the elderly grandmother could enforce.

A couple of months later, a fifty-two-year-old woman, covered with blood, limped into the South Toms River Police Station and asked to speak with a police officer. She wished to file a complaint against a fourteen-year-old boy who, she said, had held her prisoner and abused her physically and sexually.

How could a fourteen-year-old boy keep a grown woman captive? It hardly seemed possible. Nevertheless, the woman's miserable condition, and the fact that she was an adult, forced the officers on duty to take heed. Her feet were so bloody and swollen she could barely walk. In addition to these fresh, bloody wounds, a dappling of purple, blue, green, and yellow covered her arms and legs. These bruises, each at a different stage of healing, attested to the fact that whatever maltreatment she had endured had taken place over an extended period of time. Just as the changing colors of leaves tell you the season, so the changing color of bruises tells you their age. The woman's story came out in gasps; each breath she took was painful—four of her ribs had been broken. In spite of her injuries, the woman was able to tell the police her name and the location of the apartment where she had been imprisoned. Her name was Anna Giusseppi. The address of the apartment was 989 Madison Avenue. Anna Giusseppi, like Amanda, had managed to escape from the apartment, to reach the police, and to ask for help. Before being transported to the hospital, she extracted a promise from the police officers to look into her accusations.

The very next day detectives from the Patterson Police Department went to the apartment at 989 Madison Avenue. The number of occupants of the apartment had dwindled since the last time police officers had paid a visit. Amanda, Anna Giusseppi, and one of the adolescent boys, Juan, had taken flight. The ménage now consisted only of a teenaged waif, Belinda Weeks; her friend, Debbie; and Debbie's mother, Marie Moore. The other adolescent boy, Tony Rogers, was an intermittent occupant, who moved back and forth between this apartment and his parents' home.

Since Belinda's previous encounter with the police, her condition had worsened. Her frame was gaunt and the joints of her shoulders, elbows, and knees stuck out. She was starving. Scars covered her back and limbs, and her arms and legs, like Anna Giusseppi's, were dappled with colorful bruises at different stages of healing. Trembling with fear, she told the detectives that the itinerant Tony, who had been staying at the apartment until shortly before the police arrived, had shackled her to a heating pipe, beaten her, and forced her to eat dirt off the floor. Now that the police had come she was even more frightened. Tony had vowed to hunt down and kill anyone who dared reveal to the police what he had done.

One person was in surprisingly good shape for an occupant of 989 Madison Avenue. Debbie, Marie Moore's daughter, had been spared the punishments inflicted on the others. Marie Moore herself, though in somewhat better shape than Belinda, was bruised and scarred. In fact, in the police report of June 10, 1982, Marie Moore was listed as a victim.

As for Tony Rogers, he was nowhere to be found. The police agreed to put out a warrant for his arrest. They then departed 989 Madison Avenue, leaving Belinda Weeks in the care of Marie Moore.

Between June 1982 and January 1983, when Belinda Weeks was killed, she was held captive at the apartment. She was thumb-cuffed and toe-cuffed to the floorboards and walls. She was kept naked and starved. Objects of different shapes and sizes were inserted into her rectum and vagina. Clothespins were fastened to her nipples. Then, on a cold January day, Belinda Weeks was killed. During Marie's trial, a newspaper described Tony Rogers's testimony regarding Belinda's death; he was a witness for the prosecution. The newspaper article read as follows: "In a flat voice devoid of emotion, the witness described the victim's death. He said that in January 1983, the girl—by then weak and bruise-covered—fell while her handcuffs were being removed. In the process, she accidentally hit her head against a bathtub, passed out, and apparently died. . . ." According to Marie, Tony had grabbed the frail victim by the hair and had deliberately smashed her skull against the side of a tub. But at the time of Marie's trial, no one much cared to hear her version of the crime.

According to Tony's trial testimony, Marie Moore's daughter, Debbie, demonstrated extraordinary sangfroid. Having just witnessed the final breaths of the diminutive Belinda (whose shackled body she had been obliged to step over each morning on her way out the door to school), Debbie turned to her mother and Tony and said, "I don't want a dead body in the apartment when I come home from school." Debbie could be imperious, and the other members of Marie Moore's household had learned to defer to her wishes. Even Marie was intimidated by her daughter. This particular request was among Debbie's more reasonable.

Marie and Tony did their best to meet Debbie's demand. According to Tony, after Debbie left for school, Marie went shopping. She bought a yellow garment bag and eight rolls of silver duct tape. Upon her return to the apartment, she and Tony managed to squeeze

Belinda's body into the garment bag. They then placed the garment bag inside a couple of plastic garbage bags and proceeded to wind yards of duct tape around the bulky package. Exhausted, the two finally hauled the corpse, which now looked like some sort of space-age mummy, to the attic, where they left it. When Debbie returned from school, the apartment was spotless.

But as the cold of winter gave way to the warmth of spring, the body in the attic began to decompose and fill the lower floors of the house with the smell of rotting flesh. Marie tried damage control. She and Tony did their best to tape up all of the holes around lighting fixtures through which the stench seeped. Marie purchased dozens of stick-on room deodorizers in an effort to cover the smell. She brought home bags of lye, which Tony poured over the body.

In spite of Marie's valiant efforts, the garbage bags and duct tape proved more porous than their manufacturers' claims had led Marie to believe. Eventually body fluids began seeping through the ceiling. January's freezing temperatures had retarded decomposition; now April's sunny weather hastened the process. The apartment at 989 Madison Avenue was no longer habitable. It was time to move.

Before leaving the premises, Marie and Tony took further precautions to hide the body. They wrapped the foul, leaky package containing the remains of Belinda Weeks in a blanket and tied it with string. Marie and Tony then shoved the thrice-wrapped corpse in a crawl space above a third-floor bedroom. They boarded up the entrance to the space and wallpapered over it. Now they were ready to move.

But as the body continued to disintegrate, so too did the bond between Marie and Tony. Theirs had been a peculiar relationship from the start. Tony, twenty-two years Marie's junior, had originally been Debbie's beau. Debbie and he were of an age. Exactly how Tony negotiated the transition from his classmate to her mother remains to this day a puzzle. It could not have been accomplished had Marie not encouraged it and Debbie not acceded to it.

Whatever its origins, the sadomasochistic romance between the middle-aged den mother and the barely pubertal boy could not survive the bizarre events of the previous year. Besides, Tony was now well into adolescence and his tastes in female companionship had changed. In July, Tony returned to his parents' home, and by fall he had a new girlfriend—someone closer to his own age. Now he would have nothing to do with his aging ex-lover.

Marie, in response, became increasingly obsessed with Tony. She drove around the streets of Paterson looking for him. She called him and sent him love letters. Tony did not respond. Finally, in desperation, Marie sent word to Tony that, if he refused to see her, she would go the police. Belinda Weeks's grandmother had reported her missing months before; Marie would solve the mystery of her disappearance. Still Tony kept his distance. Hell having no fury like the wrath of a middle-aged woman scorned by a child, in December 1983, approximately a year after the murder, Marie Moore called the police.

Then Marie got cold feet. When the police arrived, she and Debbie provided them with a cock-and-bull story about a murderous altercation between Tony Rogers and the missing girl. They directed the detectives to a patch of freshly dug earth behind 989 Madison Avenue. There, they declared, would be found the body of Belinda Weeks. The Department of Public Works dug up the entire back yard. No Belinda.

A day or two later, still obsessed with her young former lover, Marie again summoned the police. This time she said that she just happened to discover a blood stain in a crawl space above a third-floor bedroom at 989 Madison Avenue. She advised the police to look there for the body. And there it was. There was Belinda—wrapped, tied, stored, and putrefying where Tony and Marie had left her eleven months before. Tony was arrested. Shortly thereafter, Tony confessed and implicated Marie Moore in the murder of Belinda Weeks. The young man was so cooperative that the district attorney's office reached an amicable agreement with him. In exchange for his testimony against Marie, he would be tried and sentenced as a juvenile. He'd be out on the street before he knew it. It was a deal. For the next year, Tony worked closely with state prosecutors, preparing to testify against his former lover. Meanwhile Marie sat in jail, awaiting trial.

In the summer of 1984, Marie Moore's attorney called me and described her client. Would I do the evaluation?

I am a pushover for unusual cases. As I listened to the lawyer's description of the case, it was clear to me that this was no convenience-store robbery gone awry. What, I wondered, could make a grown woman shack up with a kid? Why on earth would they torture and kill a child the same age as the defendant's daughter and then stow the corpse in the attic?

To my dismay, the hourly reimbursement for my work would not be generous. This was unfortunate, since earnings from murder cases were a major source of support for our violence research. I have found that the fascination of a case tends to be inversely proportional to the fee available for services rendered on that case. (Now there's a formula for the tweedy statistician to ponder.) In fact, there are a few cases, like Marie's, that are so intrinsically riveting that, if the attorneys were smart, they would charge experts for the privilege of working on them. I am not talking about high-profile cases like Ted Bundy or Joel Rifkin. Serial murderers can be remarkably alike in many respects. Sometimes cases like Marie's, that are at best of local interest, prove the most intriguing.

Marie's lawyer was familiar with Jonathan's and my work on the neuropsychiatric aspects of violence, which is why she called. We had, in fact, already published findings on the prevalence of certain kinds of seizures in episodically violent delinquents. In the course of reviewing Marie's medical records, the lawyer had discovered that, in the past, one of Marie's doctors had diagnosed epilepsy. Since then, Marie had been treated with medications to prevent seizures. The lawyer wondered whether I thought that Marie's seizures might have influenced Marie's behavior.

A fierce controversy smolders and periodically erupts in the worlds of neurology and psychiatry regarding the relationship of seizures to violence. Whereas some doctors insist that directed violence during a seizure is an impossibility, others believe that episodic rages can be caused by abnormal electrical activity occurring in certain structures deep within the brain. There is little disagreement that between seizure episodes some patients with epilepsy may be inordinately irritable or even paranoid. Episodes of aggression at such times can occur.

Whatever the relationship of seizures to violence may be, (the issue is still hotly debated), epilepsy in and of itself does not cause violence. Most patients with seizure disorders have probably never hurt a flea. In cases in which murderers have epilepsy, Jonathan and I have found that invariably there is something in the perpetrators' early upbringing or in the immediate circumstances surrounding the violent act that turned the irritability and sensitivity from the seizure disorders into directed aggression. In Marie's case, the nature of the murder itself was inconsistent with an organic cause. The child had been tortured for weeks, then killed. Nevertheless, I agreed to check out the question of organic impairment. Jonathan was out of the country and unavailable, so I would have to find a different neurologist.

The remainder of my conversation with the lawyer focused on arrangements for getting me into the jail where Marie was being held. Getting into jails is only somewhat easier than getting into penitentiaries. We finally concluded negotiations and were about to hang up when Marie's lawyer, Columbo-style, shared an afterthought: "There's something else I should tell you, Doctor Lewis."

"Yes?"

"I have talked with Debbie, Marie's daughter, and with some of the others who lived with her at the apartment. They all say that from time to time she changes. Her voice gets deep, like a man's. They say that at those times she wants them to call her Billy."

"Yes?" I waited. There was a question in the lawyer's voice that she seemed hesitant to put into words.

"Well," she paused, almost apologetically, "do you think that maybe Marie has multiple personality?"

"I doubt it." My response was too quick. I backtracked. "At least I've never seen a case of it."

"Is it possible?" The attorney pressed me.

Clearly I had been too glib. "I'll check it out," I promised. As I hung up, I wondered how on earth I was to check out a phenomenon that did not exist.

The ivory tower is a paradoxical structure. Constructed, presumably, as a sanctuary in which original ideas and creativity can flourish, life within its confines can have the opposite effect on thinking. Sometimes its walls are so thick and high, its architecture so traditional, that they block out important ideas floating around in the real world outside. Ivy, as in the case of Yale, just adds to the insulation. When Jonathan and I did our training, as far as Yale was concerned, there was no such thing as multiple personality disorder; hence, within the walls of the medical school, it was ignored. Neither Jonathan nor I had ever seen a case of it.

The above statement, of course, is not true. We had undoubtedly seen cases of multiple personality disorder; we just didn't know it. We were not alone in our ignorance. In the 1960s and 1970s, hardly any reputable doctor in the United States admitted to having seen a case. Doctors who thought they had seen cases of multiple personality disorder, and who had the courage to say so, were looked at askance by their colleagues. The prevailing attitude then (as it still is in many academic centers) was that those who made the diagnosis either were kidding themselves or their patients were kidding them. The first and second editions of the *Diagnostic and Statistical Manual of Mental Disorders*, a reference used by almost every psychiatrist in America, did not even list it as a possible diagnosis.

The disorder did not, like smallpox, disappear in the twentieth century. On the contrary, patients continued to present all of the symptoms and signs now recognized as characteristic of multiple personality disorder. They continued to have auditory hallucinations, to hear voices in their heads talking to each other or telling them what to do; they felt controlled from outside. However, their symptoms, especially when found together, were considered pathognomonic of schizophrenia. (*Pathognomonic*, to doctors, means "couldn't possibly be anything else.")

Diagnosis in psychiatry, I have discovered, is as trendy as the cut of blue jeans or the length of skirts. The major difference between diagnosis and fashion is that diagnostic styles take longer to change. When Jonathan and I trained, schizophrenia was in and multiple personality disorder was out. In fact, in those days, in the United States, just about any patient with psychotic symptoms—that is, with delusions and hallucinations—ran the risk of receiving a diagnosis of schizophrenia. Today at least we recognize that patients with all sorts of other psychiatric disorders can suffer from hallucinations and delusions. Mania, depression, toxic reactions, organic syndromes—just about any serious psychiatric disorder you can name, including multiple personality disorder, can be manifested by these kinds of symptoms. But when we trained, as far as Yale was concerned, multiple personality disorder did not exist, and we could not see what we did not believe existed.

This was my mind-set when I met Marie Moore. To this day, Jonathan and I cannot be certain just how many patients we evaluated together and on our own prior to Marie Moore whose symptoms of multiple personality disorder we overlooked or interpreted as evidence of other neuropsychiatric disorders. I have a hunch there were quite a few.

The room in the jail was small, even smaller than my Bellevue cubicle. Marie Moore and I sat on opposite sides of a square wooden table and stared at each other. It was like looking in a mirror: dark eyes; dark hair, identically cut (short at the nape, long straight bangs flopping over the forehead); similarly oversized glasses through which we peered at each other. Every so often one of us would brush aside a wayward strand of hair that threatened our view. Before me sat a living example of my father's saying, "There but for the grace of God. . . ."

Marie Moore was obviously not your run-of-the-mill convenience-store robber cum spur-of-the-moment murderer. She was articulate, at times amusing. I sat back for a while and let myself be entertained. She regaled me with a tale of her trip to California when she had managed to become a contestant on "The Price Is Right." I laughed aloud as she described winning large pieces of furniture and household equipment and, since she had no home of her own at the time, having it shipped east and deposited on the front lawn of her parents' home. The evaluation promised to be a refreshing change from those of battered, befuddled Starke inmates.

"Tell me about your childhood," I interrupted, somewhat reluctantly. I had enjoyed hearing about her zany exploits, but there was work to be done.

With that, the tone of the interview changed. No longer coherent and articulate, Marie launched into a convoluted explanation of how she made the acquaintance of her housemates. Now, as I review my notes taken during this interlude, I see that I wrote, "on and on and on and on and on." I write that when a patient avoids a question, cannot stick to the point, and rambles from topic to topic in what, without my redirection, could be an endless stream of free associations. I suppose, were I a psychoanalyst, I would welcome these spontaneous digressions; I would allow them to continue and seek meaning in whatever emerged. Each association might provide important clues to the patient's feelings and experiences. However, in prisons and jails, with guards breathing down one's neck and where time is strictly limited, one cannot indulge in these kinds of explorations for very long. There is vital information to be obtained—more specifically, evidence of anything that might be considered mitigating for the accused. One never knows from one interview to the next whether or not further access to the prisoner will be granted. Therefore, at times I must consciously set aside my analytic training (and genuine curiosity) and push on. Sometimes, because of the rush, I miss things.

"I was asking about your childhood. What were your folks like?" Marie was no longer loquacious. Her sentences became halting, confused. Then, to my amazement, she completely lost track of her own words. Was it a thought, a memory perhaps, that shut down communication? She simply stopped speaking. We sat together in silence for a minute or so. Then she seemed to shake herself awake. She looked at me as though suddenly remembering my presence.

"Now I've lost you," she explained with a self-conscious smile. Since that day in 1984 I have observed this kind of lapse again and again in my conversations with traumatized, severely dissociative patients. Sometimes they simply blank out an intolerable memory. Sometimes voices in their heads caution them to shut their mouths and not trust me with their secrets. But on that day, in that year, in that prison, sitting opposite Marie Moore, I did not know what to make of what I had just observed. Now I can look back at my notes and recognize what was happening.

In those days, as I have explained, my perceptions and understanding were limited by my training. I had been taught that blocking, which is what I had just seen, was a characteristic of schizophrenia. However, the woman seated across from me who had related warmly just minutes before and had amused me with her zany exploits was obviously not schizophrenic.

I had also been taught that these kinds of lapses could be evidence of a seizure disorder. If the electrical activity in certain parts of the brain misfires—becomes irregular—it can cause discontinuities in thought and awareness. When this happens, patients cease talking and stare into space. That must be what I was observing, I told myself. I had to fit what I saw into the models I had been taught. In retrospect, Marie Moore's "Now I've lost you" had much in common with Lucky Larson's "Where'd I go?"

"Your childhood," I prompted. The remainder of the afternoon I devoted to trying to obtain a picture of Marie's life prior to the death of Belinda Weeks. It was not easy. Like Lee Anne Jameson, Marie Moore had secrets. And, like Lee Anne, she was not about to spill them to a psychiatrist she had just met. Something told her that she had to be careful. Was I really trustworthy? Was I on her side? That remained to be determined. As the afternoon wore on, Marie decided to let down her guard a bit. She provided me with a slim, cloudy window into her past.

Marie was the daughter of elderly parents. At the time that I saw Marie, they were well into their seventies. They had managed to complete only eighth grade, whereas Marie had attended college for a couple of years. Her father had held a variety of different low-paying jobs: office boy, mill worker, truck driver in his youth. Eventually, in his thirties, he had obtained a job in the shipping department of a large company—a job he held for thirty years, until retirement. He had made an adequate living and Marie recalled that from time to time he showered her with expensive gifts.

But Marie's father was not always loving and supportive. When he drank, he terrorized the household. I can hear Marie's words: "My father used to drink. He went out every Saturday night. There would be yelling. . . ." She paused, this time obviously remembering but unable or unwilling to share the pictures in her head. She continued, "He could throw things. He'd break anything in his way. I used to say to my mother, 'Can I sleep with you?'" Another pause. "He'd strike my mother."

"What would you do?" I asked.

"My mom would say, 'Don't come into the living room when he's like this.' He would break the things I got my mom."

"Did you see what happened?"

"Not really." She stared off, lost in thought. "I had an imaginary brother and sister. I would send my sister to watch."

"Uh-huh." I tried to act as if I knew what she meant. I did not.

Suddenly Marie's feelings changed, and out of the blue, she volunteered, "I loved my father more than my mother. If I got hurt I ran to my father."

"What about your mom? What was she like?" My question was gentle. I expected to hear a tender description of a long-suffering, protective mother.

To my amazement, Marie's first words were, "My mother told me my grandfather was in jail for a murder he never committed." Then, she added blandly, "She said that my grandfather cut off a man's ear. He gave him a choice of his ear or his nose." In an equally matter-of-fact voice, Marie proceeded to provide me with the name of her maternal grandfather's victim and his town of residence. So, I discovered, violence was not foreign to the maternal side of the family. No sooner had I absorbed this piece of news than Marie spontaneously shared with me the fate of her mother's sister.

"My mother's sister was murdered."

"Murdered? By whom?"

"My grandmother's best friend. She took her to the river and told her to pray and then she drowned her."

I was speechless. After a while I asked, "What happened to the woman? To the murderer?"

"She was convicted and deported to Italy" came the response. Then, as an afterthought, she volunteered, "My mother wasn't loving. No hugs. No kisses."

My efforts to verify what Marie told me about her family came to naught. Her father flatly refused to allow his wife to speak with me alone. In her husband's presence, all that the frightened, rambling, incoherent woman would say about her own mother was, "My mother was nervous. She couldn't sit still. She would pace. She was very meticulous." Shortly after conveying this information, Marie's mother turned to her husband and said, "You want to go home?" So ended our one and only conversation with each other. Marie's mother and father would subsequently testify for the prosecution against their own daughter.

It was easier for Marie to talk about the murder she had been party to than to talk about her childhood. She never denied her involvement in the murder. She and Tony had kept Belinda captive, starved her, and tortured her. The only discrepancy between her story and Tony's was whether Tony had deliberately smashed Belinda's head against the tub or Belinda had fallen accidentally.

"What was Tony's life like?" I asked Marie. Tony's household, I learned, was much like Marie's. His father drank heavily, beat his wife ferociously, and batted around his children. Marie said that Tony had scars on his body from beatings and bumps on his skull from times when his father had dropped him on his head. Tony, in turn, tortured his younger sisters. When his mother caught on, she refused to let him baby-sit. When Tony's father threatened him with a machete and a gun, Tony fled his parents' home and took shelter with Marie and her flock.

"Tell me about your daughter. Who is her dad?" I asked. To my amazement, I discovered that Debbie's father was the very same age as Marie's father, seventy-eight years old. Marie had left her home when she was eighteen and had gone to live with an old man who was later to father her child. He proved to be a violent man. Marie moved out after he tied her up, raped her, and cut her leg. A scar on her knee attested to that event. But when she left, Marie did not go far. She simply moved downstairs to a different apartment in the same house—the apartment in which Belinda was imprisoned.

Visiting hours were almost over, but I could not leave without posing an essential question. As delicately as I knew how, I asked: "Marie, most people who do things like what you and Tony did to Belinda have been through a lot. I mean sticking things into her vagina, her rectum. What happened to you as you were growing up?"

"Nothing, Doctor Lewis. Nothing at all."

"Did anyone ever bother you sexually?"

"I was raped."

"Raped? What happened?"

"I don't know. I was in my twenties. It was a stranger. My father found me unconscious. He took care of me."

What followed was definitely a leading question, but I had to ask it. "How about your dad? Did he ever touch you? Bother you sexually?"

"Nothing, Doctor Lewis. I told you, nothing." And from her earnestness, anyone would have had to believe her.

CHAPTER 13

I sat at the oversized desk in my Bellevue cubicle, encircled by white powder. The previous week, enraged at the vermin war I was once again losing, I had tossed handfuls of baking soda into every nook and cranny. Fallout from my attack was heavy. A fine white powder covered the books and papers on my desk, and I had to dust off the seat of my chair before sitting down to work. But I had won. Not a single cockroach had dared to cross my path since my offensive. And my trustworthy mouse machine buzzed away at frequencies inaudible to my ears but sufficiently irritating to rodents to send them scampering to my colleagues' offices. I would be safe behind my powdery moat for the next two years until we moved into modern quarters.

The rest of Bellevue Hospital, the Departments of Medicine, Surgery, and dozens of subspecialties that permeate modern medicine, had long since moved to higher ground down the street. They inhabited the shiny, white corridors of the New Bellevue. Their floors bore some resemblance to the polished corridors of the penitentiary at Starke. But the Department of Psychiatry remained in the old building, its move to the top floors of New Bellevue delayed by a variety of misfortunes. The latest obstacle presented itself in the shape of newly installed parquet flooring. Shortly after installation, the elegant wooden squares started to buckle, and within weeks the floors took on the configuration of a frozen turbulent stream. I recall my first visit to the area to get a look at what would be my new quarters. I made the error of wearing shoes with one-inch heels. I steadied myself by hanging onto walls or grasping the outstretched hands of colleagues wearing sensible sneakers or flats. According to inside sources, the flooring company had skipped an essential step in the installation and had glued the lovely wooden squares directly on top of the cold, damp concrete. A year or so later, when we finally moved to our offices in the New Bellevue, white linoleum and industrial-strength carpeting covered the floors and all traces of the rippling parquet had vanished.

The Old Bellevue Psychiatric Hospital, now a men's shelter, had enormous charm: high ceilings, marble inlaid floors, a double set of marble staircases leading from the entrance to the first-floor offices, an enormous wrought-iron chandelier over the stairs. So quaint were our quarters that Woody Allen had chosen the old building as a set for his period movie, *Zelig*.

I recall the morning I climbed out of a taxi at Thirtieth and First (just opposite the city morgue) to find the Old Bellevue Psychiatric Hospital and the street in front of it transformed. The lampposts at the entrance, which since I had arrived in 1979 had been crowned with bare electric bulbs, now sported elegant, turn-of-the-century frosted globes. The date inscribed on a stone slab on the front of the building, like the mileage on a used automobile, had somehow been rolled back a decade. And the assortment of compact cars with MD plates that usually could be found higgledy-piggledy along the curb in front of the hospital were nowhere to be seen. In their place I saw a museum of antique cars, neatly parked one behind the other. The population, too, had changed. In place of the doctors, nurses, patients, and vagrants usually milling about the premises stood a small cadre of men dressed in long, dark woolen coats. It looked to me at first as if a minion of Hassidim had descended on our facility to pray for a stricken friend.

I walked toward the entrance, trying not to stare. Then I saw him. Right there in the street in front of Old Bellevue, right under my office, stood Woody Allen, dressed in a luscious camel-hair coat that came well below his knees; there he was, gesturing to cameramen, who seemed to hang on his every word. I was no farther from him than I had been from Old Sparky. From that distance I could see that his hair really was red. I stood and gawked like a 1940s teenager who had unexpectedly bumped into Frank Sinatra while on her way to the orthodontist. The funny thing is, as I walked through the set no one stopped me. No one even noticed me as I made my way past the cameramen and actors, past the tall iron gates, down a short path, and into the refurbished entrance. For years my taste in winter fashion has been long, straight skirts and high boots. I must have fit in. Only when I paused at the entrance and looked back did I see the hoard of white-coated doctors, nurses, and technicians lined up behind barricades across the street in front of the morgue, staring at the spectacle through which I had walked.

That evening, when I left for Grand Central Station, I stepped out of the building and found everything gone. The bald light bulbs were back, their frosted globes nowhere in sight. The date on the building again proclaimed its 1930s vintage. The beautiful coaches had disappeared and the pumpkins with their MD plates once more lined the street. As I walked up Thirtieth Street toward First Avenue, I caught a glimpse of a long, double-decker truck headed uptown with its cargo of exquisite antique cars. Events like this kept me at Bellevue and gave me the energy to keep up the battles with my rodent co-tenants.

I blew the white powder off the notes of my first meeting with Marie Moore and studied them. What could have possessed a thirty-six-year-old woman to shack up with a barely adolescent boy? Why then would they together kidnap, torture, and kill a young girl? It made no sense. Granted, Marie and Tony were not your everyday, impulsive convenience-store bunglers; but they were no Bonnie and Clyde, either. I struggled to make sense of what the dark-haired, dark-eyed woman in the oversized glasses who reminded me of me had said. Marie's account of her life was confusing. Her symptoms and behaviors didn't quite fit any of the syndromes in the *Diagnostic Manual*. Sometimes I managed to convince myself that she was manic depressive. Her wacky excursion to California certainly seemed manic. I riffled through my notes, looking for evidence of other manic episodes or for indications that Marie fell into depressive moods. Marie had made several suicide attempts, but it was unclear what had provoked them. There were periods when Marie reported that she would not leave her bed and go to work. She did not sound depressed at these times. During these interludes she simply abdicated all responsibility for her care to Anna Giusseppi and Tony. Anna Giusseppi would dress her, feed her, pamper her, while she remained helpless and immobile. Like a young child, Marie did as she was told.

Anna Giusseppi took advantage of these times to play doctor. Daily, week after week, Anna would shepherd her helpless charge into the bathroom. There, a docile Marie would bend over the side of the tub, remove her pajama bottoms, and permit Anna to administer enemas. Sometimes, Marie said, Tony would participate; he added a sadistic touch to the already perverse procedure by taping the nozzle of the tube to Marie's buttocks and forcing her to retain the fluid until it pleased him to allow her to empty her flooded bowels. Sometimes he forced her to sit on a chair or on the floor, the nozzle still inside her. How, I wondered, did a grown woman permit herself to be so tortured, so infantilized, and so humiliated?

I struggled to manipulate these bizarre signs, symptoms, and behaviors into the framework of the diagnoses I had been taught. They did not fit. Marie's moods and behaviors were changeable. But were they really the peaks and troughs of a bipolar disorder (the term used by then for manic depressive illness)? I was not convinced. I had treated many bipolar patients and Marie was definitely different from them. Exactly how I was not sure.

I had promised Marie's lawyer that I would "check out" her alleged seizure disorder. I love to grapple with mind-brain issues, and I looked forward to exploring this aspect of the puzzle. The task, of course, would not be as much fun as if Jonathan had been involved. Nevertheless, it would be interesting.

Marie, like Lee Anne, had managed to generate a fair amount of medical paperwork over her lifetime. Ever since my explorations of Lee Anne's hospital charts, I have relished the prospect of foraging through old medical records and reports. The question to be answered was straightforward: What were the signs and symptoms in the past that made some doctors think that Marie suffered from epilepsy? Did she really have a seizure disorder?

Something bad had definitely happened to Marie Moore's brain; of that there could be no doubt. Results of a CAT scan were unequivocal. According to the neuroradiologist, the pictures revealed "a very striking pattern of frontal lobe atrophy with widening of the inter-hemispheric fissure and some lesser atrophy of the vermis of the cere-bellum." Marie had something in common with Lucky Larson: she and Lucky had both damaged those parts of their brains that are vital for judgment and the modulation of primitive impulses. Whether this damage was caused by a car accident in which Marie's head hit the windshield or it was the result of an earlier whack in the head with a baseball bat could not be established. What mattered was that her frontal lobes had been damaged badly, and that the injury was in-flicted prior to the murder of Belinda Weeks.

Marie's EEG, however, was normal. Over a decade before the mur-der, in about 1972, Marie had sought help from a neurologist. She had come to him complaining of blackouts and memory lapses. People told her of things she had done or said, places she had gone, and she would have no recollection of them. She explained to the doctor that the problem was not new. As a child she was blamed for deeds she swore she had not done. Other children's toys or clothes would be found in her room, and she would insist that she had not taken them. Playmates called her a thief.

Marie told the neurologist about episodes in adulthood when her behaviors were so violent and uncontrollable that they caused her to be fired from her job at the telephone company. At times, she said, she wet her pants. Given this picture, in spite of a normal EEG, the neurologist diagnosed epilepsy and prescribed antiepileptic medications. He tried, sequentially and together, phenobarbital, Dilantin, and Mysoline. Nothing helped. Marie continued to badger the neurologist with a variety of new and different complaints: buzzing in the ears, "passing out," numbness on one side of the body, "difficulty with her legs." Finally the frustrated neurologist decided that Marie's problems were more emotional than neurologic. His notes reflected his uncertainty about what was causing her peculiar symptoms. The differential diagnosis he gave (*differential diagnosis* to doctors means "I'm not sure what's wrong, but these are my hunches") was of "psychomotor seizures vs. psychosomatic symptoms." The doctor thereupon tried to cover all bases by renewing Marie's prescriptions for seizure medications and ever so gently steering her in the direction of a psychotherapist. Marie's daughter, Debbie, was probably a more astute clinician than all of us doctors. When Marie went into her amnesic states, Debbie would say, "Mom, you're hypnotized."

The more I studied the old records and reports, and the notes from my first session with Marie, the more I found myself leaning toward the neurologist's initial diagnosis. It looked to me as though Marie did have psychomotor seizures. They would explain her lapses, her memory loss, her violent, uncontrollable episodes, her incontinence. The normal EEG could mean nothing—half the time the EEGs of epileptic patients are normal. Her brain had certainly received more than its share of buffeting, and any injury could have created scarring and a focus of abnormal electrical activity. If the scarring was deep enough, a surface EEG might not detect the abnormal electrical activity it caused. If I squeezed them hard, I could fit almost all of Marie's signs and symptoms into the diagnostic framework of psychomotor seizures.

When I evaluated Marie Moore, my frame of reference included such diagnoses as schizophrenia, bipolar mood disorder, and psychomotor seizures. It did not encompass multiple personality disorder. My frame of reference, like the walls of the ivory tower, delimited my thinking. If I learned one thing from Marie Moore, it was that ivory towers need better ventilation and more windows.

I had another promise to keep. I had promised Marie's attorney that I would "check out" multiple personality disorder. I set aside my notes and pondered what seemed to me an impossible task: the exploration of a nonexistent phenomenon. The lawyer might just as well have told me to study the mating patterns of the phoenix or the hormonal status of Peter Pan.

In 1984, I was probably, with one exception, the only citizen of the United States above the age of twelve who had read neither *The Three Faces of Eve* nor *Sybil*. Because it took me so long to get through a book, I had to be selective. When I went on vacation and had the luxury of reading fiction, my taste ran to spy novels—Ken Follett, John le Carré. In my mind I had filed *Eve* and *Sybil* somewhere between fantasy and science fiction, neither of which interested me. Marie Moore was the other person who had not read either of those books. This fact, I hope, exhausts once and for all the similarities between us.

A colleague, with whom I shared my diagnostic predicament, suggested that I use hypnosis. He said that if an alternate personality existed, under hypnosis he or she was more likely to make an appearance. But this was a forensic case. Because patients under hypnosis are especially suggestible, findings gleaned from hypnosis are suspect in a court of law. However, even if I had wished to, I could not have followed my friend's suggestion. I did not have the faintest idea how to hypnotize someone. At Yale, when Jonathan and I trained, hypnosis (like multiple personality disorder) was out, psychoanalysis was in. Freud had long ago given up hypnosis and so had Yale.

When I trained, the Department of Psychiatry was steeped in psychoanalysis. Its influence had spread from the Medical School all the way crosstown to the Law School. In fact, Anna Freud had been invited to teach a course at the Law School. Her visiting professorship corresponded in time with the brief period of my life devoted to creating the Abstract Design Test to measure a person's capacity for intimacy. I was also undergoing the final phases of my own training analysis. I was, in short, a true believer. I even managed to wangle a place in one of Miss Freud's small seminars on psychoanalysis and law.

I was fascinated, not with what she taught but with her. She was a tiny woman, no more than five-foot-one or -two, with gray, frizzy, uncolored, and uncoiffed hair. She dressed in a cotton T-shirt and full black or navy skirt that fell to her ankles. She was not pretty. And yet from the time she walked in the door of the seminar room to the time she left, I could not take my eyes off her. There was a seriousness and intensity about the way she focused on whoever was speaking—an utter absorption that endeared her to me. She was opinionated. When she disagreed, her eyes flashed—but she did allow others to be heard.

One day I discovered that Anna Freud was being housed in an apartment above mine in the building where I lived. Mel, to whom I was engaged at the time, suggested that we invite her to tea. She declined, but her gracious note of regret remains to this day in my safe deposit box.

Though she refused my invitation to tea, Anna Freud did accept Mel's invitation to visit the residential treatment center, Highland Heights, where he has consulted for years. It is a Catholic institution, and at the time of Miss Freud's visit, the teaching sisters wore long, dark habits. They covered their heads with wimples, underneath which their faces barely showed. On the way back from the treatment center, after a morning filled with conferences and case presentations, Miss Freud turned to Mel and stated with satisfaction that this had been one of the most pleasant experiences of her stay in New Haven. "I really felt comfortable there," she remarked.

"Really?" Mel was delighted. "What pleased you most?" Mel waited to hear how much she appreciated the fact that the center was using her "metapsychological profile" to conceptualize the children's problems and needs.

"I like the way they dressed," she declared. "For the first time I did not feel out of place." Mel glanced down and saw that Miss Freud's black skirt and the black habits of the sisters were of a length.

I was not certain exactly how I was going to "check out" multiple personality disorder, but I was certain that I did not want to be alone when I did. I therefore prevailed on one of the investigators working on Marie's case to accompany me to the jail and sit in on the interview.

I opened my second interview by introducing Marie to the investigator. Then, since I was not sure exactly what to do, I allowed Marie to take the lead and I tried to follow. Her thoughts turned to the octogenarian upstairs, the father of Marie's child, Debbie.

Marie volunteered, "He used to make me have sex when I didn't want to. . . . He made me bend over and try to have sex in the rectum. . . . He had an obsession with sex. . . . He made me pose nude. The pictures are in a safe deposit box. . . . We had to run away from him." Now, reviewing the monologue, my eye rests on the words, "We had to run away from him." What did she mean by "we"? But in 1984 the pronoun flew by unnoticed.

Then, straight out of left field, she commented, "In the beginning my father didn't accept my baby." I figured that most fathers would not be ecstatic to learn that an only daughter had been impregnated by a man more than twice her age. I did not need analytic training to realize that Marie's choice of mate had something to do with the old man's resemblance to her father. On the other hand, normal women often choose to marry father figures. I refused to make too much of Marie's May-December union. Think of Picasso, of Casals, I told myself. In spite of my efforts to remain open-minded, the thought of Marie's relationship with the sadistic old man upstairs made me queasy.

Marie's thoughts turned to sex. She began to talk about other male relatives—uncles who had "made advances," "tried to kiss [her]," "asked [her] to meet [them] in hotels." One uncle, she said, "was impotent. He told us when we visited Florida." Again I did not ask the meaning of "us" and "we."

Marie tended to dismiss her mother with brief comments: "My mother was not smart." "My mother says, 'Debbie, tell your mother I love her,'" "She [my mother] was always afraid of him [Marie's father]." I already knew this. Marie's father had refused to let her mother talk with me alone, and her mother had abided by his wishes.

"Tell me more about your dad," I ventured, and at the risk of losing everything, added, "Does he have a temper?"

"He did have a temper."

"You mean when he drank?"

"No. Even when he didn't drink. He'd slam doors, get red from the neck up." Then, without skipping a beat, "My mother would tell me he wanted sex. . . . I kind of think he made my mother have sex when she didn't want to. . . . She was always afraid of him." Marie continued, "When I came back from California she had a big slash on her shoulder. For a short time she came to live with me. . . . He gets mad."

Her words had barely had a chance to register in my brain when, again from left field, came the remark, "Once he called me into the cellar and said, 'I'm a man, I have needs.'"

I tried not to sound too curious. "What did you do?"

"I told him to go to my mother."

"What did he say?"

"He said, 'She has someone else.' "

So Marie's father had made sexual overtures to her. The question in my mind was whether these whining complaints of a frustrated old man could possibly have driven Marie into the arms of a barely adolescent boy. It seemed unlikely.

Marie began to speak of Tony and his sadistic ways. She described in greater detail than I felt the need to hear how he forced her to bend over, taped her thumbs to her toes, then proceeded to administer enemas. Once started, Marie could not stop. She seemed compelled to describe the many ways Tony had tortured her and the other residents of 989 Madison Avenue.

"He would pick up a hammer and go to hit Belinda. . . . He would say, 'I have to eliminate these people.' I asked him if he meant to kill them."

"What would you do?"

"I would blank out." She paused. "I think Billy would be there."

At last Marie had given me the opportunity to try to conjure Billy. I interrupted. "Marie, how did Billy get there? What made him appear?"

"I'm not sure. Sometimes Tony would say, 'Make Billy come.' "

"Run that by me again."

"Tony. He would say, 'Make Billy come,' and he came."

I sat still, trying to figure out my next move. Finally I asked, "Would Billy talk with me?" I felt like an idiot. It was like asking if Santa would answer my letter or the Tooth Fairy put money under my pillow.

"I don't know." Obviously Marie did not think my question idiotic.

"Is it O.K. with you if I talk with him?"

"I guess so."

"Great. Let's try."

I sat back, took a deep breath, then in my most hypnotic tones, spoke the words. "Make Billy come."

I waited. The investigator waited. Marie waited.

Nothing happened.

"Let's try again," I suggested, trying to appear confident and optimistic. Slowly, distinctly I intoned: "Make Billy come."

We waited. And waited.

Nothing happened. I was beginning to feel ridiculous. Slowly, calmly, with an air of great authority, I spoke the magic words for the third time: "Maaake Billy Cooome."

We waited.

I was a failure. Nothing happened.

There was no point in keeping the investigator prisoner. Obviously I was not going to be attacked by a violent alternate personality. I was not even going to have the pleasure of making his acquaintance. He did not exist. I had kept my word. I had "checked out" multiple personality disorder. Now I could move on. I told the investigator that he could take off, smoke a cigarette, whatever. I did not need protection. He left, agreeing to return at five o'clock to pick me up and drive me home.

I spent the remaining time talking with Marie about her unusual household and about the peculiar hold that Tony had over everyone, especially over Marie. Tony had threatened to expose her, to tell the authorities about her bizarre changes in behavior. He convinced her that if they knew of her peculiar switches, Debbie—whom Marie held dearest—would be torn from her and placed in foster care.

During what I expected would be the final hour of this, our second meeting, I tried to make sense of Marie's trip to California. From Marie's medical records and from the notes of her brief skirmish with a psychotherapist, it was evident that "The Price Is Right" was but one aspect of her motivation. Marie wanted to get away. Once in California, she actually set up housekeeping. In fact, I discovered, a few of the residents of 989 Madison came west to join her. Anna Giusseppi, Debbie, and others whose names were unfamiliar had put in appearances. Even Billy showed up. Marie said that someone she called Helen had tortured her with enemas, and tried to take over her life.

Helen tied her to bedposts and imprisoned her. Helen took Anna prisoner and tried to kill her. Or was it Anna who tried to kill Helen? No, it was Marie who wanted to kill Helen. Someone tried to kill herself. I struggled vainly to make head or tail of this sadomasochistic *Alice in Wonderland*. It was like trying to keep track of a grotesque "Who's on first?" routine. I could not figure out who had done what to whom. After almost an hour, I did not much care. I asked myself how this woman managed to become entangled over and over again in the same kinds of messes. She was forever running into the very situations she attempted to flee. I recalled the words of one of my college professors when, during an especially depressing period senior year, I confessed that I couldn't wait to leave Cambridge. He said, simply, "You take yourself with you." Marie had taken herself to California. At that point I hadn't an inkling of who else within her had come along for the ride.

I was relieved when, at five on the dot, the investigator poked his head in the door and exclaimed, "Time to go!" As I straightened my papers and prepared to leave, I told Marie that I would come back and talk with her again. Now that I had squared away Billy, I could focus on real issues; learn more about Marie's moods; get a better understanding of the neurologic consequences of the many blows to her head.

I picked up my papers and pens and started to rise when, in a quiet, plaintive voice, Marie said, "Don't go. There's something I have to tell you." I sat down. The investigator would just have to wait. Marie stared at me through her thick, oversized glasses. Something was on the tip of her tongue. I waited.

After a minute or two I again started to rise. "Don't worry, Marie. I'll be back. We'll have plenty of time to talk," I reassured her.

Marie continued to stare at me, but was having trouble speaking. Her eyes, peering out through their monstrous frames, grew larger, as if they were trying to express what her lips could not. Once more, in soft, pleading tones, Marie repeated, "Don't go. There's something I have to tell you."

I remained in my seat and waited. "What is it, Marie? What is it you want me to know?" I sat, determined to allow Marie all the time she needed. A minute. Two minutes. Three minutes went by. I snuck a look at my watch. It was well past five and the investigator was waiting.

Eventually I had to accept the fact that Marie was not going to share whatever the secret was that she so desperately wanted me to know. I rose. "Don't worry, Marie, I'll be back soon." Clearly no more would be accomplished that day. I picked up my papers and walked to the door, turning my back on Marie. I placed my hand on the doorknob and started to turn it.

Suddenly from behind me came a voice the timbre of which I shall never forget. It was deep. It was male. And it had the menacing quality of a lion about to strike. Low, guttural came the familiar words, "Don't go. There's something I have to tell you." I could not move, even to turn around. My hand was fixed to the doorknob, but I could feel the fine hairs on my arms rise, and I shivered. Then slowly, so as not to ruffle the beast behind me, I turned and stared.

Marie was gone. In her place, knees spread wide apart, elbows bent, a hand on each thigh, sat a tough young man. After a second or two the young man lifted his right hand from his thigh and reached toward me. "Hulloah," came the throaty greeting. I reached for his hand and shook it.

"Billy?" I whispered.

He nodded.

I stood staring. Then I turned, stuck my head out the door, and called to the investigator, whose name and face I do not recall. "I think you'd better come back. I don't think you want to leave now. Someone has arrived."

CHAPTER 14

I know that "Billy" shook hands with the investigator. The image of Billy is crisp and clear. As for the investigator, I saw only his arm extended toward Billy. Everything else about the investigator—his face, his build, his age, even his name—is gone. Billy filled the room, his presence eclipsing all and everyone else. I saw Billy's face, his firm, set expression, his authoritative carriage. The face before me was tough and streetwise. Marie's doe eyes, round and enlarged by her thick lenses, were gone; in their place hard, dark, calculating circles sized me up. Their intensity made me glad that I had summoned Mr. What's-his-name.

"You got a cigarette?" Billy did not ask. He ordered. Mr. What's-his-name reached into a shirt pocket and produced an open pack.

"Got a light?"

A lighter appeared. Mr. What's-his-name's hand flicked it on and extended the flame. Billy inhaled deeply and the tip of his cigarette glowed.

———

Billy took a few drags on his cigarette, holding it between the thumb and index finger of his left hand.

"Do you know who I am?" I asked. I was relieved to discover that I could speak. Billy waited for me to explain. If he had been in the shadows, listening to my conversation with Marie, he was not letting on.

"I'm Marie's doctor. I'm Doctor Lewis." No response. "Her lawyer hired me to see if I could help." Billy nodded. The ball was obviously still in my court. "And this is Mr. (What's-his-name). He's also working on Marie's case." A nod. Still the ball was on my side of the net. I tried a gentle serve.

"Tell me, Billy, how well do you know Marie?" I waited.

"I know her very well" came to the slow, careful response.

"How well?" I tried to conceal my fear, but my throat felt tight and my voice was high-pitched. (My mother always told me never to play poker.) Now I decided to wait. It was a fair return and I had placed the ball well within Billy's reach.

"I know everything about her," he responded. I scampered to keep the volley going.

"How old was she when you came?"

"Young, very young."

"How young?"

"Two, three years old."

"Two or three years old." I hate when psychiatrists just repeat the last words of a patient; it seems so patronizing. But at that moment that was all I could think of to say. To my surprise and delight, my moronic repetition did not put an end to the exchange.

"Maybe four. Before she went to kindergarten."

"Great!" Now I was too friendly, too upbeat. I just couldn't seem to strike the right tone. The struggle to get things right reminded me of our efforts to dress for death row. Jonathan and I always wound up too preppy or too hippie.

I continued, hoping that in time the pitch of my voice would return to normal. "You know, Billy, I'm really glad that you've known

Marie since she was little. (Too sweet). You see, Marie doesn't remember a whole lot about her childhood. Maybe you can help."
(Better. I was relaxing.) He nodded. Billy was not about to volunteer anything. On the other hand, for the first time I had the sense
of his willingness to continue the give and take. What remained unclear was just how long Billy would play. Nor did I know if he would
ever come back once this set ended. After all, he had not been visible for months. This might be my only chance to learn what
he knew about Marie's past. Therefore, at the risk of frightening
him away and losing him forever, I asked what had to be asked.
"Marie told me that her father called her into the cellar. He said to
her, 'I'm a man. I have needs.' She also told me that no one ever
bothered her sexually. Tell me, Billy, did her father ever fool around
with her?"

The room was quiet. Billy shifted in his seat until we were face to
face, directly across the table from each other.

"Sure he did," Billy growled, but for some reason I was no longer
frightened. Something about Billy's tone or expression filled me instead with a terrible sadness.

"What happened?" I asked. Billy stared straight into my eyes, his
gaze so fixed and piercing that it blinded me to the lenses and frames
that must have been there. This man, this beast, this man-beast in a
woman's body seemed familiar. Then I knew where I had seen this
picture before. It was a word picture, but I had seen it. I was looking
at Billy, but superimposed were fragments and images of a Yeats poem
I had read in college.

> *Surely some revelation is at hand;*
>
> . . . .
>
> *A shape with lion body and the head of a man.*
> *A gaze blank and pitiless as the sun,*
>
> . . . .
>
> *. . . centuries of stony sleep*
> *Were vexed to nightmare by a rocking cradle,*

And what rough beast, its hour come round at last,
*Slouches towards Bethlehem to be born?**

A revelation was at hand, and I knew that if I listened, I too would be vexed to nightmare, not by a rocking cradle but by images of a small, helpless child. What had Billy said? Two? Three? Maybe four years old? After this revelation I would never again see people as I had before. My innocence, which sprang from ignorance, would be stripped away, and I would learn things about human beings that I had not been taught in medical school or even during my training as a psychiatrist—things most of us would rather not know.

"Sure he fucked around with her. From the time she was four years old. That's when he started."

"Started what?"

Billy sneered, "He took pencils. He stuck them in her vagina. He stuck them in her rectum."

"He did that to her once?"

"Once?" Billy glared at me contemptuously. "He did it four times a week. Her mother went to work. He stayed home. He used to put his fingers inside her."

Billy paused and looked me in the eye. I tried to look neutral, interested but neutral. I did not want to appear shocked (which I was) for fear of turning him off. I did not want to appear overinterested and risk encouraging fabrications. Billy continued. "He would give her a bath. That's when he used to take it out. Then after, he would put it between her legs. He'd say, 'Now don't tell Mama. Don't tell Mama what we did.' Then he'd give her presents. Lots of presents. Games. Toys. Money."

Billy paused.

"How about sex? Did he ever have sex with her?"

"He'd put Vaseline on his penis. He'd put Vaseline in the vagina.

*W. B. Yeats, "The Second Coming."

Put it in the vagina. She bled. She was only ten. She bled so bad she had to throw her underwear outside. She told her mama she got her period. But that wasn't her period. She didn't get her period 'til she was twelve." Again Billy paused. He was thinking, talking to himself. "Sometimes he would have sex with me. That's so's it wouldn't hurt her."

"How is that possible?" I asked. "You're a boy."

"I was in a woman's body," came the immediate response. Billy's was the logic of dreams.

"You're telling me Marie's father had intercourse with her? I mean with you?" I wasn't quite sure what I meant.

"Sure he did," the growl was deep, the words enunciated slowly as if the speaker relished his listener's discomfort.

"When she was in high school, maybe she was twelve, he came to her room. He said, 'I wanna do more for you, Marie, but you gotta do more for me.' He took her into her bedroom."

"Where was her mother?" I would prove him wrong. This could not have happened.

"Her mother? Why her mother worked. Hannibal Electronics. Her mother worked. Seven A.M. to seven P.M. her mother worked. Seven A.M. to seven P.M. she was out of that house."

Now the voice was cruel.

"So he takes her in the bedroom. Then he says, 'I'm just gonna ask you to take off your panties.' He was tryin' to be nice and gentle. Then he says, 'I'll ease on in. We'll just take the Vaseline.' "

"What happened?"

"Gradually. Gradually, over a period of time, he got in. They had intercourse." Then, as though it were an afterthought, an insignificant detail, Billy added, "You know Marie had an abortion in 1972. You know that. She went to a clinic in New York."

"Why did she have an abortion?" I asked. "Marie already had one child. Why not another?"

Billy looked at me with an expression that asked how I could be so stupid.

"She had an abortion 'cause she thought it was her father's baby."

And that is how I learned that Marie's incestuous relationship that began at age two or three or four had continued into adulthood, first with her father, then with the old man upstairs. Only her escape to California had brought it to an end. Now Marie's symptoms started to make sense. It was at the time of the abortion that Marie began to experience the blanking-out spells, the so-called seizures. Around that time she started seeing doctors, complaining of numbness, of headaches, eventually of paralysis. Something else also fell into place. Marie had told me that in 1972 she was raped by a stranger. She said that when she awakened she saw her father. She said her father had taken care of her. These years coincided with a period during which her father bought her three cars. The stakes were now higher. Toys and games no longer bought silence.

"Did her mother ever know? I mean, did she ever find out what Marie's father was doing?"

"Sure she did."

"How do you know that?"

"I know 'cause her mother used to yell at her father. She used to say, 'Leave her alone. You've got me.'" So this was why Marie's father refused to allow her mother to see me alone. This was why her mother became so confused and illogical when I tried to speak with her in her husband's presence.

Billy had said his piece. He was finished. Nowadays if something like that happened I would handle things quite differently. I would know enough to take the time to thank Billy profusely, not only for all the pain he had taken on himself in order to spare Marie but also for having the courage and trust to confide in me. But right then all I really thought about was talking with Marie and sharing with her what Billy had told me.

"Billy, it's been really good talking with you, but now I need to speak with Marie again," I explained. He had been so reluctant to come, I figured he'd welcome the chance to leave.

A look of loathing crossed Billy's face, and he snarled, "You can't talk with Marie."

"What do you mean, Billy? I have to talk with Marie."

"I won't let you."

Billy was obviously enjoying the game. He smiled, but it was not a friendly smile. It was the smile of a young Caligula just beginning to enjoy his power. I have discovered since then that violent alternate personalities are usually caricatures of evil; they are characters created in the minds of tormented children to take their pain and defend them against real or imagined enemies. They embody the strength, courage, and wiliness needed for a tortured child to survive. They also keep the memories. Nevertheless, they are the constructs of child minds. But then, in 1984, I saw only a fierce, intimidating young punk, determined to thwart my efforts to help Marie.

Billy was not done with me. He had an uncanny way of knowing exactly how to unsettle me.

"You know I could kill her."

"What did you say?"

"I said I could kill her. I could kill Marie."

"What do you mean?"

"I could make her take pills. I've done it before." He paused and smiled. Marie had told me of her suicide attempt with phenobarbital. "I could make her hang herself," he threatened.

Now I was scared. "Oh, Billy, please don't do that. Please promise me that you won't do that," I pleaded. But Billy refused to promise.

"Billy, at least let me talk with Marie," I begged. Billy was adamant. I had conjured the malign genie and now could not stuff him back into his lamp. In desperation I tried the technique Marie had taught me. Over and over again I chanted the words, "Make Marie come. Make Marie come."

I watched with relief as the face before me slowly changed, softened; Marie was back. She removed her glasses and, like a small child, rubbed her eyes with her fists, as though she were awakening from a nap.

Visiting hours were over. We had overstayed our welcome. As a guard ushered me from the room, I did the best I could to explain to Marie what had transpired during her absence. She had obviously been absent, dissociated during my talk with Billy. When I asked her to promise not to kill herself, she looked puzzled. Why would I make such a request? She had no intention of killing herself. There was no time to explain Billy's threats. Not long thereafter I was told that guards discovered a sharpened plastic implement in her cell and feared she might be planning to harm herself.

On the way home in the car, seated next to the investigator, I reflected on the events of the day. I was satisfied. I had kept my promise to Marie's attorney; I had "checked out multiple personality." I was also grateful for the company of Mr. What's-his-name—not so much for protecting me but rather for bearing witness. Without him, I was convinced, nobody would believe me.

How could I expect a judge and jury to believe in a phenomenon I, a psychiatrist, had so recently questioned? The only witnesses to Marie's tragic childhood were her parents. Marie's mother was a potential resource, but her father refused to allow the woman to speak with me alone. There were, of course, several witnesses to Marie's dramatically changeable demeanor and behavior, but the motley crew from 989 Madison Avenue was not about to come to the aid of the fiendish woman who had terrorized them.

Today, a decade later, I know what I should have done. Alternate personalities leave evidence of their existence all over the place. Jonathan and I have been able to trace clues of multiple personality disorder all the way back to early childhood. Teacher reports, social service records, medical charts, letters to friends and relatives, journals, diaries, drawings—all are pieces of the puzzle that, when fitted together, reveal the picture of a divided, often fragmented mind. School records attest to widely fluctuating academic capabilities. Homework samples from the very same week or month of the child's schooling look as if they were the work of different students. Handwriting in journals and diaries can vary markedly from one entry to the next. Sometimes it looks like the writing of a "righty"; sometimes its slant suggests that a "lefty" wrote it. Styles of drawing differ. One day drawings appear to be the work of a preschooler; the next day they show the sophistication of an adult. Driver's licenses, hospital admissions, job applications, and letters to friends and family reveal different signatures, even different names. These constitute the evidence needed to show that multiple personality disorder existed years before the diagnosis was even considered. They are proof that the interviewer did not create the disorder.

Old medical records can be gold mines of information about abuse: inexplicable accidents and injuries; vague complaints of illnesses for which no causes can be found; repeated urinary tract infections; rectal pain and bleeding. (As I write this I think back to Lee Anne and wonder just how much Jonathan and I missed.)

Friends. Acquaintances. Employers. When families are mute, sometimes near-strangers can help; they have observed the memory lapses, the changing demeanors, the inconsistencies. We once saw a patient with multiple personality disorder who, in an alternate personality state, suddenly took off for Las Vegas with a girlfriend of the moment. No one, including his boss, knew where he was. A week later, dressed in his usual lab coat, he returned to work, oblivious to the events of the prior week. The man was flabbergasted when his boss fired him on the spot. In the patient's mind, he had never missed a day. Employers tend to remember these kinds of episodes.

In short, there are numerous ways a sophisticated clinician can document multiple personality disorder objectively. Unfortunately, in 1984, when I saw Marie, not only was I unsophisticated, I was downright ignorant.

The first thing I did on returning to Bellevue was go to the library and look up what had been written on multiple personality disorder and who had written it. I found that the number of clinical investigators whose work had passed the scrutiny of reviewers and whose papers had appeared in the scientific literature could pretty much be counted on the fingers of one hand. I called them. Two returned my calls. The secretary of one of these gurus informed me that for $150 her boss would return my call. Clearly his expertise was in demand. I left my number. He did call back. To date, and it is now over ten years, I have not received a bill. If two can be considered a consensus, then there was a consensus: judges and juries were not likely to believe what I had witnessed unless they saw it for themselves. Both consultants were adamant. An interview with Marie/Billy had to be videotaped and shown in court.

I presented the advice I had received to the attorneys. They were adamant. Videotaping was out of the question.

"Why?" I asked.

"Why? Because Marie might incriminate herself," came the answer. I was dumbfounded. Here they had a client who had already admitted to participation in the murder—she had to admit to it in order to mount an insanity defense. Now her lawyers were worried about self-incrimination? The very reasoning behind this decision sounded insane to me.

The attorneys could not be budged. There would be no videotaping. How, I asked myself, was I to present to the jury in words a phenomenon that even I had not believed existed until I saw it? It could not be done, and I said so. Eventually I would come to recognize the limitations even of visible, tangible, objectively verifiable evidence. By 1986, I would realize that videotapes could be insufficient proof. Other psychiatrists had to see for themselves a mental condition that they were convinced was bunkum. In Marie's case, all I wanted to do was videotape, and her lawyers said no.

Very few mental illnesses can be confirmed by laboratory data. There are a few rare ones for which biochemical tests clinch diagnoses. For example, acute intermittent porphyria, the illness thought to be responsible for George III's episodic madness, could today be confirmed in a biochemistry laboratory. Some forms of mental retardation can be demonstrated through biochemical tests and chromosomal studies. But for the most part, those psychiatric disorders that fill our mental hospital beds—those categorized now as schizophrenia—have defied intense efforts to document their biologic underpinnings.

Multiple personality disorder, too, has no laboratory test to validate its existence. The illness, however, is especially interesting because different personalities or personality states tend to have different physiologic responses. Temperature and blood pressure may vary; different personalities may have different visual acuities; there have been reports of personalities with different allergic responses; performances on certain psychological tests may vary markedly, and even encephalographic recordings of brain wave activity may differ. However, fascinating as these findings may be, they are still research findings. They are considered experimental and not yet accepted as diagnostic proof of the disorder. Trained method actors, adopting a variety of roles, have been able to call forth or duplicate many of the physiologic changes that occur spontaneously when patients with multiple personality disorder switch from one personality state to another. Thus, none of these physiologic tests could be used to document Marie's condition.

Neurologic testimony is always more believable than psychiatric testimony. You can see the brain; the mind is invisible. Fortunately, in Marie's case, the jury would be able to see her damaged brain. They would be provided the next best thing to X-ray vision: CAT scan pictures. These pictures showed atrophy of both frontal lobes—graphic evidence that the parts of her brain on which she had to rely for judgment and modulation of sexual and aggressive drives were in poor repair. If Marie's neurologic deficits did not explain or excuse her acts, at least they might be accepted by a jury as mitigating her responsibility. Mitigating factors are the difference between a life sentence and being condemned to death.

Marie's seizure history was also important. If any of her lapses of consciousness, her long periods of memory loss, were the result of seizures rather than dissociative states, then perhaps a case could be made that she was in an altered state at the time of Belinda's murder. However, Marie's EEGs in the past were always normal. The outside possibility existed, however, that the previous EEGs had been performed between seizure episodes. The lawyers decided to obtain a forty-eight-hour electroencephalogram. Maybe at some time during this lengthy procedure her brain waves would go awry.

I was delighted with this decision. I could meet once more with Marie, elicit Billy, and determine whether, when Billy materialized, his brain waves differed from Marie's. It would not prove Billy's existence. As mentioned, actors can modify their own brain waves. It would still be an interesting finding.

The forty-eight-hour electroencephalogram was conducted in a hospital, which is where my third and final interview with Marie took place. No seizure activity was found. Unfortunately, the strip of paper containing all of the electrical activity of the brain recorded during the period of time when Billy emerged was inexplicably lost or destroyed, and those data were never analyzed.

When I entered her hospital room, the Marie Moore I saw looked like no one I had ever seen before. The metamorphosis was not because another personality had emerged. Rather, a garden of electrodes had sprouted from Marie's head. The combination of Marie's oversized glasses and her electrical antennae produced to my eyes a cross between an extraterrestrial and a surprised grasshopper. I tried not to stare. Or laugh.

We had work to do. As usual, it was best to begin with something relatively nonthreatening. I opened with questions about the real-life characters that populated Marie Moore's 989 Madison Avenue world.

"Tell me about Tony," I started off. "What was he really like?"

"Tony?"

"Yes. Tony."

"He was slow. He was really slow."

She thought for a moment. "He could only print. I had to teach him how to write."

Another pause. She seemed to be counting in her head.

"He repeated eighth [pause] twice."

So Tony was no genius, or if he was, it didn't show academically.

Then, unsolicited, she volunteered, "He threw a chair at a teacher."

"How about his family? What were they like?" I asked.

Expressionless, as though catching me up on the latest episodes of a boring sitcom or the new characters in a soap opera whose first appearances I had missed, Marie proceeded to provide me with a précis of Tony's family life. Marie was a woman of few words.

"Tony's brother Mario tried to rape him."

"The father beat him with a belt."

"Sometimes they were undressed."

"The father had weapons. A machete."

"The father had a handgun near the bed."

"The father was in jail for something."

"That's what the mother told Tony."

"That's what Tony told me."

Not the flicker of an eye, no hint of a grimace, no pause or fleeting hesitation suggested a trace of anxiety. The words emerged from Marie's mouth devoid of inflection. She could have been reading a grocery list: avocado, celery, American processed cheese slices, rape, belt, machete. . . .

On and on she droned.

"Tony'd beat up his little sister. He'd beat up Louisa."

"He'd lock Louisa out of the house. He'd lock her out in the cold."

"The mother was afraid to leave Tony with Louisa."

"Tony's mother said she hated to leave Louisa in the house alone with Tony."

"I met the mother."

"She told me that."

The grocery list continued, but now Marie was telling me about Tony's mother. It was as though we had turned down the next aisle of the supermarket: soap flakes, detergent, Mop 'n Glo, rape, beat, lock out in cold. . . .

"Tony had bumps on his head."

"Tony said his mother deliberately dropped him on his head when he was little."

No wonder Tony "repeated eighth twice," I thought. In her unrelenting monotone, Marie provided a picture of the grotesque household out of which her juvenile paramour had crawled.

This was as close to Tony as I would come. I would never be allowed access to him or his family. He was going to be the state's prime witness. But Marie had given me a pretty good sense of the forces that had propelled Tony toward the apartment on Madison, and the enticements or stimuli that kept him there. Had the helpless Belinda taken the place of Francesca or Louisa? When he tortured Belinda and Marie and Anna Giusseppi, did he become his brutal father—the man who, Tony told Marie, beat his mother and threatened Tony himself with a gun and a machete? Certainly the intensity of Tony's maliciousness, his relentless persecution of the members of his surrogate family, far exceeded anything Marie and the others might have done to invite this degree of brutality.

Tony brought his fury with him when he moved into 989 Madison Avenue.

Marie continued, sounding ever more like a robot. I began to feel as though each time I asked something I had pressed "play" on a tape deck or answering machine. I took off my glasses and sat for a minute or two, elbows on my knees, hands over my eyes, trying to figure out what was going on. In our first meeting Marie had been lively. I had laughed at her story of the quiz show, at the mental picture of a washer-dryer and breakfront on her parents' lawn. Now her voice was dead. It was as though Marie could talk with enthusiasm about anything—anything, that is, that did not matter to her. As emotions stirred within her, her voice lost all trace of feeling. The events that she described had been stripped, separated from any emotions that might once have been attached to them; information and feelings had been dissociated, one from the other. When Marie did not retreat entirely from painful events and memories, fall into a waking sleep, and allow Billy to handle them, she simply split off the feelings from the events. I asked for pictures of flesh-and-blood people in her life. She showed me skeletons.

"Tell me about Anna Giusseppi."

"Anna Giusseppi." Marie repeated the name. The computer registered the name; a pause while it sought the data file.

"Anna Giusseppi was born October 4, 1923."

"Anna Giusseppi was very slow. She had no high-school diploma."

"When Anna Giusseppi's mother died, Anna Giusseppi was hospitalized at Middletown."

"Anna Giusseppi was hospitalized when she was twenty years old."

"Anna Giusseppi's sister Rosetta says, 'If Anna's nervous or peculiar it's 'cause she's been through a lot.' "

"Anna had shock treatment."

"Rosetta said she had shock treatments."

"Anna Giusseppi's father was a drunk. He beat her mother."

"Anna didn't like men."

"Anna said, 'Men hurt you.' "

"Anna had hallucinations."

"Anna thought she saw her mother."

"Anna said, 'Oh, Ma, you're here. Ma. Ma.' "

I stopped asking questions. Again, I placed my glasses on the table and sat, my hands over my eyes, pondering the lives of Marie's entourage, the battered brood that sought shelter under Marie's roof.

For years Jonathan and I had been puzzling over the question of how the mothers and fathers of our incarcerated delinquents and condemned murderers found each other. We had pictured encounters on shuttle buses transporting visitors from bus stations to prison yards; mixers between male and female wards of state hospitals; chance meetings at police precincts, while awaiting fingerprinting. But what forces of nature or society could have conspired to draw together this benighted group of castoffs? I reviewed in my mind what I had learned about each: Belinda, orphaned, in the care of an aged grandmother who lacked the energy to cope with a teenager; Tony, his violent father and brothers, his victimized mother. Anna Giusseppi, her drunken father, the death of her mother, her psychosis, her shock treatment, her sister's cryptic, "she's been through a lot." And, of course, Marie. Marie who practically from infancy knew nothing but pain, sexual abuse, and humiliation; Marie, who had run from her father to the bed of a sadistic man her father's age. Chance may have brought them all together; I now understood what kept them together. Long before any of them had met each other, torture and humiliation had become a way of life; for all of them pain and degradation were an old pair of curiously attractive but excruciatingly uncomfortable shoes. Whenever they slipped into them they hurt, and yet they could not bring themselves to get rid of them. Over and over again, unaware of what they were doing or why, they reinvented the only lives they had ever known. For each, Marie provided a home away from home.

In spite of my efforts to think scientifically and avoid making inferences I could not prove, in order to understand the situation I found myself drawn back to my psychoanalytic roots. Freud had described the way we all tend to repeat or perpetuate the relationships we know. He called it a repetition compulsion. He labeled it, but could not explain it. We drag out the old game board, choose the most familiar pieces with which to play, and arrange and rearrange them in familiar patterns. Sometimes we find ourselves playing against ourselves. If we have been tortured as children, we do not merely root for the opposition; we become the opposition. We, the aggressors, try to beat ourselves at our own game. No one knows why we do this, but this is what we do.

And so the forlorn, sadomasochistic clutch of misfits at 989 Madison Avenue stuck together. They could not tear themselves away from the place or from each other. They fulfilled each other's needs, alternating roles. They took turns. Today I am my abuser; you are the child; you are me. Tomorrow I shall be the child; you will torture me. Over and over they replayed the events of childhood as if these painful reenactments could somehow exorcise the past and set the players free. Even Belinda, tortured by all, and prostituted to Marie's aged common-law husband, could not stay away. She kept coming back. Eventually she was held captive, thumb-cuffed to the floorboards. But the others stayed by choice; they stayed until the games got too rough or the apartment began to stink.

As for Marie, she too floated from one role to the next: now a nurturing mother; now a cruel tormentor. The residents of 989 were made for each other.

I do not remember whether I summoned Billy or whether he came on his own. Suddenly he was there in the hospital room. My notes state in large print: BILLY ARRIVES!

At our previous meeting I had an agenda. What did Billy know about Marie's childhood? What memories did he keep? What did Billy do for Marie? At this, my third meeting with Marie and second and final encounter with Billy, *he* was determined to set the agenda. There were things he wanted me to understand. First and foremost, he wanted me to know how powerful he was. In retrospect I can appreciate how vulnerable Billy felt after our first meeting. Until Billy and I had spoken to each other, no one outside the bizarre little household at 989 Madison Avenue had met him; or if they had, they did not know it. No one even suspected he existed. I had suddenly put an end to that secrecy. As Billy saw it, I had jeopardized everyone's safety. Secrecy and safety, I have learned, are synonyms to protector personalities. Billy was taking no chances. He would scare me into silence.

"My business is violence," he began, puffing himself up like a superhero balloon at a Macy's Thanksgiving Day Parade. The more Billy tried to intimidate me, the crazier he sounded.

"I am the Mafia," he declared. That would show me.

"Really?"

"I have guys who work for me," the voice was streetwise, menacing.

"Oh?"

The first time I met Billy, he frightened me. This time I was curious, not scared. He was not a threat, but was, rather, a two-dimensional cartoon of evil. Billy was the construct of a frightened child's mind. Marie's brain at two or three or four years of age had fashioned him, brought him into being to protect her from her father. He had not matured much since then.

Over the years Jonathan and I have met a lot of Billys. What I mean is that we have made the acquaintance of many protector personalities; they are entities called forth in early childhood by tortured children unable to endure their pain alone. How these beings are created, no one really knows. It looks to observers as though certain chronically abused children self-hypnotize; they remove themselves from the situation. They see what is happening, but do not feel it. It is as if it were happening to someone else—someone else feels the pain and is strong enough to endure it. In time that someone else becomes a protector. Over the years, we have come to appreciate the ambivalent relationship that exists between protector personality states and the helpless children who created them. These protectors boast, "I took the pain." Then in the very next breath, they threaten to hurt, maim, even kill the "wimp" whose pain they endured. They are contemptuous of the child they saved. It has taken us a while to understand this problematic relationship. Now I can see that the first time I met Billy, when he threatened to kill Marie, he was giving me a crash course in the psychology of protector personality states. I was too scared and inexperienced to catch on just then.

"I have ten men under me." Billy was determined to impress me, but the more he boasted, the crazier he sounded.

"You do?"

Billy continued, "Uncle Ricciola, he got me in the Mafia. He was in the Gambino family."

It sounded to me as though Billy or Marie or someone were pulling my leg. But the speaker was deadly serious. Billy was providing me with a picture of the imaginary universe that he inhabited when Marie was out in the real world. Billy's was an underworld in every sense of the word. While Marie lived out her tortured days in the apartment with Debbie and Belinda and Tony and Anna Giusseppi, and the others, Billy led a parallel life surrounded by a hierarchy of gangsters and thugs.

This kind of imaginary or delusional system, so new to me in 1984, I know now to be commonplace. Over the past decade, Jonathan and I have encountered many patients whose protector alternates function somewhere beneath conscious awareness, within the hierarchies of fantasy worlds. The nature of these inner worlds—their structures, their complexities—are bounded only by the limits of the human imagination, by the individual's singular frame of reference.

Time was running out. Now *I* had an agenda. I had to know more about the murder of Belinda Weeks if I were to be of any help to Marie or Billy or anyone else. I interrupted Billy.

"Billy, I have a question. Does Marie know all about the murder?"

"No." The response was immediate. I sat very still and listened to Billy's account of the murder. He enjoyed describing it.

"Tony said he would starve Belinda. But Marie tried to sneak food to her. When Tony found out she did that, he punished Marie. . . . November, December, January. That's when the heavy beating started. That's when the burning started. He set fire to her. . . ."

Whom was Billy talking about, Marie or Belinda? Maybe both. Both had started out as sex partners and ended up as victims. This explained why, when the police visited 989 Madison Avenue, they listed Marie *and* Belinda as victims. In the end, Tony killed Belinda and came to loathe Marie. What, I wondered, was Tony's relationship with Billy?

"Tell me about the murder." I tried to keep my voice even and as unemotional as Marie's had been when she gave the grocery list account of her housemates. I did not want to stop Billy, just focus him. I waited, hoping my question had not put an end to his revelations.

He continued. "That morning Belinda was handcuffed to the kitchen floor. Marie woke up early. It was cold. She went to the kitchen. She said, 'Belinda.' There was no response. . . . Marie took a barrette and opened the handcuffs. She got a blanket. . . ."

Then, according to Billy, Tony woke up. Annoyed at the disturbance, he marched into the kitchen and became enraged at the sight of Marie, leaning over the pitiful girl. Belinda was his to do with as he pleased. Tony grabbed Belinda by the hair. Now Billy's voice was excited.

"He dragged her toward the bathroom. He stomped on her chest. He stomped on her face."

"What did Marie do?" I asked, careful to avoid any expression of reproach.

"Tony pushed Marie. Marie fainted. That's when I came." The last sentence was said with pride. Billy was the strong one. He wasn't squeamish like Marie.

"What happened next?"

"Then? Then Tony flung the kid against the tub. Even after he stomped her face, he flung her against the tub."

"And Marie?" I interjected, "What did she do?"

"Marie was gone. She disappeared." I was not surprised at this piece of news. Marie knew how to remove herself from ugly situations. She had had lots of practice.

"I tried to get Marie back, but it didn't happen," Billy smirked contemptuously. There he was, Billy, left to clean up a mess Marie could not tolerate.

In the end, it was Billy, not Marie, who went to the hardware store for the duct tape and garbage bags. Together the men, Tony and Billy, wound the corpse, lugged it upstairs, and stashed it in the attic. They had become fast friends, partners in crime. They didn't need Marie or Belinda. Marie could die, too, for all they cared.

"Where was Marie during all of this?" I asked.

I never got an answer. Billy had shared all he intended to share. He had made clear that Marie did not participate in the murder or its aftermath. I wondered where she was. Asleep? In a world of her own? Or had she been watching from some safe place in the wings? If so, did that make her an accessory to the crime?

Regardless of her role, I knew it would be hard for a jury to empathize with a tormented, divided soul like Marie when a fourteen-year-old girl had suffered so hideous a death while held captive under her roof. Could a jury separate Marie's acts from Billy's, her responsibility from his? Would they even believe in

Billy's existence? Had I not met Billy, I surely would not have believed it.

Direct testimony is usually straightforward. The defendant's lawyer asks all the questions that you want to be asked. There is little tension and, hence, it is rarely memorable. I remember little of the first hour or so of my testimony. It must have included a review of my credentials and an account of my interviews with Marie. I have a vague recollection of explaining to the jury the phenomenon of multiple personality disorder and providing a description of Marie's personality states. What followed I recall vividly. Those two or three minutes have the clarity for me of Billy's first appearance.

"Doctor Lewis," Marie's attorney asked, "was Marie Moore ever sexually abused?" I paused and considered the question. How could I answer this question accurately? I didn't know for sure what had happened to Marie. I knew only what Marie's protector, Billy, had told me. That is what I would have to tell the jury. I began:

"Marie has no memory of having been abused sexually. She denies it. However, according to Billy, Marie's father abused her sexually. Billy said that when Marie was about four years old, her father used to stick pencils in her rectum and vagina. He did it several times a week. Later on, when Marie was ten . . ." I got no further. In a flash the mousy, bespectacled Marie jumped up from the defense table where she was seated and shouted, "That's not true!"

What happened next is a blur. I could see people around Marie, trying to quiet her. I could hear the judge's gavel as he tried to call the courtroom to order, then cleared the court. A recess was called, guards circled Marie, and she was led out of the courtroom. Marie had demonstrated for the jury better than any videotape the phenomenon of multiple personality disorder. Marie had no memory of what Billy said had happened to her. Decades of stony sleep had protected her from the knowledge.

Either the jury did not understand what they had seen or they did not care. They found Marie Moore guilty of the murder of Belinda Weeks. They sentenced her to death. Tony completed the remaining months of his sentence and was set free.

CHAPTER 15

"At approximately 7:00 A.M. on October 31, 1981, the nude body of the victim was found on the floor of her room in St. Francis Convent by a nun who had noticed the deceased missing at chapel earlier that morning." So reads the opinion of the Potter County Court of Appeals. The opinion continues: "Another nun testified that she passed by the deceased's open bedroom door at midnight the night before and heard her breathing. She further testified that although there was blood on the deceased's face when the body was found that morning, the nuns did not suspect foul play and had the body removed to a funeral home."

So unthinkable was the crime—the murder of a nun—that when the sisters of St. Francis saw the body, naked on the floor of her tiny cubicle, they could not grasp what had happened. They took it for granted that Sister Catherine had died of natural causes. So heinous was the crime that the appeals court could not find it in its heart to spare Johnny Frank Garrett's life, even though he was but seventeen, a juvenile, at the time of the murder.

Five years after the murder, in June 1986, Jonathan and I would come to Huntsville, Texas, to study juveniles condemned to death. There we would examine Johnny for the first time. And like just about everyone else who had seen Johnny before us, we would fail to understand the murderer or grasp the forces that came together that night and generated the grisly act. What we thought we saw was a schizophrenic fellow, convinced that he had been placed on earth to save the Native Americans from extinction. Johnny hallucinated; voices whispered reassurances. He, Johnny, like the braves of old, would be saved from death. Sometimes Johnny's Aunt Barbara, long dead, came to him in his cell and soothed him. Suddenly she would appear; just when he felt all was lost, he would find her perched at the foot of his cot. Gently she would approach him and breathe words of comfort in his ear. "You're not gonna dah, Johnny. Ah won't let that happen."

Johnny Frank Garrett heard voices; he saw visions; he had delusions. Jonathan and I agreed that Johnny was psychotic. This was also one of the few instances in which our diagnostic opinion was in agreement with the prison staff's. Even the prison psychiatrist called Johnny schizophrenic. We have learned over the years that you have to be really crazy to be called schizophrenic by a death row psychiatrist.

Johnny was also brain damaged. There was no question about that, either. According to medical records, his brain had been oxygen deprived at birth. The number of functioning neurons that remained under his calvarium after his traumatic entry into the world had been diminished further by a series of injuries. By the time Jonathan and I met Johnny, there was no way for us to distinguish the relative effects of birth trauma and the effects of repeated blows delivered to his head by a sequence of unfriendly stepfathers. Thus, in addition to his psychosis, Johnny had the impulsiveness, labile moods, poor judgment, and paranoia of a prizefighter who has weathered too many rounds. But as we were to discover many years later, neither his psychosis nor his brain damage accounted entirely for Johnny's murder of the aged nun in the Convent of St. Francis. However, in 1986, we thought they did, and we said so.

Johnny was a research subject, but his deficits were so severe and pervasive that I felt it my duty to furnish his lawyer with a clinical report of his condition. Johnny was the sickest death row inmate I had ever examined. I figured that his lawyer would be able to make use of our findings in the course of the appeals process.

I felt confident about my grasp of Johnny's neuropsychiatric condition. But what never quite made sense to me, what continued to puzzle and trouble me long after our return from Huntsville, was Johnny's choice of victim. Had Johnny killed a man—someone who reminded him of his brutal stepfathers—I could have made sense of his crime. But why kill a harmless old lady? And then there was the rape to explain. What would make a seventeen-year-old boy sexually assault a seventy-six-year-old nun? I just couldn't see it.

The nuns, who at first attributed Sister Catherine's unexpected demise to a heart attack, and we doctors, who at first attributed Johnny's behaviors to a combination of psychosis, brain damage, and batterings by some less than nurturing stepfathers, were doing exactly what we all do every day of our lives: we see what we expect to see. With a little ingenuity we manage to fit new data into old mind-sets. Anything that doesn't fit we filter out as extraneous noise.

When an event is frightening and bizarre, when it challenges our notions of reality and assaults our sensibilities, it blinds us. We block it out. Had we paused, reconsidered—had Jonathan and I taken a second look—we might have begun to see the picture. When we don't even believe that something is possible or that it exists, we fail to see it at all. That is exactly what happened to us in the case of Johnny Garrett.

The nuns were quicker than we to rectify their error. The body of Sister Catherine was already at the funeral parlor, and plans for a requiem mass were well under way, when the nuns first began to suspect foul play. A couple of facts did not sit right with Sister Agnes. She paused. Reconsidered. If Sister Catherine had succumbed to a heart attack, she reasoned, why was so much blood splattered about her room? And why was she naked? Surely, had she been on her way to the bathroom, she would have taken the time to put on a robe, no matter how urgent her calling—Sister Catherine was known for her modesty. Sister Agnes, a ruminative soul, was reluctant to dismiss her friend's sudden death so easily. She paced the convent halls. She stopped from time to time to gaze out the windows and reflect on the horror of the previous night. Sister Agnes was, therefore, the first to notice the broken pane of glass and the cut window screen in the recreation room. Someone had broken in. Her ability to wait, reflect, take a second look at an event that at first had seemed simply an act of God brought to light the murder.

Years would pass between the time Jonathan and I first examined Johnny and our pausing to take a second look. The first time we saw Johnny we were in a hurry. There were seven condemned juveniles in Huntsville who had to be examined. We had no time to sit around and think. Besides, in Johnny's case, the clinical picture was pretty obvious. Johnny was schizophrenic. Sadly, we had not yet learned to practice what we preached. For years we had been teaching doctors in training about the dire consequences of being in a hurry. We had stressed the importance of asking questions thoroughly, in many different ways and contexts. We had taught our students the extraordinary responsibilities inherent in evaluating delinquents and criminals, how easy it was to miss a diagnosis and dismiss a disturbed inmate as a mere sociopath. And yet Jonathan and I allowed ourselves to hurry.

It did not take a psychiatrist to recognize that this crime was not the work of a brilliant criminal mind. Minutes after the police arrived at the convent, a blood-covered serrated knife was found beneath the bed of the deceased. Not long thereafter, a second knife, the kind usually used to cut tough meat, was discovered outside, in the convent driveway beneath a broken window. Its condition suggested it had been used to cut the screen. Fingerprints on the headboard of Sister Catherine's bed matched those on the bloody knife found under the bed and on the handle of the knife beneath the window. Whoever had visited Sister Catherine during the wee hours of the morning was either unconcerned with the possibility of being caught or ignorant of such fundamental forensic procedures as fingerprinting. What kind of monster would break into a convent, cut through a screen with one knife, drop it on the ground, climb to the living quarters, rape a helpless, devout, senior citizen, stab her with a second knife, and take off into the night? What kind of moron would leave both knives behind and not even bother to rub off his fingerprints?

Shortly after the knives were discovered, Johnny Frank Garrett, a scrawny teenager who lived close by, was arrested. Just a few weeks before the crime he had been released from a state school for delinquents. On the day prior to the murder, he had been seen skulking around the premises of the convent. Finally, his fingerprints matched those on the two knives, as well as those on Sister Catherine's headboard.

The detectives who interrogated Johnny swore that they had apprised him of his rights. The Potter County opinion states emphatically, "It is undisputed that appellant was given Miranda warnings prior to interrogation." "You have the right to a defense attorney," he was told. For two hours after receiving this offer, Johnny said nothing. He sat silently before his accusers, staring into space; his lips moved occasionally but no sound emerged. A couple of times he asked to talk "to a district attorney," but this request was refused. There would be time enough for Johnny to get acquainted with the D.A. It never occurred to the detectives, or the lawyers who were called upon later to represent Johnny, much less to any of the appeals courts through which his case slowly made its way, that when Johnny asked to speak with a "district attorney" he was responding directly to the Miranda admonition, "You have the right to an attorney." The fine legal distinction between a defense attorney and a district attorney had escaped "appellant's" limited powers of reasoning.

Then, out of the blue, to the interrogators' surprise, "appellant" did an about-face. He confessed. The Potter County opinion reads as follows: "Later appellant admitted going to the convent, breaking the window, and going inside." Johnny dropped the aw-shucks, hayseed facade he had maintained since his arrest and, in chilling detail, described the crime. What a switch! The detectives breathed a sigh of relief. One of the ugliest murders in the county proved one of the easiest to solve.

A cynic might say that the police chose to misunderstand Johnny's request to speak with an attorney. After all, following his confession, they caught on pretty fast. Now they got it. Johnny wanted a lawyer? Sure. And, presto, a public defender materialized. On the other hand, as Jonathan and I would learn eventually, it was not always easy to understand Johnny Garrett. He was forever changing.

For example, according to the records, shortly after confessing to the murder, Johnny did another about-face. With a childlike innocence that apparently fooled no one, he insisted, as he had at the start, that he had nothing to do with the murder. Hence, he refused to sign the confession he had just provided. What was going on? The detectives figured that the kid had suddenly wised up. But to the lawmen who had witnessed Johnny's sudden change of heart, it made no difference. The stenographer had taken it all down; Johnny's account of entering the convent matched the facts of the case. What is more, the treads of Johnny's boots had imprinted the soft mud outside the convent window, leaving a cuneiform signature at the scene of the crime. Later on, the autopsy revealed that hairs found between Sister Catherine's legs matched those plucked from Johnny's pubic region. And, of course, there were the fingerprints. Authorship of the work was never in question. Given this overwhelming body of evidence against him, Johnny's subsequent protestations of innocence came across as ridiculous.

From then on Johnny stuck to his guns. Throughout his trial, he insisted that he had been framed. Somebody else had killed Sister Catherine and, as usual, he was the patsy. Sure, Johnny admitted, he had wandered around the convent grounds the day before the murder. He had never denied that. Johnny loved to go "creepy crawling," as he put it—to slip into places, unseen, and steal things. But he never hurt anyone. He was sure of that.

This was not the first time that Johnny had been blamed for things he had not done. Ever since he was a little kid people had been picking on him. Someone kept setting him up. Johnny never forgot the time he got sent to reform school. The teachers at school said he threw a water glass at a kid's face and almost killed him. Johnny knew that he didn't do it, but as usual he took the heat. Things like that were always happening to him. Someone had to be going around pretending to be Johnny Garrett, deliberately getting him into hot water. Sometimes he was convinced he had a double. Johnny sat in his cell thinking maybe they should do one of those lie detector tests he had seen on T.V. It would prove he didn't kill that nun. Everyone knew that Johnny didn't do things like that. Sure he was kind of sneaky; he would be the first to admit that. But he wasn't violent.

And, in fact, had a lie detector test been administered, Johnny probably would have passed with flying colors. There were times when, if hooked up to the machine and asked whether he had killed the nun, Johnny could have said no, and his response probably would not have raised an incriminating blip.

The trial court, unlike Johnny's own lawyers, had no problem understanding Johnny's ever-changing stories. He was a liar, pure and simple. A stupid one at that. But such glaring lies! The boy didn't seem all that retarded. He should have known that no one would believe him when he changed his story so many times. Now I did it. Now I didn't. Now I did it. Now I didn't. His chances might have been better had he just pleaded guilty, looked contrite, and thrown himself on the mercy of the court. After all, he was only seventeen years old. His youth and a little remorse could have gone a long way toward softening the hearts of a judge and jury. But to rape a nun, choke her, stab her, leave cutlery monogrammed with his bloody fingerprints all over the place, and then deny everything—that was just too much. Johnny Frank Garrett, thief, rapist, murderer, liar, was not crazy. He was bad.

The verdict: guilty. The sentence: death. Johnny was dispatched to death row in Huntsville to await execution. And that's how things stood until 1986, when Jonathan and I visited death row in Texas for the very first time. By the time we examined Johnny, we had done research on violent inmates in Connecticut, Florida, California, and states in between and we could easily have written a *Michelin Guide to Death Rows and Detention Centers in the United States.*

CHAPTER 16

Over the next four years Johnny Garrett paced his cell, conversed with his voices, and waited to be executed. And waited. And waited. Johnny may have inhabited the cell in Huntsville, but he did not really live there. Johnny lived apart, in a personal universe peopled by Indians, Nazis, and dead relatives.

As far as the guards and inmates were concerned, they were more than happy to leave Johnny alone. He was too unpredictable. Usually he was fine. Months on end could pass without incident. Then, out of the blue, something would set Johnny off, and anyone who witnessed the explosion that followed would forever keep his distance. One never knew what lit Johnny's fuse. There was the time a guard said something—no one ever figured out what it was. Seconds later a radio came flying straight for the guard's head. Only the bars on Johnny's cell interrupted the heavy missile's trajectory, thus coming between Johnny and a possible second murder charge. The very next day, when Johnny was dragged before a disciplinary panel, he denied everything. As usual, he was being framed. He had done nothing. And, oddly enough, Johnny seemed to believe what he was saying.

In 1986, when Jonathan and I came to Huntsville and first examined Johnny, the guard who ushered him into the examining room whispered to us, "That'un there's a strange'un." Prisoners must be pretty strange for guards to take notice.

Ever since the advent of Thorazine and the like, with the slow demise of the state hospital system, prisons have become repositories of disruptive, impoverished, mentally ill men. Psychotic, aggressive men who just a few years ago would have lived out their days muttering quietly to themselves or raising havoc on the back wards of state hospitals now make the rounds of prisons, shelters, and a dwindling assortment of available public psychiatric institutions. About a third of their nights are spent tossing and turning on prison pallets; another third in shelters, on the streets, or "depending on the kindness of strangers"; and another third struggling to keep warm between the thin mattresses and polyester blankets of mental hospitals. Because so many poor, sick men now make their homes in prison cells, their keepers get lots of clinical experience—more, perhaps, than many psychiatric residents. As the guards become increasingly accustomed to this clientele, even their most psychotic charges start to look relatively normal.

Not Johnny. Johnny may have looked sane to the trial judge and jury, but to the experienced eyes of the Huntsville guards, Johnny looked crazy. That says something. Johnny's wariness far exceeded the adaptive suspiciousness necessary for survival on death row. He trusted no one, least of all his attorneys. (Then again, as will become clear, not all of his attorneys were trustworthy.) Johnny heard voices. Actually, he did not just hear them, he kept up running conversations with them. His nocturnal altercations kept the other inmates awake. "Go to bed, already, ya crazy bastard!" they shouted. Sometimes Johnny became these voices; he turned into Yoni Red Eagle or the Nazi Commandant. When this happened his tiermates knew that they were in the company of a bona fide "loony." "Shut the fuck up, ya Nazi bastard, or I'll do it for you." "If you don't cut that out, Chief, I'll tell you where I'm gonna stick one of them arrows!" came hoots from the far ends of the cell block. Fortunately, Johnny's excursions to Never Never Land, or wherever he went, were relatively infrequent. Usually Johnny was just a naive kid, a hayseed, who had not aged a day since the murder of Sister Catherine.

Johnny was one of the only death row inmates whose hallucinations, delusions, paranoia, and excursions to fantasy land caused the prison psychiatrist to make a diagnosis of schizophrenia. When a death row psychiatrist calls a condemned man schizophrenic, you can be sure the inmate is very, very sick. The doctor prescribed Thorazine. Thorazine proved useless. No amount of it, or for that matter of any of the other chemicals the prison doctor prescribed, put a damper on Johnny's voices.

A death row psychiatrist's allegiance is torn between Hypocrites and the state. If a condemned person is insane, he cannot be executed. However, if the doctor treats him properly and brings him back to his senses, that patient will be put to death. How should a prison doctor interpret the medical injunction, "Above all do no harm"? As Koko, the *Mikado*'s Lord High Executioner, once said, "Here's a pretty mess." In Johnny's case, the psychiatrist opted to treat, but since the medication never even touched Johnny's hallucinations, the doctor was never faced with the guilt of hastening Johnny's demise. His conscience was clear.

Jonathan and I had not come to Huntsville just to see Johnny Garrett. Johnny was but one of more than thirty young murderers in the United States who had been condemned to death before their eighteenth birthdays. We would be studying fourteen of them in prisons from coast to coast.

Over the preceding years we had evaluated fifteen adult

condemned murderers. Those we examined were nothing like the cold, calculating thugs we had seen on the silver screen—the ones who ground toothbrushes into shivs and slid them between the ribs of wholesome, clean-cut, all-American prison guards. (Nor, for that matter, did the guards fit their Hollywood images, but that's another story.) We met no Jimmy Cagneys or Robert Mitchums among the inmates in the prisons we visited. We found ourselves, rather, in the company of a pathetic crew of intellectually limited, dysfunctional, half-mad, occasionally explosive losers. Long before these men wound up on death row, their similarly limited, primitive, impulsive parents had raised them in the only fashion they knew. They battered them. They used them sexually. They sold their child bodies to buddies in exchange for drugs or food or money. They neglected them. Sometimes they even tried to kill them. These brutish parents had set the stage on which our condemned subjects now found themselves playing out the final act. It was a drama generations in the making. The mothers and fathers of our subjects had held their children out of the open windows of moving cars; they had set them on fire; they had shot at them; they had slashed them with knives and machetes. But in spite of their efforts to destroy them, the children had lived to adulthood. They had lived to perpetrate on others the violence that had been visited upon them. That's how traditions get started. Now the state, in loco parentis, was about to finish the job the mothers and fathers had bungled.

During our study of condemned adults, Jonathan and I learned to our surprise that, in certain states, children—minors—could be sentenced to death. In some states, a child as young as age thirteen could be put to death. In others there was no lower age limit. What sorts of children, we wondered, could be deemed so vicious and depraved as to warrant a death sentence? We decided to try to find out. Since, in the mid-1980s, Texas housed the largest number of condemned juveniles in the United States, it was the obvious place for us to start. Johnny was just one of fourteen research subjects.

Most people don't realize that the United States has a death penalty for juveniles. We are one of the few countries in the world in which such a sentence is possible. In all Western European countries the death penalty for adults as well as children has been abolished. Most countries in which the death penalty is still an option exempt minors under the age of eighteen years. In 1983, our own American Bar Association adopted a resolution opposing "in principle, the imposition of capital punishment upon any person for any offense committed while under the age of eighteen." Nevertheless, the sentence of death for juveniles has remained on the books in many states. At the time of our study, over thirty youngsters were actually awaiting execution in fifteen states, extending from New Jersey and Pennsylvania in the East, to Florida in the South, and all the way west to Texas. The United States shares this tradition with such countries as Iran, several emerging African nations, and an island or two in the Caribbean.

The Supreme Court has articulated the principle of "evolving standards of decency." Given that concept, one might assume that in the United States these kinds of sentences would never be carried out. After all, few juveniles, homicidal or otherwise, give the death penalty a second thought when they commit their crimes. Maybe the option is left on the books in the vain hope of deterring a few potentially violent youths from acting on their homicidal impulses; such, we discovered, is not the case. In fact, during a twelve-month period in the mid-1980s, a period that coincided by chance with the start of our study of condemned juveniles, three young adults were executed in the United States for crimes for which they had been convicted and condemned as juveniles. Two of these sentences were carried out in Texas. Prior to 1985, the last person executed in the United States for a crime committed when he was a juvenile was James Andrew Echols. James, a black youngster, was electrocuted in Texas on May 7, 1964, for the rape of a white female. Thus Texas has the distinction of having terminated one era of juvenile executions and inaugurated the next.

———

I doubt that Jonathan or I will ever forget our first sight of Johnny Gar-rett. He was the very caricature of a madman: long, light brown, un-combed, wavy, shoulder-length hair; a brown, untrimmed moustache and beard; dark, sunken hollows for eyes; and a lethal glare.

Given Texas's Draconian record, Jonathan and I expected the young condemned inmates we saw to exhibit fear, or at least a little anxiety. Johnny did not. The wild mystic who came before us expressed more concern about his spiritual being than about the prospect of losing his corporeal one. Johnny, we discovered, had created his own Jehovah-less religion in which he was a messiah. (Of note, his mother was a Je-hovah's Witness.) Johnny explained that he was what he termed an "Odious." (Neither Jonathan nor I smiled.) An "Odious," Johnny said, was a worshipper of the Norse god, Odin. Johnny was also an Aryan and a Hitler fan. The Holocaust, Johnny declared, was a hoax perpe-trated by the Jews. (Jonathan and I had heard that one before.) Just when we thought we understood who Johnny was, or thought he was, he would volunteer another piece of information to confuse us. Johnny, it seems, was also a Cherokee.

"How's that, Johnny?" I asked. "Run that by me again."

"Inside me, I tell the white half to go to Hell," Johnny explained. We had no idea what he was talking about. Time being of the essence, we would not even try to clarify that issue. Other prisoners were wait-ing to be evaluated. In those days, Jonathan and I had a marvelous ca-pacity, when we didn't understand what a patient was saying, to dismiss it as gibberish. Therefore, while Johnny was laying his cards on the table, trying to tell us who he was, we were telling him to put his cards back in the pack and set the deck aside.

Every so often during our examination Johnny would pause, fall silent, and look away, as though he were listening to something Jonathan and I could not hear. "Johnny, you seem to be hearing voices that aren't there," I ventured. This is one of the dumber statements psychiatrists are taught to make. Jonathan and I have since dropped it from our repertoire for reasons that will become obvious.

Johnny shook his head vigorously. No. No. No.

"You mean you don't hear voices that aren't real?"

"No. Of course not. The voices are real!"

(Jonathan and I now ask, "Can you ever talk to someone in your head?")

"What do the voices say?"

"They tell me what to do."

"Like what?"

"I can't tell you."

"Do you know who they are?"

Johnny paused and his eyes flitted back and forth.

"Whose voices?"

"I can hear Aunt Barbara." Johnny sounded softer, less angry.

"She told me to trust you. To confide in you."

Lots of people who are lonely and scared find comfort in imaginary conversations. We promptly dismissed Aunt Barbara as a normal, expectable phenomenon. In spite of Johnny's having Aunt Barbara's blessing to talk with us, every so often, in the midst of recounting tales about his childhood, Johnny would suddenly fall silent and stare straight ahead. At these times, his features would harden and his eyes would glow with the fury we had seen at the start of our meeting. Had Aunt Barbara changed her mind? Was she now telling Johnny to keep his mouth shut?

Gingerly we approached the topic of Johnny's crime. To our amazement, Johnny was unfazed by our questions. His explanation was straightforward. Someone else out there, on the other side of the prison walls, had killed Sister Catherine; he, Johnny Garrett, was taking the rap. What is more, he knew who it was, but he couldn't say. If he told, something bad would happen to his family. In fact, he decided that he probably had said too much already.

The diagnostic picture was obvious. Delusions, hallucinations, feelings of being controlled from outside. Jonathan and I were convinced that Johnny was schizophrenic. For once we were in agreement with the prison psychiatrist.

Getting a history from Johnny Garrett was a challenge. A voice in his head kept interfering. He would start to answer, think better of it, and shut down. It was an art to overcome this obstacle—an art that, in those days, we had not fully mastered.

"Tell us about your childhood, Johnny." There, that was a pretty simple question. Johnny's voices allowed him to respond.

"When I was born, the welfare was gonna take me away. They said my mother was unfit."

"Why was that?"

"She had some of these here nervous breakdowns."

We learned that between her bouts of madness, Johnny's mother had allied herself with a series of violent partners; each proved more abusive to her and to her children than the last. We also learned that when Johnny was very young, while his mother was psychiatrically hospitalized, Johnny's grandparents took care of him. This arrangement sounded like a good thing. But when Johnny was three and a half years old, and his mother emerged from one of her hospitalizations, she wanted him back. She got him. A battle for custody ensued, and throughout his childhood and adolescence Johnny was pulled back and forth between the two households, his mother's and his grandparents'.

Johnny had lots of fathers. In order to keep track of them, Johnny numbered them chronologically, one through four. Johnny was uncertain which one was his real father, his biological father. Some folks said it was father number one; others said father number two was his daddy. Father number one, a fierce man, was not around long, and Johnny felt lucky to have escaped the brunt of his rages. "He beat my mom and my brother. . . . He beat my brother with a baseball bat. . . . He liked beating women. I seen him." When it came to father number one, Johnny thought he had gotten off easy compared to his brother. The next three fathers were a different story.

"My second father, he beat me real bad when I was small," Johnny explained. "I have marks on my behind. They say that he sat me on a hot stove because I wouldn't stop crying."

"Can we look?" Johnny nodded assent. Johnny bent over and lowered his pants. A deep scar, about three inches long and a half inch wide, extended diagonally outward, starting from Johnny's anus and terminating in the middle of his left buttock—a shiny canyon where seared muscle and flesh must have slowly knitted together.

Scars on Johnny's back and arms, clearly the results of beatings, attested further to the quality of Johnny's relationships with his fathers. But it was the relentless assaults of father number three, not just upon his body but also on his very soul, that fractured forever whatever had made Johnny a whole person. Now, in a monotone reminiscent of Marie Moore, Johnny described what had happened to him when father number three moved into his mother's trailer.

"Him and a friend came home. Mom was at work. My baby sisters and brother were asleep. My big brother was with my uncle. I just came home from the lake. I had a cat with kittens. I heard my baby cats. I found one of the kittens in the garden. I picked it up. I went over to the basket. I bent over to put the kitten in the basket. Then he came over."

"Who?"

"My stepfather. My third dad. He was with his friend. He gave me a choice. Suck him and his friend or be beaten up." Johnny paused and cleared his throat. "He made me swallow it."

The crazy, illogical utterances had stopped. As he related this event, Johnny was coherent, clear as a bell.

"Did it ever happen again, or was that the only time?"

"He did it every chance he got. He'd come check me out of school. He'd take me home. He'd make me strip." Now, the feelings caught up with the words. Johnny was unable to continue. He paused, took a deep breath.

"He made me bend over on the floor. . . . He made me spread my legs and entered me that way . . . he fucked me in my ass."

The words were familiar. Billy had said pretty much the same thing.

In fact, in the decade since our first meeting with Johnny, we have seen more than a dozen violent men whose rage could be traced back to early, repeated experiences of being sodomized.

I did not know what to say.

Finally Johnny broke the silence. "After they got the divorce, they kept coming back."

"They?"

"Different dudes. He, my third father, brought friends over. They took pichurs. They made fewums."

"Fewums? What's that?" I asked.

"You know. Fewums with a camera."

"What kind of films?"

"One was called *Big Brother Gets Banged*. There was one called *Mother's Lover*."

I had nothing to say. Fortunately, I did not have to because Johnny continued. "They used animals. In one fewum a donkey had sex with a woman."

"That's impossible," I challenged, as though I knew what I was talking about.

"No, it's not impossible!" Johnny was definite. It was obvious to him that I knew nothing about making porn films. "They had to lift its front part up on a pulley. She was laying back on the bed. They lowered it down on her." Then he added, as if to supplement my education, "They used lots of different animals."

I tried to sound casual as I asked questions Yale had never taught me to ask about practices I had heard of but only half believed ever really happened.

"Johnny, were you ever in those films?" I asked.

"Not with the donkey. There was this big collie. This male collie. They had it fuck me. They took pichurs."

Silence again. I decided to skip the details.

"Who else was in these films?" I asked. I wanted proof.

"I remember a dark-haired prostitute. They called her Sunshine. . . . I saw children as young as seven years old having sex with adults." Johnny did not know the names of most of the adults. "They never showed their faces. Just the kids."

So the identity of the adults was protected. Only the kids were exposed. What Johnny told me rang true. I had once heard a lecture by an FBI agent. He talked about how children used in pornography fear for the rest of their lives that their identities and the perverted acts they were once forced to perform will some day come to light.

"Didn't you tell anyone?"

"No. I was ashamed."

Johnny was more terrified of being recognized in the pornographic films he had made as a child than he was of his impending execution. He had not even told his attorneys about the films.

Johnny was not the first death row inmate, and would not be the last whom Jonathan and I saw, who preferred death to disclosure of his past. At the end of our examination, I asked Johnny to allow me to tell his attorney what he had told me. Johnny hesitated. "It could help your case," I encouraged.

Johnny was not convinced.

"They might use it. They might humiliate me," came Johnny's response.

"No, it won't be used that way. The lawyer will use what we share with him just for your appeal," I reassured. Patiently, I explained that the judge should have known about these porno movies at the time of Johnny's trial. These experiences could have been used for purposes of mitigation. It might not be too late. I assured Johnny that he could trust his lawyer to use the information only to try to save Johnny's life. He would not use it to humiliate him. Reluctantly, Johnny agreed to let me share the secrets of his childhood with his lawyer. As I left, I repeated my assurances that Johnny could trust his own lawyer.

I was wrong. Actually, I was right and I was wrong. I was right that Johnny's lawyer would not make public Johnny's humiliations; he kept them secret. I was wrong that he could be trusted to use them to help Johnny. Johnny's court-appointed attorney kept those secrets so well that, as far as I could tell, he never even bothered to read about them himself. When I sent him my report about Johnny, I assumed that he would run with the information. I provided him with evidence of brain damage, psychosis, torture, child pornography. All of these issues should have been raised at Johnny's trial, if not at the guilt-innocence phase, then at least at the sentencing phase. These were important appeals issues. But this lawyer did not run with the information I sent him—nor did he walk. He sat on it. When my report arrived on his desk, he shoved it into a cardboard file box with the rest of the papers pertaining to Johnny's case, and promptly forgot about it. The beatings, the burn, the sodomy, the psychosis, the brain damage, the pornography—everything that Jonathan and I identified that might have been of help remained secret, locked in Johnny's mind and stuffed in a file box in the attorney's office.

CHAPTER 17

For two years Johnny's secrets lay undisturbed in the lawyer's file box. No one knew about what had happened to Johnny and, for that matter, no one much cared. During that time, the only one who gave Johnny's case a second thought was the governor of Texas. For some reason, amid the hundred and fifty or so death warrants on the governor's desk awaiting signature, Johnny's caught the governor's eye. Or perhaps the governor just flipped a coin. Whatever the explanation, one day the governor saw fit to sign Johnny's death warrant. Johnny was to be executed on October 6, 1988.

On September 14, 1988, twenty-six months after Jonathan and I evaluated Johnny Garrett, and less than a month before the execution was scheduled to take place, I received a phone call from someone who identified himself as Johnny Garrett's lawyer. Would I please prepare an affidavit, documenting the findings of our clinical evaluation? I was cool but polite. Certainly. I would need a little time to refresh my memory, to review all the materials. I could get a draft to him in a week or two, three at the outside. Would that do?

Obviously I did not understand the situation. A death warrant had already been signed. In three weeks Johnny would be dead. At that point, the lawyer suggested, I could keep my affidavit (and, he implied, use it as I saw fit). The lawyer needed it now or never.

I bristled. Why on earth had he waited two years to call? The initial report with all the documentation had been sent to Johnny's lawyer in 1986. With it went a cover letter, offering our help. Johnny was the most impaired and abused juvenile we evaluated, and I had gone out of my way to make sure his lawyer knew that.

Finally I caught on. The man I was speaking with was not the attorney to whom I had sent the report. As far as anyone could determine, Johnny's previous court-appointed attorney had done nothing on his case between the time of our evaluation and the time that the governor signed Johnny's death warrant. At that point, Johnny's case was transferred to the Capital Punishment Clinic of the University of Texas. The voice on the other end of the phone belonged to a brand-new lawyer from that clinic. His discovery of my report was almost serendipitous and attested to his diligence. He had spent the seventy-two hours between receiving the case and telephoning us, foraging through file boxes, seeking material to form the grounds for a last-minute appeal. It was in this context that he came upon the report. Were it not for his efforts, Johnny would have gone to his death on October 6, 1988, our findings and his secrets undisclosed.

What relevance did our clinical findings have to Johnny's case? Johnny's brain damage impaired his judgment as well as his ability to control his behaviors and appreciate their consequences. He was also psychotic. He mistook fantasy for reality, felt mortally threatened when he was not even endangered, and lashed out at real and imagined enemies. How responsible could such a person be for his violent acts?

Historically, almost all civilized societies absolve insane people from full responsibility for their criminal acts. Johnny, with his hallucinations, delusions, and intense paranoia, was clearly insane—even the prison psychiatrist thought so. Moreover, the nature and relentlessness of the abuse he had sustained as a child should have been raised at the time of sentencing for purposes of mitigation. We were not sure why Johnny's madness was expressed by raping and murdering an aged nun; that would remain a mystery for another four years. Given his history of repeated sexual abuse by "father number three" and his sidekicks, we would have expected Johnny's victim to have been male. But no matter what influenced Johnny's choice of victim, the very nature of the crime—the rape and murder of an old woman—said something about the mental state of its perpetrator. You don't have to be a psychiatrist to know that raping and murdering an old nun is not a normal thing to do.

I addressed all of these issues—brain damage, psychosis, and abuse—in a hastily drafted five-page affidavit. On September 15, 1988, twenty-four hours after the lawyer's phone call, the document was on its way to Texas. The affidavit concluded with a paragraph indicating that Jonathan and I were: "prepared to testify and to be cross-examined regarding the contents of this affidavit if Johnny Garrett were to be granted a new trial or a new hearing regarding sentencing."

In death row cases, no news is good news. When October 6, 1988, came and went, and Johnny's name did not appear in the newspapers, we all breathed a sigh of relief. Although we never spoke to that attorney again, we assumed that there must have been a stay of execution. When 1989 and 1990 came and went, and we heard nothing, we assumed that Johnny's death sentence had been commuted and that it would not be necessary for us to testify at a new trial or even a new sentencing hearing. We assumed. We assumed. Johnny's case taught us that in death penalty cases, you assume nothing.

Over the next three years, when I thought of Johnny Garrett at all (which was infrequently), I pictured him spending his days in an institution for the criminally insane, weaving baskets and messianic fantasies, and growing his hair longer and longer. I was buoyed by the knowledge that our clinical findings had been of some use to at least one subject in our study of fourteen death row juveniles.

The next three years were eye-openers. As Jonathan and I learned more about multiple personality disorder, our skepticism regarding its existence began to melt away. Marie Moore had convinced us that the phenomenon of multiple personality disorder could occur. We assumed, of course, that it was a rare phenomenon. Those were busy years. There was so much to do, to learn, that we rarely looked back. After all, we reasoned, multiple personality disorder was uncommon. How many times could we have missed it? Such was our assumption.

In 1991, the television show "48 Hours" devoted a program to juveniles condemned to death, and who should appear on screen but Johnny Frank Garrett. Barbara Bard, the expert who had conducted the educational assessments of the juveniles on death row, was watching. The next morning the phone rang at Bellevue. It was Barbara.

"Dorothy, we missed it."

This phrase has become familiar. Barbara explained that the Johnny Garrett she saw on television was nothing like the person she had met in Huntsville. Barbara also reported that, in the course of the television interview, Johnny's eyes widened and his whole demeanor changed. He looked quite different from the old man of the mountain we had examined five years before. Barbara was also struck by Johnny's insistence on his innocence.

"I think he's a multiple," Barbara concluded.

Shortly thereafter, Jonathan called me. Jonathan and I like to tease each other with observations or insights that one of us has made and the other overlooked.

"Dorothy, we missed it," boomed Jonathan, a certain amount of glee in his voice. I was the psychiatrist—clearly *I* had missed something. In preparation for a lecture, Jonathan had been reviewing the clinical data we had gathered on all of our death row subjects. As he pored over Johnny Garrett's neurological and psychiatric reports, in the light of what we had recently learned about multiple personality disorder, Johnny's clinical picture started to look different. Symptoms such as blackouts, memory lapses, staring spells, which, given Johnny's history of brain injury, we both had interpreted as symptoms of possible psychomotor epilepsy, began to look more like dissociative episodes. Other symptoms—Johnny's auditory hallucinations, his belief that he was a Cherokee, his becoming a Nazi—symptoms we had previously attributed to schizophrenia, began to fit more and more the picture of multiple personality disorder. In this context, even Johnny's phrase "I tell the white half to go to Hell" started to make sense. I reviewed all of Johnny's records; I got hold of the "48 Hours" videotape and watched as a Johnny I barely recognized spaced out and changed demeanor. I had missed the diagnosis of multiple personality disorder in Johnny Frank Garrett.

So what.

Johnny was still psychotic and brain damaged, and I had said so. There was plenty of evidence that he was out of touch with reality. Furthermore, Jonathan had amassed ample neurologic evidence that his brain did not function normally. So what if he also suffered from multiple personality disorder? Granted, multiple personality disorder would explain certain aspects of Johnny's behavior. It would explain his switches from confessing to murder one minute, to pleading innocent the next. It would explain the Cherokee and the Nazi Commandant. The important question was whether, in the long run, the diagnosis of multiple personality disorder would help Johnny now. Should we share our insights with Johnny's attorneys?

Johnny's lawyers already had ample documentation of his psychosis and brain damage. It didn't take a psychiatrist to see how crazy he was. Everyone knew that the state did not kill crazy people; therefore, I assumed, Johnny's life was not in danger. Why muddy the clinical waters? It seemed to me that to examine Johnny again would be more a time-consuming, academic exercise than a service. We decided to let sleeping personalities lie. Even if I documented their existence, the chances of Johnny's ever getting treatment in prison for multiple personality disorder was minimal. Johnny was probably better off with the prison psychiatrist's diagnosis of schizophrenia.

Once again Johnny slipped to the back of my mind. When I did think about him, it was to regret my lack of clinical sophistication when I first examined him.

On January 8, 1992, a brief article appeared on a back page of the *New York Times*. It caught my eye because, for the first time in recent memory, the governor of Texas had granted a stay of execution to a condemned prisoner. According to the newspaper, this almost unprecedented action had taken place in response to a request by Pope John Paul II. The paper pointed out that the Pope's intervention was especially magnanimous and would carry special weight because the prisoner in question was not Catholic. Furthermore, he had murdered a nun.

The governor of Texas found herself in a quandary. According to the materials she had read, the condemned was obviously demented. Texas was about to execute a crazy man for an act committed as a crazy boy. If ever there were a case deserving of clemency, this was it. On the other hand, Texas was still the no-nonsense state. In fact, Texas was running neck and neck with Florida for the distinction of executing the greatest number of criminals since the death penalty was reinstituted in the United States in 1976. No governor of Texas who granted clemency outright could rely on reelection. It was as simple as that.

Perhaps there was another way to "do the right thing" and still maintain a law-and-order reputation. The governor would convene a clemency board. It would act as another jury. It would hear the death penalty arguments, pro and con. If, after pondering all the evidence, it voted to spare the prisoner, so be it. Nobody could then accuse this governor of being soft on crime. Who was the political pawn whose life hung in the balance? Johnny Frank Garrett.

When our system is shocked, we sometimes remember insignificant details of an event. I recall lying in bed reading the newspaper, the light over my right shoulder; my husband asleep to my left, his light out; the placement of the article on the inner column immediately to the right of the middle fold.

At first I could not believe what I was reading. I had assumed that, thanks to our clinical report, Johnny's life was no longer in danger. After providing his lawyer with my hastily prepared 1988 affidavit, I had not heard from the lawyer again. Therefore, I took for granted that our documentation of Johnny's mental impairment and his history of abuse had been sufficient—that his sentence had been commuted. Suddenly nothing made sense. I resolved to call the lawyer the next day and clarify the situation.

But when I called his office, I discovered that the lawyer with whom I had spoken in 1988, the one for whom I had rushed to complete an affidavit, was no longer Johnny's attorney. At some time between the 1988 affidavit and the 1992 death warrant, Johnny's case had again been transferred, this time to the Texas Resource Center. I suspect things would have turned out differently had one attorney sustained an interest in Johnny.

The Texas Resource Center, I discovered, consisted of a group of minimally paid but maximally dedicated young attorneys, whose job it was to take on the usually futile, often last-minute appeals of condemned prisoners in Texas. Johnny's case was now in the hands of two bright young women.

The decision whether or not to contact Johnny's new lawyers was not easy. Jonathan and I have made it a practice never to offer our services in notorious cases (fascinating though the newspapers sometimes try to make them sound). Our examinations of those few notorious murderers we have seen, such as Mark David Chapman and Theodore Bundy, were serendipitous. Chapman had been admitted to the Bellevue forensic unit at a time when we were doing a study of violent young adult offenders, and his lawyer had allowed him to participate in our study. Bundy was evaluated almost by chance. His lawyers had learned that we were on our way to Florida to evaluate a group of condemned juveniles. Would we please evaluate their client, since we were going to be in the neighborhood?

When we first evaluated Johnny he was but one of fourteen subjects in our study, a nonentity as far as the rest of the world was concerned. Johnny had become the focus of world attention only because of the Pope's efforts on his behalf. Should I offer my services where they might not be wanted? On the other hand, Jonathan and I did have some new insights into the case, and we felt we owed it to Johnny to share them with his lawyers. After a lengthy telephone conversation, Jonathan and I agreed that I should call the Texas Resource Center. I would let Johnny's new lawyers decide whether or not our hunch regarding multiple personality disorder was worth pursuing. I think Jonathan and I both felt a little guilty at not having recognized the disorder in 1986. Here was a chance to try to make amends and set the record straight. I called his new attorneys.

Johnny's lawyers listened attentively as I explained our initial involvement in Johnny's case, and why we now suspected our initial diagnosis had been wrong. I made clear that even if I saw Johnny again, I couldn't be certain what I would find. Moreover, even if Johnny turned out to suffer from multiple personality disorder, would this determination so late in the case have any relevance? Might it not seem like a ploy? Would such a controversial diagnosis be suspect? The attorneys decided to ponder the question, consult colleagues, and get back to me.

I never learned their reasoning. I only learned their verdict: Come. So I packed my overnight case and came.

A psychiatrist who suspects the existence of multiple personality disorder needs time to make the diagnosis. Usually the first few sessions with the patient are spent simply taking a history and establishing rapport. Marie Moore taught me that. Trust is essential if alternate personalities are to make themselves known. These entities, hidden for years, have managed to protect their host by remaining secret. They perceive exposure as dangerous. If Johnny did have alternate personalities, how was I to gain their trust quickly, especially with a death sentence hanging over their heads?

Then there was the issue of hypnosis. I did not want to use it. Granted, it could hasten the determination of multiple personality disorder, but subjects under hypnosis are notoriously suggestible. In legal cases it is important to avoid any possible accusation of suggesting or creating alternate personalities. If alternate personalities existed, I had to gain enough trust in the short time available to me to enable them to make their presence known of their own free will. To heighten the tension further, the entire session with Johnny would have to be videotaped. If Johnny had the disorder, others would have to see it to believe it. Even then, there was no guarantee that a clemency board would appreciate the implications of what they saw.

The state penitentiary at Huntsville is a study in paradoxes. Like just about all of the prisons Jonathan and I have visited, its walls are surrounded by coils of razor-sharp barbed wire, guaranteed to mince anyone foolish enough to attempt exit or entry through it. Two parallel, electronically controlled gates interrupt the bramble of metal knives and thereby give potential access to the prison. Once through these gates, however, one finds a secret garden. A pathway, lined by rows of bright, colorful flowers, leads pleasantly to the glass doors of the Huntsville prison proper. It was a bit like the salad bar Jonathan once discovered in the Starke, Florida, greasy spoon.

The inside of the Texas prison, at least the part we were permitted to see, is also less forbidding than the inside of other prisons we have visited. A room directly to the left of the entrance, past the glass doors, displays items made by the prisoners; they are for sale to the public. Years ago, on our first visit, we bought beautifully crafted miniature leather cowboy boots, each with its singular shape and design. To the right, behind what looks like a bank teller's window, sits a guard.

On our first visit to Huntsville, I was among friends: Jonathan, Barbara Bard, Marilyn Feldman. This time, except for the attorney who accompanied me, I was alone. As we entered the building, the guard behind the window inquired graciously how he could be of service. You can say one thing for the guards at Huntsville. They may have helped dispatch a record number of inmates, but they are unfailingly polite.

The prison was expecting us. Another guard escorted us through a maze of corridors to an interview room, a narrow rectangle containing a long rectangular table that filled almost the entire space. Outside the door, relaxed, awaiting our arrival, we found a pair of uniformed guards leaning against a wall and a young man in prison garb, standing with his arms shackled behind his back.

"Hi, Johnny. How're you doing?" the lawyer greeted the prisoner.

Johnny?

This was surely not the person I had examined six years before. The scraggle-toothed youngster before me could not possibly be the bearded hermit of 1986. First of all, this man was much younger than Johnny would have been. He could not have been much more than twenty, maybe twenty-one. He looked more boy than man. Furthermore, this was not the face of the ageless mystic we had evaluated. Even the eyes were different. The Johnny Garrett I remembered had brooding eyes that flashed occasionally with sparks of rage. His cheeks were hollow, filled in with a long, wispy brown beard. The youth before me had a rounder, clean-shaven face, wide childlike eyes, and lank brown hair, parted in the middle, that fell over his eyes and that he kept brushing back from his forehead.

"Do you remember Doctor Lewis?" the lawyer asked.

"Shoore Ah do," drawled the prisoner. The guards removed his handcuffs, and the youngster held out his hand in greeting.

It was Johnny.

Precious minutes ticked by as the lawyer and I set up the camera, trying to focus it on Johnny's face. Facial expressions are invaluable clues to the appearance of alternate personalities. Seeing our struggle to secure the video camera to its tripod, one of the guards graciously offered to help us. He said that he had a similar camera at home. We accepted his offer. Time was running out.

At last we were ready to begin the interview. As I sat down at the table, I noticed that the guard, who had been so helpful, was now standing at the doorway, inside the room. Erect and uniformed, he looked to me a bit like a liveried chauffeur. Obviously I could not conduct a sensitive, personal interview with Johnny with this guard monitoring our every word. I objected. He had to leave. A slew of discussions ensued as the lawyer explained my situation to the guards, the guards called their superiors, their superiors contacted the deputy warden, who in turn called the warden. On and on, up and down the chain of command, back and forth, went the negotiations. Impossible. Prison regulations. A guard had to be in the room. The attorney stuck to her guns. This was to be a confidential interview between an inmate, his attorney, and the doctor she had chosen to evaluate her client. Eventually we won. It was our only victory.

Reluctantly the guard stepped outside the door and closed it. He and his partner, who had been waiting outside, would observe the interview from a rectangular, eye-level window that extended the length of one wall of the room, the wall opposite where Johnny was seated. If Johnny were to look up, he would be able to see the tops of the guards' heads and four eyes peering directly at him. What a way to establish an atmosphere of trust! We closed the door. Johnny and I moved to the far end of the table and took seats at the corner, on a diagonal from each other. The attorney readjusted the focus of the camera. Then she pressed "record." The interview began.

Before a word could be spoken, Johnny's expression changed. Fleetingly, the muscles of his face hardened, and he fixed me with a glare so intense, so fierce, that I felt myself in the presence of the mad mystic I had met in 1986. Then it was gone. As quickly as it appeared it vanished, and I found myself looking once more into the eyes of the bumpkin with whom I had shaken hands.

"Johnny, what just happened?"

No answer.

"Johnny, what just happened?" I repeated.

Johnny paused, as if listening for permission to answer me. Then he responded. "Sometahms Ah push things back."

"What do you mean?"

"Ah refocus."

"How do you mean?"

"Ah bin doin' it faw yeahs. Even on the street. Mah juvenile parole officah asked mah mom if Ah was on drugs."

"Were you?"

"No."

"Last time we talked, you told me what a hard time you had as a kid. How your stepfathers beat up on you and all. Many kids who go through tough times like that can sort of space out, get away from it, go to a special place in their heads and not feel anything. Could you do that?" I asked an important question I had learned to ask during the six years between our two interviews. Some children who are tortured can sort of self-hypnotize and not feel the pain. It was awfully early in the interview to blow one of my favorite multiple personality questions, but Johnny's fleeting, menacing expression had definitely invited it. I could not properly ignore what I had observed.

"Sure Ah can. The first tahm Ah did it, Ah remembah Ah was in trouble. Ah don't know what faw. Ah knew Ah had a whippin' comin'. Ah focused out. Ah put mahself at a party."

"What happened then?"

"Ah don't know. The next thing Ah know Ah heard a cat meowing. Ah was still at the party, but Ah heard this here cat."

"And?"

"It brought me back. Ah sort of woke up. And, you know, there was a cat on mah lap."

"Where were you? Were you at the party still?"

"No, of course not. There was no party. Ah was at home. Ah was back from the party."

I was puzzled and I looked it.

"Ah think Ah just had a good imagination." So, I gathered, Johnny had gone to an imaginary party, a party in his head.

He continued. "Sometahms Ah could project mahself." Johnny's vocabulary was more sophisticated than I remembered it to have been.

"Project yourself?" I needed only to repeat his last few words and he could continue.

"Ah could put mahself a few blocks away. That way Ah could see what was happenin', but Ah didn't have to feel it."

"You could just decide to do it and make it happen?"

"Sometahms Ah could do it on purpose. Sometahms it just happened."

"How do you mean?"

"Ah'd get them blackouts. Ah told the doctors about them." Then I recalled that I had read in one of Johnny's old records that, when Johnny was a child, a doctor had told his mother that he had seizures. Johnny Garrett did not have seizures. But he, like other chronically tortured children, could space out and anesthetize himself to pain.

"Sometahms Ah'd get these headaches. Sometahms Ah'd get dizzy and then get them blackouts. When Ah come out of them, Ah'd have a headache." I had learned over the years that headaches often occurred when alternate personalities were in conflict with each other, when they argued with each other in the patient's head.

"You mean you didn't always decide to refocus? To black out? It wasn't always up to you?"

"No. Sometahms it just happened. But sometahms Ah could make it happen."

"How's that?"

"Ah call it astral projection."

There was a concept with which to grapple. Johnny seemed to be saying that he literally "spaced out." "Why astral projection?"

"That's the only name Ah know for it." Johnny looked sheepish.

"What happens then?"

"Ah go into the void."

"When would you do that?"

"When mah stepfather—you know, mah third father—when he did that-that-that-thing to me."

Johnny paused and looked toward the ceiling. Something or someone kept interrupting his words. He seemed to be looking to a being above him for permission to continue. His eyes got wide and he continued to stutter. I have noticed that many patients with multiple personality disorder stutter when switching from one personality state to another or when one personality tries to stop another from speaking.

"When he ha-had sex with me. Ah would go i-i-into the void."

Now I knew that Johnny, like many of the other tortured children I had seen over the previous six years, could space out and separate himself from painful situations. This did not necessarily mean that Johnny suffered from multiple personality disorder. It simple meant that he had acquired the ability to dissociate.

"Johnny, you know how people switch channels on a T.V. set?" Again, it was early in the interview to ask my other favorite question. It might be too soon to get an honest reply, but the timing seemed right.

"Uh-huh."

"Well, Johnny, some kids can do something like that. If they need to be big and strong for some reason they can switch into someone else, someone big and strong. If they just want to goof around, they can switch and become a little kid. It's like switching channels on T.V. Could you ever do that?"

"Ah always acted older." I blew it. He didn't even know what I was talking about. A highly intelligent, sensitive patient at Bellevue, Max, had taught me to ask abused children this question. It had proved to be one of the most effective ways of eliciting dissociative experiences, and I had just wasted it by asking too soon. Or so I thought.

"Could you ever actually become older or stronger?" I asked, lamely.

"That's the Vulcan mind transfer."

"The what?"

"Ah could make mahself into somebody else."

"What do you mean?" (Thank you, Max, I thought. Thank you. Thank you.)

Johnny continued. "Ah call him Aaron Shockman."

"How's that?"

"Ah'm not sure when it happened. Ah think it started in fifth grade. Ah used to get beat up a lot. When that happened Ah became Aaron Shockman. Then Aaron Shockman started winnin' for me."

"Did he ever talk to you?"

"Not so's you could hear him. But Ah could hear him."

"What else did he do for you?"

"You remember Ah was telling you about what mah third father done? It would be A-A-Aaron Shockman he was doin' that with. Not me."

"And you?"

"Ah told you. Ah would go into the void."

So Johnny, like other children who have been tortured beyond endurance, was able to escape; he could remove himself and let someone else endure the pain. "Did you ever tell anyone about Aaron Shockman?"

"Ah wrote it to someone. Ah wrote to a woman named November. She stopped writing to me after that. Ah don't know if she just lost interest or thought Ah was nuts."

"Tell me more about it." (Another psychiatric cliché, I thought.)

"He was mah twin. But he was older. He's older than me mentally, intellectually. He's smarter than me." Now Johnny was speaking in the present tense. He seemed to be saying that Aaron Shockman was still around.

"How old is he?"

"Nobody knows. Ah think he maht be nineteen." Johnny was really twenty-seven years old. But the person I was speaking with was a seventeen-year-old kid.

In Johnny's world, not only were past and present one, but also twins of different ages could exist side by side. I nodded, as though Johnny were making perfect sense.

"What else did he do for you?" I returned to the past tense.

"He took a lot of pain. Physical pain mostly."

There it was, the phrase I had heard over and over again since 1984 from the protector personalities of just about every patient I had ever seen who suffered from multiple personality disorder, including Marie Moore. When the patients or their alters could not say it, sometimes they wrote it. Sometimes it came in barely audible whispers: I took the pain. Their tone was often matter-of-fact, sometimes even a little contemptuous. *I*, not he, took the pain. I took the pain when he couldn't stand it. That was their tacit message.

"Who is stronger, Johnny, you or Aaron Shockman?"

"Ah never thought about that." Another long pause as he looked up and pondered the question.

"He's got to be stronger. He takes the pain." Then, as an after-thought, "He lahks it."

Part of Johnny had somehow come to relish the pain. So many of the patients with multiple personality disorder whom Jonathan and I have seen have perpetuated in adulthood the kinds of painful experiences visited upon them as children. Marie Moore, sexually abused in childhood by her aged father, later became pregnant by a seventy-eight-year-old sadist just like him.

Johnny continued to reflect on Aaron's prowess. "Aaron would faht. He knew preshah points. He could take the pain."

Again and again he repeated the words: take the pain.

"Did he do anything else for you?"

"He can make me do things." Once more Johnny lapsed into the present tense.

"How do you mean?"

"Lahk rearrange the furniture. Sometahms Ah'd start out. Then Ah'd have one of them blackouts. Then Ah'd be at the other side of town." Clearly I was expected to understand what Johnny was saying, follow a train of thought that defied logic. It all seemed so obvious to Johnny. How come I didn't seem to get it? Johnny thought for a moment. "When he did that in mah cell, mah radio would be moved."

Now the incident with the prison guard began to make sense. The guard probably had said something or had done something that threatened Johnny, that reminded him or one of his alters of something from childhood. Maybe it was just the way the guard carried himself, maybe something in the tone of an order he gave. Then Johnny spaced, went into the void, and Aaron took over. Aaron flung the radio at the guard's head. Then Aaron vanished, leaving Johnny holding the bag. Little wonder that when Johnny was charged with the assault on the guard, he denied it so vehemently.

My questions had started Johnny thinking.

"You remember that tahm Ah was tellin' you about when Ah got burned?" I recalled the deep scar on the flesh of his buttocks. "Ah told you how Ah was livin' with mah grandparents. Ah think it was mah second father who did it. Ah know somebody set me on one of them heaters. Ah assume Ah was nekked. Ah musta felt it. Ah got burn marks on mah buttocks. But Ah don't remember cryin'."

So someone had taken the pain before fifth grade, before Aaron's arrival, or else Aaron had been around far longer than Johnny knew.

It was time to ask. "Tell me about the night of the murder, Johnny."

Johnny started out in a tone I found surprisingly matter-of-fact. "Ah remember first Ah was at mah granny and granpaw's place. Ah remember there was some sort of argument there. It was in front of mah granny and granpaw. Ah know Ah got humiliated." Now Johnny was struggling to explain what went on at his grandparents'. The words just didn't come and the story was getting garbled. I looked at my watch. Time was running out; I had to move things along. There just wasn't time for irrelevancies. If we saved Johnny's life there would be plenty of time to hear about dear old Granny and Granpaw.

"Tell me about the convent," I interrupted.

"After mah granny's, Ah went to mah mom's."

"What happened there?"

"Ah don't remember. Ah was drunk on Lord Calvert. Ah remember mah mom, standin' in her slip. Mah sister Janet says she saw me that night, in the doorway of mah mother's house. Ah don't remember that. When Ah left mah mother's house, Ah remember goin' to the convent. Aaron had taught me to creepy crawl. Ah like to creepy crawl. Ah remember goin' through the fields."

"What made you go there?"

"Ah don't know. Somethin' musta happened at mah mom's. Ah know Ah was upset. When Ah get upset, Aaron tells me to creepy crawl and Ah'll feel better."

With these words, Johnny's eyes grew wide, at once frightened and frightening.

"Johnny? Johnny!"

There was no response. Johnny stared blankly at a point in space. He had entered the void. Johnny was gone, and I still did not know what had happened on the night Sister Catherine was murdered. Well, if Johnny had left, maybe someone else would be good enough to fill me in.

"Aaron? Aaron are you there?"

No answer.

"Aaron, I need to talk with you." His was the only name I knew, and so I called upon him. Nothing happened. I waited.

"Aaron, Johnny doesn't remember what happened that night. Aaron, were you there? Aaron, help me." Again, I waited.

Was it really happening or was it my imagination? Later, when I viewed the video, I saw that it was true. The muscles of Johnny's face tightened. Then he fixed me with a hard, pitiless stare. I had seen that gaze before, somewhere else. For a moment the picture of the menacing Billy flashed across my mind, of Marie Moore's protector.

"Who are you?" I asked.

No answer.

"I need to know."

Still no answer.

"Please tell me your name." I tried to sound firm and confident. I was neither.

It felt like hours. It was only minutes. At last he spoke. The voice was more mature than Johnny's; the hick accent was gone.

"What's so important about a name?"

The words were familiar. I had heard them before and have heard them many times since. Powerful alters are reluctant to reveal who they are. I tried to sound businesslike.

"I need to know whom I'm talking to," I persisted. "Do you know who I am?"

"I know who you are," came the icy reply. "You are Doctor Lewis." Then, turning to the woman behind the camera, he said, "You are one of Johnny's new lawyers."

For a moment the attorney seemed unsure of what to say. Johnny had pretty much ignored her presence. But not this entity; he took in everything. If she was anxious, she did not show it. A few seconds later, calm and composed, she responded, "That's right. Now that you know us, tell us who you are."

"Here's a pen," I offered. "You don't have to say it. Just write it." Often alternate personalities will write what cannot be spoken aloud. Sometimes that is the only way they will communicate. Often the child has been threatened with death if he or she "tells" what was done. Writing is a way some alters have of getting around that obstacle. Alters can be extremely literal.

Cautiously, the figure before us lifted the pen and formed the letters: Aaron Shockman.

The writing was distinctive, almost artistic, unlike Johnny's boyish scrawl. At last I was making the acquaintance of the elusive, omnipresent Aaron Shockman. I tried to sound nonchalant. "How did you know my name?"

"I was there. You remember, the last time you came. You asked him what he was looking at. That was me." Then, disdainfully, he added, "It wasn't always Barbara he was listening to." Aaron fairly spat the name Barbara.

Everything Aaron said made sense. It was true. Years before, when Jonathan and I interviewed Johnny, he was obviously hearing voices. When we asked him what he heard, he told us that he was talking with his Aunt Barbara. But she was not alone. The figure before me had also been there, had witnessed the interview, had orchestrated its content.

"Why didn't you speak with us, with Dr. Pincus and me, when we saw Johnny six years ago?"

"Because I didn't trust you."

"Why?"

"Because you weren't there when he needed you."

"What do you mean?"

"When he was being fucked. You weren't there." I could not argue with that. The fact that Jonathan and I did not even know of Johnny's existence when Johnny "was being fucked" did not matter. Alternate personalities are sometimes maddeningly illogical. If Aaron could help when Johnny was little, then why couldn't I?

I wondered how old Johnny was when, as Aaron so graphically put it, "he was being fucked." Powerful alters come when pain is unendurable.

"How long have you known Johnny?" I asked.

"Since he was little. He needed a friend."

"What was happening to Johnny then?"

"Too much love. Too much love," came the enigmatic reply.

"Huh?"

"His mother and his grandmother. They both wanted him." I knew from records that Johnny's mother and grandmother had fought for custody of him. But as far as anyone knew, Johnny's problems stemmed from too much torture and too little love. Aaron was not making sense. He continued. "He needed me. He made me. He was being fucked. He needed someone to take the pain."

"How come you could take the pain?" I interrupted.

"I took the pain cause he can't," came the illogical reply. How was it that I could not understand something so simple? "I taught him how to release the pressure. When he masturbated he wouldn't want to finger himself. I'd take over. A finger. Sometimes thin bottles."

The situation was obvious, at least to Aaron. Johnny, the child, had been stimulated sexually beyond endurance. Sure, at first it had hurt him, but eventually it excited him. The stimulation engendered fantasies and urges he couldn't allow himself to gratify. Johnny had been taught that it was wrong to stimulate himself, so when he felt excited, Aaron would take over and shove bottles into Johnny's rectum. Aaron was doing it to Johnny so it wasn't really masturbation.

"He's sexually confused. He doesn't know if he's a homosexual. That's 'cause his stepfather raped him."

"And before that?"

"Before that there was his brother. Johnny sucked his dick willingly. He loved him." As I think back on Aaron's words, I think I understand the sequence of events. Those fathers and stepfathers probably raped his older brother as well as Johnny. Then his brother did to Johnny what the fathers had done to him. Tradition.

"Anyone else?" I asked.

Aaron paused. "Then a neighbor, Joey. Then Steve."

"Anyone else?" I sensed that Aaron was being evasive. What was he not sharing?

Aaron continued. "There were other men. Boys. We were being filmed." I noticed Aaron, unlike Johnny, pronounced the *l* in "filmed." Something else about the way Aaron spoke caught my ear. Aaron referred to himself and Johnny as "We." They were a team. Whatever happened to Johnny happened to Aaron; whatever happened to Aaron happened to Johnny. Aaron had two functions: he took the pain; and when Johnny's urges became intense, when unacceptable sexual feelings bubbled up and threatened to overwhelm Johnny, Aaron either provided the means for release by masturbating Johnny or he sent Johnny creepy crawling in search of other objects to quench his desires.

Now Aaron's voice was haughty. "Johnny was raped by socialites. Judges. Cops. A doctor. People prominent in Amarillo. Never by people from the streets. Johnny never fucked with no one from the streets." Aaron's highfalutin tone was at odds with his street vocabulary and grammar. If nothing more, Aaron took pride in the caliber of Johnny's clientele.

"What were their names?"

Aaron froze. His eyes flashed. Now something or someone was stopping him. Even Aaron had a boss.

"I can't tell you that."

"Why not?"

"They'll hurt his mother."

After all he had said, it was hard for me to imagine that Aaron had any other secrets worse than those he had already revealed. So many of the abused patients Jonathan and I have seen were threatened as children. If they told what was done to them, their loved ones would be harmed. Silence bought survival for them. But Aaron had already told me about what his stepfathers had done. Why all this secrecy?

Aaron continued. "Besides, no one will believe him."

Again Aaron spoke in the present. It was as though it were all still happening.

"It's safe to tell me now. Who were they? Who threatened Johnny?"

"I can tell you that one of them, Judge S., was the man who sent him to a state school. When he sent him away, he didn't even realize Johnny was the same boy he had fucked." Was Aaron saying that Judge S. was one of Johnny's customers? One of Johnny's fancy clientele? No, Aaron must mean that Johnny was done in, "fucked over," by the judicial system.

"You mean the judge screwed Johnny by sending him away?"

"No, I mean the judge was one of the men who fucked him in the ass in the apartment at Pucket Place." Aaron was quite definite. His memory was clear.

Once started, Aaron could not stop. He, like Billy, spoke without feeling, as though he were narrating a movie he was watching for the third or fourth time.

"Kids. There were kids there younger than Johnny. There was a nine-year-old girl. She was fucked in the ass while the film was being made. Just like Johnny. Johnny couldn't take it. I could."

"Did Johnny bleed?"

"His ass? Sure. He had to put toilet paper in his ass so blood wouldn't stain his pants. It's like when a woman loses her virginity."

Now I understood Johnny's confusion about his sexuality. He felt that he had been made into a woman. Someone—some man, some men—had shoved their organs inside him and Johnny bled; he bled like a woman. I sat silently, trying to take in what I was hearing, trying not to weep. Then, out of nowhere, a non sequitur: "His grandmother and grandfather put all their love into Johnny."

Where did that thought come from, I wondered. Maybe it was Aaron's attempt to lighten the atmosphere, to introduce a fond memory. Maybe he, too, was having a hard time with these memories. Sometimes Aaron just didn't make any sense at all. I had heard just about all I could take of Johnny's career in pornography and prostitution. I decided to return to a less upsetting topic: the murder.

"Tell me about the convent."

"Johnny didn't do it."

As Aaron described Johnny, he sounded as though he were describing the behaviors of a mildly retarded relative. "Johnny broke into the convent because of what had happened earlier."

"Tell me more about that night."

"He didn't do it. I told you. It was because of what happened earlier that night. That's why he went to creepy crawl. The convent was the nearest place. He went into the nun's room. He already had an erection. Johnny broke in because he needed to release pressure. But she woke up."

I was still puzzled. What had happened that night to so stimulate Johnny? The four stepfathers were a thing of the past. According to Johnny, he had just visited Granny and Granpaw. Then he had stopped by his mother's trailer. He had spent the evening with the people who loved him.

"So?"

"When he got into her room, he blacked out. I took over. I put my hand over her mouth so she wouldn't scream. I raped her."

"You raped her? Why?"

"Johnny needed it."

Alternates have a marvelous way of recounting the most bizarre, the most grotesque acts, as though they were describing the facts of life. Johnny needed sex; Aaron raped a nun. It was as simple as that. Sometimes Aaron shoved a bottle in Johnny's behind. Other times he found Johnny a woman.

"I know Johnny better than Johnny does. He had an erection. I knew what he wanted. But he wouldn't be able to do it. I put him to sleep. I took over."

"Who killed her?"

Again Aaron's eyes widened and fixed me with a wild, untamed look. He was afraid. He fell silent. The powerful Aaron Shockman was frightened. I thought, maybe Aaron is not as powerful as Johnny thinks. Aaron remained silent, listening, anxious.

"What's happening?" I waited. "Is someone talking to you?" Still no answer. "Is someone stopping you?" The silence continued as Aaron remained wide-eyed, in a trance.

Since that day I have seen this phenomenon many times. I have thought that I was speaking with someone's most violent protector alter, only to discover weeks, even months later, the existence of a more powerful and dangerous personality.

"Aaron, if you didn't kill her, who did?"

"I don't know," came the reply. I could tell he was lying. "When I got off her she wasn't dead. It all happened on the bed. When I left, she was on the bed."

"But Aaron," I interrupted. "They said they found her on the floor. What happened?"

"I don't know. All I do know is that I did not kill her. Johnny did not kill her. I did not kill her." I believed him.

When I reviewed the tapes of this interview, it was clear that Aaron was speaking the truth as he knew it. Back at Bellevue, away from the prison, in the relative calm of my office, I watched Aaron periodically freeze in fear, stop talking, and listen to something or someone I could not hear. Someone else—someone behind the scenes—was calling the shots during my interview with Aaron. It was evident that someone stronger, crueler than Aaron Shockman had finished off poor Sister Catherine, and if Aaron knew who it was, he was not about to tell me.

The question remained: Who had wielded the knife? And why had he murdered an aged nun? Why should Johnny, or one of his surrogates, choose a victim who was four times Johnny's age?

"Aaron, you told me about Johnny's stepfathers. You told me about the socialites. What about women? Did women ever bother Johnny?"

"They loved him," came the simple response. At times I felt as

Dorothy Otnow Lewis, M.D.

though I were talking to an ancient Chinese sage, whose cryptic utterances required years of reflection to be fathomed. "Who loved him? What do you mean?"

"His neighbor, Sharon, was the first. She was nineteen. I think he was eight. I know it was before he sucked his brother's dick. She told him, the more he played with himself, the sooner he'd have a real erection. She taught him to play with a woman's vagina, to do the tongue."

"How about other women?"

"There were different ones." Aaron was evasive.

I had to ask. Johnny had visited his mother's trailer just before he went to the convent.

"How about his mother?"

No answer.

"Aaron, you said something happened earlier that day, the day Sister Catherine was raped," I pressed him for a response.

Aaron was mute. His eyes widened, then turned upward. He was listening.

"Aaron, what's happening? Who is talking to you?" By this time I was pretty good at recognizing interference from an uninvited alternate.

"That bitch, Barbara. She's trying to make me stop."

"Aaron, it's okay. Maybe I should talk with Barbara directly."

Years before, Johnny had told Jonathan and me that he could talk with his Aunt Barbara. We had dismissed the experience as wishful thinking at best, evidence of schizophrenia at worst. Now the picture looked different. Johnny was not schizophrenic. He had alternate personalities that spoke with him. Barbara was one of them. Hence I stood a fair chance of being able to speak with Aunt Barbara directly.

I tried to sound authoritative, kind but strong. "Aaron, I want you to go back into the void with Johnny. I want to talk with Barbara. I need to talk with Aunt Barbara."

Please come, Barbara. I prayed silently for her appearance. Please don't make me use hypnosis to conjure you. Hypnosis causes so many credibility problems. If you're there, just come out and talk with me. Please don't force me to compromise this interview. People under hypnosis are so suggestible. I don't want to use it. Such were my thoughts and prayers as I waited to see whether or not Barbara, like a Vonnegut space traveler, would materialize.

Gradually Aaron's chiseled features melted, and I watched the softer lines of Aunt Barbara's face emerge. The eyes turned in my direction, then looked past me and seemed to focus on a point behind me in the distance.

"Barbara?" A nod.

"Barbara, I want to talk with you." Her gaze remained fixed on a faraway point.

"Barbara, why don't you look at me?"

"I can't see you. You're blurred." Barbara fumbled, as if seeking a pair of glasses with which to see me better. I had read about cases in which alternate personalities had different visual acuities from each other and from the host. This was the first time I had witnessed the phenomenon. Now, as I think back, I recall that several times during the interview, Johnny removed and then replaced a pair of horn-rimmed glasses.

"Barbara," I sounded too sweet, cajoling. I went on, trying to rid my voice of its saccharine, "I need your help. Tell me about the women."

Her voice was soft, with just a trace of the Southern accent.

"There were girls. There were women. There was this woman. She baby-sat for him when he was little. When he got older she picked him up in her car. He looked so nice, walking down the street. He had no ass at all. They liked that, the women." It was obvious from her tone and inflections that Barbara, too, enjoyed Johnny's physique.

"Did they pay him?"

"That wasn't 'til later," came the matter-of-fact response. "Men and women. They both paid him. Of course, he had to give the money to his stepfather. You know that his stepfather was his pimp."

No, I did not know that, but I was not about to admit that to Barbara. I knew about the porn films when Johnny was a small child. I did not realize that throughout his teens Johnny Frank Garrett had also been forced to be a male prostitute. Aaron had tried to tell me earlier that day, but I could not hear. I was in too big a hurry.

"What about his mother?" I asked.

Unlike Aaron, Barbara spoke easily. She acted as though she had nothing to hide.

"His mother? Johnny doesn't want to admit it. He wanted his mother. After she got her divorce from her fourth husband, one night he got her drunk."

Johnny got his own mother drunk? That seemed improbable. His mother had been an addict and an alcoholic for years. Barbara had to be mistaken, but that's how she saw things.

Barbara continued speaking. "Mind you, he didn't rape her. He had sex with her. He knew how to please a woman with his mouth. It was good for her, too."

Barbara's tone, once soft and gentle, was now devoid of feeling. She could have been describing the plot twists of a somewhat tedious romantic novel. Incest, to Barbara, was no big deal.

She continued. "Later on, Johnny thought he had sinned against God and his mother."

To this day, I do not know whether or not Johnny Garrett ever had sexual relations with his mother. I do know that part of Johnny was certain that he had.

"How do you know about that?" I tried not to sound overinterested. I also did not want to appear to question Barbara's statements. The quickest way to cut off communication with alters is to challenge their veracity. Usually there is time later on to explore in detail what is fantasy and what is reality. One can seek out charts and records and friends and relatives to confirm or refute what patients or their alternates tell you. In Johnny's case, whether or not there would be time for such explorations remained uncertain.

Barbara scoffed at my question.

"He told me. After it happened, he came around to my house. He started crying. I asked him why he was crying. He said because he had sex with his mother."

Keep going. Don't stop talking, I thought to myself.

"When was that?" I ventured, trying not to put a ripple in the stream of words flowing from Barbara's lips.

"Johnny was seventeen." Then, as an afterthought, Barbara added, "It was right before he got arrested."

It was making sense, or so I thought. Johnny had told me that, on the night of the murder, he had been humiliated at his grandparents' home. It wasn't clear what had happened there, but he said that he left their house and went to his mother's trailer. He had described his mother. She was in her slip. Then a blank. The next thing he knew, he was walking through the fields to the convent. Had he slept with his mother that night? Or had the mere sight of her, clad only in her slip, created the pressure that then propelled Johnny to the convent?

Barbara continued. "If Aaron hadn't taken over that night, that woman wouldn't have been raped. Johnny couldn't do such a thing." What woman? Whom did Barbara mean? Johnny's mother? Sister Catherine? Did Sister Catherine remind Johnny of his mother? That hardly seemed possible. Johnny had a young mother. What was Barbara trying to tell me?

Before I could ask another question, a tap on the window signaled the end of the interview. I had completely lost track of time. I begged the guards to grant me a few more minutes to try to put things together, literally. Grudgingly, they agreed. Ten more minutes.

The time for questions was over. Now I had to retrieve Johnny from the void. I hoped the task would be easier than the first time I had to bring back Marie, the time Billy refused to leave. Before even trying to locate Johnny, I made sure to thank everyone: Aaron, Aunt Barbara, and anyone else who might happen to be lurking in the recesses of Johnny's brain. I thanked them all for helping me understand Johnny.

I also asked everyone and anyone within earshot not to hurt themselves, each other, or anyone else. My technique had come a long way since my first encounter with Billy. I knew what I was doing.

"We are going to be working hard to save Johnny's life," I reassured. "Now I want you all to promise not to hurt each other or anyone else. And, above all, I want you all to promise that you won't let Johnny hurt himself. I want you to nod your head to show that you all have promised."

I waited. No nod.

"Who doesn't want to make that promise?" I asked.

Johnny's facial muscles tightened. His eyes grew hard, pitiless, and cold. Aaron made his final appearance of the day. I did not have to ask who had arrived. Aaron was unmistakable.

"I'll do what Johnny wants. Besides, wouldn't it be better if Johnny killed himself than let them kill him?"

Aaron had a point. I was not about to admit that.

"Aaron," I was firm. "I want you to promise."

"We'll see," came the reply. Again he said "we." The decision would not be unilateral.

Then, spontaneously, the features of the face before me softened. Everyone seemed to have something to say to me about Johnny's impending demise. This time the voice belonged to Barbara.

"I'm not going to let them execute Johnny," came the syrupy words. "I'm not going to let that happen to him."

"How's that?"

"They will put the poison in my veins." The voice was sweet and loving, the syllables lilting, like a lullaby.

"What do you mean?"

"They will kill me, not Johnny. Johnny will live. I promised him. Then they will have to give Johnny a life sentence. Maybe release him."

Aunt Barbara believed that she could sacrifice herself so that her helpless nephew might live. Her logic was familiar. An alternate was, as usual, incapable of linking her own mortality to that of her host. The logic of alters is the logic of dreams. In the realm of the unconscious, opposites exist side by side. Alternates just can't seem to comprehend that their minds are inextricably attached to their host's brain. Tired of taking the pain and pulling the host's chestnuts out of the fire, alternates often attempt to murder the host. Sometimes they whisper suicidal messages in the host's ear. "Jump in front of that car." "Take those pills. All of them." "Cut your wrists. Go ahead." It was this kind of primitive reasoning that led Billy to threaten Marie's life. He took for granted that he, Billy, would survive. In Johnny's case, I was seeing a reversal of this scenario: an alternate personality was volunteering to sacrifice her own life in order to save the host.

I did not even try to reason with Aunt Barbara. There was no time. She would not have believed me anyway. Besides, my task was to try to keep everyone alive. Barbara's self-sacrifice was not a major problem. I worried, rather, that Aaron would beat the executioner to the punch and convince Johnny to hang himself.

Johnny's clemency hearing was just two weeks away. Now it was up to Johnny's attorneys to decide whether or not to make use of the fact that he suffered from multiple personality disorder. Should they try to explain to the board that his alternate personalities had committed the offense for which Johnny was to pay?

It was a tough call. I knew from a review of legal cases in which the issue of multiple personality disorder was raised that courts tended to hold hosts responsible for the acts of their alters. I can't really blame lay people for having that attitude. There is, after all, one body, one brain. But what boggles my mind is the stance of my colleagues who specialize in forensic psychiatry. They may recognize the phenomenon of multiple personality disorder. They may see that a defendant's mind has been divided, shattered by early, ongoing, unendurable pain. They know that in these cases a defendant's left hand does not know what his right hand is doing. They are aware that much of the time the defendant lives in a fantasy world. He is out of touch with reality. Nevertheless, these psychiatrists indulge in the exercise of trying to determine whether a defendant's homicidal, protector, alternate personality—the primitive product of a tortured child's imagination— can distinguish right from wrong. Amazing.

That Johnny was psychotic had long been established. His sense of reality was marginal. There was also ample evidence of damage to his brain. Perhaps it was best to leave well enough alone. The lawyers had already lined up a series of relatives and friends who were prepared (some, admittedly, reluctantly) to testify before the clemency board to the abuse Johnny had endured. Even Johnny's mother was willing to admit that she had not provided the most wholesome of home environments. The constellation of psychosis, brain damage, physical abuse, and child pornography and prostitution would almost surely be sufficient to soften the hearts of the clemency board. Why introduce a diagnosis like multiple personality disorder that many people, psychiatrists included, doubted even existed?

On the other hand, the diagnosis of multiple personality disorder explained why Johnny kept protesting his innocence; it also clarified why he had no clear memory of the murderous act. Was it even ethical to execute Johnny for a crime he truly believed he had not committed? The law states clearly that a condemned prisoner must understand the nature of the crime for which he is being executed. In this case, Aaron had confessed to the rape, and we really were not certain who within Johnny had committed the murder. Surely if anyone we had met were to pay for the crime, then it should have been Aaron. He was the rapist. If the clemency board believed the diagnosis, then they would have to wrestle with the problem of executing the innocent Johnny along with one of the culprits, Aaron.

The clemency board had another legal principle with which to contend. Not only must a condemned person understand the nature of the crime for which he is being executed, he must also understand the fact that he is about to die for it. In Johnny's case, Aunt Barbara had promised repeatedly that Johnny would not die. She would take the poison for him. Therefore Johnny was convinced that he would not die. Johnny's lawyers felt that they had to reveal his condition to the clemency board and force the board to struggle with the ethical, psychiatric, and metaphysical issues raised by Johnny's psychiatric condition.

The evening before the clemency hearing was a frenzied time as lawyers from the Texas Resource Center prepared reams of documentation for the next day's tribunal. The lawyers had prepared an eloquent, fact-filled argument for sparing Johnny's life. They had buttressed it with psychiatric evaluations, neurologic examinations, psychological test results, and affidavits by family members confirming the fact that Johnny Frank Garrett had led a tortured existence from infancy until his arrest at age seventeen. The attorneys spent the final hours before the hearing putting together a thick looseleaf notebook containing these data for each clemency board member. They had also prepared a videotape of excerpts of my psychiatric interview—the one in which Johnny's alters revealed themselves. Tapes of the full interview were also made available to the board if they wanted further documentation of his condition. To read through the materials, review the tapes, ponder their significance, and come to a decision would require hours. A life was at stake.

On the morning of January 18, 1992, for two hours, the clemency board listened as the defense lawyers presented to them the reasons for sparing Johnny's life. The forty or so board members watched segments of my psychiatric interview with Johnny et al. They saw Aaron describe the torture that Johnny could not recall. They witnessed Aunt Barbara declare that Johnny would not die. She would die for him.

Then it was the prosecution's turn to speak. The board heard the district attorney dismiss the psychiatric findings as poppycock. They listened intently as he read to them a disparaging letter about me, written by a San Quentin inmate. I was a phony. I was not to be believed. What the district attorney failed to share with the board was the fact that the letter he read aloud was sent by a serial killer who, on occasion, kept the heads of his victims in his freezer. The board also was not told that this disgruntled death row inmate was currently in the process of bringing suit against his own dedicated attorney, several state officials, and the past and present governors of the state of California. As I watched the expressions on the faces of the clemency board, it looked to me as if they were according this bizarre letter as much credence as they had the Pope's plea for clemency, perhaps more.

Arguments by both sides completed, the members of the clemency board filed out of the courtroom. Each lugged the heavy tome that the lawyers had prepared. Johnny's life was literally and figuratively in their hands.

I gathered up my own materials and rose to leave. There was obviously no way that the board would be able to get through the data provided them in less than three or four hours. If they decided to review all of the taped interview, deliberations could extend for another day. I might as well grab a bite of lunch, pack my bag, and fly home.

Nobody else moved. I looked toward the defense attorneys for guidance. Hand signals told me to remain seated. I did as I was told. Then I waited. I figured that perhaps the presiding judge was about to return and comment on the proceedings. But he was nowhere to be seen. He had vanished along with the clemency board.

I did not have to wait long. In less than an hour the judge returned to the bench, and shortly thereafter the clemency board filed back into the courtroom. Having seen my share of T.V. courtroom dramas, I assumed that they needed clarification on a point or two of law. Perhaps they had returned to request formally to see the tapes of the entire psychiatric interview.

I was astonished. They had reached a verdict. Clemency would not be recommended. It took them just about forty-five minutes to come to that conclusion.

On February 11, 1992, Johnny Frank Garrett was executed in the death chamber of the state prison in Huntsville, Texas. To no one's surprise, Aunt Barbara's plan did not come off, and the poison flowed into Johnny's veins. From witnesses' accounts of his death, Jonathan and I were convinced that, at some time before the poison was injected, Johnny entered the void. Someone far tougher than Johnny came to help him through his final ordeal. According to observers, whoever took Johnny's place sent love to Johnny's mother, then turned to the warden and to the ever-courteous guards and declared, "The rest of you can kiss my ass!"

Like the clemency board members, I was given a copy of the thick looseleaf notebook containing what I now think of as Johnny's remains. Since, after the hearing, its contents were irrelevant to Johnny's fate, I set it aside with the rest of the case materials. After the execution, the entire record was transferred to what my office refers to as the dead file drawer. That drawer was filling up rapidly.

During the weeks to come, when I thought back on the case, I still found myself puzzling over Johnny's choice of victim. Even if, as Aunt Barbara said, Johnny had been intimate with his mother, his mother was still a relatively young woman at the time of the murder. Sister Catherine, the victim, was an old lady. In my experience, I have found that victims tend to resemble abusers. But the only old lady in Johnny's life had been his granny. She, it seemed to me, had rescued him from his mother. Granny and Granpaw had raised Johnny until he was three or four years old. Over the years he had been returned to their household periodically for safekeeping when his mother could not care for him. According to Johnny, if anything, there was "too much love" in that household. Thus the murder of seventy-six-year-old Sister Catherine made no sense to me.

In September of 1992, in preparation for writing this chapter, I resurrected Johnny's file with the heavy looseleaf notebook that his attorneys had prepared. I had lots of time and so I decided to read the seven affidavits from relatives, parole officers, and caseworkers that had been appended in the final days preceding the clemency hearing. Among them was a sworn statement by Johnny's cousin, Kathalene. Her affidavit was dated January 30, 1992, ten years after the murder, five days prior to the clemency hearing, and twelve days before the execution. I had never read it before. It went as follows:

> I am Johnny Frank Garrett's cousin. Johnny and I were raised together by our grandparents. . . . My mom dumped me at their house just like my aunt did Johnny. . . . My mom and my aunt didn't care too much about Johnny and me 'cause they left us there with Grandma and Grandpa to go through the same things they went through when they was kids.
>
> We lived in a house at 604 North Hayes Street in Amarillo. It was an old stucco building that was real run down. There were vacant lots all around our house. We didn't have any neighbors. I can remember lying in my bed and seeing the stars between the crack where the ceiling and the wall met. I had lots of dreams about Jesus coming to save me and Johnny when I looked at the stars through that crack. I was always cold in that old house. . . .
>
> Grandma didn't do any housework to speak of. Grandpa did the little bit of cleaning that was done. . . . Grandma would take me and Johnny to the Dumpster at the Piggly Wiggly store. She made us go through the Dumpster to get food. . . . She would make us eat old tomatoes or other garbage before we got back home to Grandpa. . . . Grandpa did the cooking when we had food. Mostly he would cook taters and beans up into a stew. Everywhere in the house you looked there was roaches.

The roaches would just fall off the ceiling into the stew. Johnny and I called it roach stew. Johnny would eat anything. He would just pick out the roaches and keep eating because it's all we had. . . .

Sometimes Grandma would lock me and Johnny in a room all day. That's when Johnny and I would start playing with our imaginary friends. We used to have those little bitty dolls that won't fall over and we would play like we were the grandparents. Johnny and me would beat them and do awful things that our real grandparents did to us.

Grandma would always tell Johnny and me there wasn't any place for us in this world because our parents didn't want us. . . . She would always call Johnny a little bastard because he didn't have a dad. Sometimes she would tell us that she loved us, but turn right around and beat the hell out of us and make our nose bleed. When she blacked our eyes she would powder our face to hide it. She always made us wear long sleeve shirts and we never got to wear shorts unless they didn't know about it.

Grandma had different personalities. She would be real nice when other people were around, but as soon as the grown-ups would leave Grandma would get real mean to us kids. My earliest memory of Grandma was when I was about two. Grandma hit me in the head with a pipe. It knocked me out. I only remember her standing over me with the pipe and I felt the pain in my head over my ear. I remember rags with blood on them. I now take Dilantin for seizures that the doctor says was caused by Grandma hitting me in the head with that pipe. When I was three years old she ran over my hands with the car. . . .

Grandma hit Johnny in the head a lot of times. . . . She would just up and hit him with whatever she had close by. . . . Once Grandma grabbed one of those things that you put in shoes to keep them straight. Johnny was sitting in the front seat with Grandma and she hit him in the head with that thing until he went to sleep. That's what she did when she wanted us to go to sleep. She would hit us in the head until we passed out.

I will tell you the truth about how Johnny got burned. . . . Johnny wouldn't stop crying. There was a gas heater in the bathroom and Grandma took Johnny in there and turned the gas heater up until the flames were touching the top. She waited until it got real hot and then she took off his pants and jerked him up and sat him down on the heater. She held him there for what seemed like a long time. I'd never heard someone scream like that before. It burned his bottom real bad. . . . I know it was Grandma who burned Johnny. She did the same thing to me. I have scars on my arms, legs, and feet from her burning me on that same heater. . . . I heard Grandma and Aunt Charlotte talking about how Johnny's stepdad was going to prison for sitting Johnny on a stove, but I know it was Grandma who did it. . . .

Grandma never did take a bath and she stunk horribly. . . . Johnny and me we stunk like her 'cause we had to sleep with her. . . . She wouldn't get up to use the bathroom. Grandma would take a scoot in a glass or pee in a glass and just leave it in the sink for us kids to drink out of. Grandma and my mom scooted in their beds at night until the day they died. . . .

Grandma would take me and Johnny 'Goodwillin'. We wouldn't go to the store to do it. Grandma would drive us around to the Goodwill boxes and throw us in to look for things. Johnny and I was so scared one of the kids from our school would see us and tell the other kids. . . .

When Grandma found little girl clothes she would dress Johnny up like a girl. That would happen at least twice a week. She would make him act prissy like a little girl, too. If he didn't she would hit him with her fists in the face and head. . . .

Usually after Grandma had dressed Johnny up like a little girl Grandma would make Johnny parade around in front of Grandpa and then Johnny and Grandpa would go into his room. Grandma and Grandpa never slept together in the same room. Grandpa always had a separate bedroom. Grandpa sexually abused Johnny. I would hear them and Johnny would be crying.

So the rape and murder of Sister Catherine was not an act of random violence, an indiscriminate expression of pent-up fury. The choice of victim, which had puzzled Jonathan and me for the six years of our involvement in the case, was no longer a mystery. The act had been programmed years before, in a house on North Hayes Street. It had been rehearsed in childhood behind closed doors, with tiny dolls who were made to take the pain; and it had been reinforced by a series of brutal stepfathers and a mother oblivious to intergenerational boundaries.

Johnny had struggled to describe for me the precipitant of the evening's violence: some sort of humiliation at his grandmother's house; a visit to his mother's trailer; his mother, clad only in a slip; stimulation; erection; an urge that had to be satisfied. But the words did not come out fast enough for me. Johnny had become confused; he stuttered, hesitated. And I, in a hurry, in an ignorant hurry, dismissed his faltering attempts to communicate as digressions. I pushed ahead, intent on hearing about the murder itself; intent on hearing about what I assumed was important.

Now it was clear. Whatever happened that night at his grandparents' place and at his mother's trailer had kindled in Johnny an old, excruciating, sexual arousal; it also ignited in him an old, murderous, uncontrollable rage. When Johnny could no longer tolerate these feelings, as in childhood, his alternate personalities took over. Aaron sent Johnny creepy crawling. Together they made their way to the convent. Then Johnny entered the void and Aaron raped Sister Catherine. To that Aaron willingly confessed. We shall never know for sure who among Johnny's alters actually murdered the aged nun. Was it Aaron? Aunt Barbara? My own guess is that it was the powerful, controlling figure with the fiery eyes—the one who most intimidated Aaron, the one who refused to give me his name. We can be fairly certain, however, that whoever committed the murder, whoever slashed the throat of the innocent nun, did not see Sister Catherine's face when he did it. He saw instead the face of Granny. Alters, stuck in time, are always mistaking one situation for another, forever confusing someone with someone else.

At last I understood Aaron's enigmatic non sequitur, the one I was in too big a hurry to pursue: "His grandmother and grandfather put all their love into Johnny. . . . Too much love. Too much love."

CHAPTER 18

In courtrooms, reason prevails over passion. In courtrooms, fair, principled prosecutors and sane, capable defense attorneys present their cases before wise judges and impartial juries. Right? Wrong. Maybe that's how it's supposed to be, but that's not the way it is, not by a long shot. When judges, juries, lawyers, and, yes, psychiatrists set foot in a courtroom, something peculiar happens. They often park their common sense at the door.

Years ago, further back than most readers will be able to recall, we did not watch T.V.; we listened to the radio. My favorite program was "The Shadow." The Shadow, who was "in reality Lamont Cranston, wealthy young man about town," had the ability "to cloud men's minds so that they cannot see him." The concept that someone or something was powerful enough to addle people's minds until they couldn't see what was right under their noses intrigued me. How did he do it? Could he do it to me?

Well, courtrooms do that to people every day of the week. It's true. Individuals of above average intelligence who ordinarily think logically and whose judgment is usually impeccable lose these powers, or at least temporarily mislay them, upon entering court. I am speaking now about what often happens to people in murder trials. Civil actions may be another story entirely. I don't know. I am thinking especially of capital murder cases.

Capital murder trials are unlike any other criminal proceedings. They deal with life and death. With so much at stake, one would assume that only the sanest, wisest, and most experienced legal minds would be allowed to play the game. By "play" I mean judge, prosecute, or defend. Wrong again. For example, I have known some of the craziest, most immature, and least experienced individuals to be permitted to represent accused murderers in capital trials. I am not thinking about lawyers, although there are well-documented cases in which capital defendants were represented by drunk, felonious, or totally inexperienced court-appointed attorneys. I am speaking rather of capital defendants who have been allowed to represent themselves, to proceed *pro se*. They don't win, at least not in the cases on which I have worked. I should modify that statement. Defendants don't win if they wish to plead innocent. Guilty pleas are much more likely to prevail.

Capital murder trials are hard enough for seasoned jurists to handle. Everyone knows that. So you have to ask yourself, what on earth would possess a defendant in a capital murder case to represent himself? Most of the capital defendants whom I have examined who have pleaded innocent have been high as a kite, not on drugs but on their own juices or neurotransmitters, when they decided to represent themselves. Even after a death sentence has been passed, they have seemed oblivious to their plight. I think again of Ted Bundy and his cheerful words regarding execution. "Don't worry, Doctor Lewis. It's not gonna happen!" Those who have represented themselves and pleaded guilty have, by and large, either been depressed and eager to die or psychotic and certain they wouldn't.

Judges should know this. They should at least ask themselves why anyone in his right mind would represent himself in such a situation. But here's where that peculiar power of the courtroom to cloud men's minds kicks in. Judges who, every day of the week, outside the court in their roles as fathers or husbands or whatever, easily distinguish children from grownups and crazy people from sane people, in court lose this ability to make such simple distinctions. A particularly lethal strain of this disturbance of reason filtered into the Missouri courtroom in which Heath Wilkins was tried. Heath Wilkins was a sixteen-year-old boy who stabbed to death a salesclerk in the course of an ill-conceived convenience-store robbery. He hadn't planned it that way—it happened. Heath, like his father and brother, had spent a good portion of his life in mental institutions. At one time he was thought to be schizophrenic. No matter. When Heath Wilkins, at sixteen, asked to dismiss his attorney, represent himself, plead guilty, and be sentenced to death, all his wishes were granted. How come?

I have to assume that in everyday life the judge who heard this case was of sound mind. I figure that under ordinary circumstances that judge would have been able to recognize the differences between Heath's maturity, mental stability, and legal expertise and the maturity, mental stability, and legal expertise required of a defense attorney in the capital murder trial of a juvenile. The point is, he didn't. The mysterious courtroom atmosphere that clouds men's minds took over. From behind the bench, Heath's incoherent muttering (and I saw the transcript of his rambling statements) sounded O.K. to the judge. He found Heath both competent and guilty and forthwith sentenced him to death.

Of course a few years later, when Heath matured, his depression lifted, and his head cleared (thanks, perhaps, to appropriate medication), he no longer wished to plead guilty and be executed. Sorry, too late. Now he was in a pickle. After several appeals and a hearing in which Jonathan and I testified before the very same judge who had sentenced Heath to death, the verdict and sentence were upheld. Today, about a decade since our testimony, an appeals court has finally overturned the verdict and sentence. But Heath is still not out of the woods. A zealous assistant D.A.—someone who obviously has breathed in a little too much of that Missouri courtroom air—has appealed to a yet higher court to reinstate the original verdict and death sentence. He must figure Heath had his chance when he was a kid and blew it. This ought to teach him a lesson.

Lawyers are not the only ones addled by courtroom ethers. Psychiatrists are not immune. Well-trained physicians—doctors who, in their everyday practices, recognize and treat properly the illogical, delusional, downright peculiar thinking of their everyday psychotic patients—also seem to suffer a sort of temporary blindness when asked by prosecutors to evaluate violent people. The very same psychotic signs and symptoms that they recognize as requiring hospitalization or at least hefty doses of Thorazine, lithium, or the like in their nonviolent patients seem to elude many psychiatrists when it comes to evaluating crazy, homicidal people. I don't think the courtroom is completely to blame. The grotesqueness of an act or the number of homicides committed can also cloud clinical judgment.

One cannot, of course, completely ignore the income factor. A psychiatrist who depends on court referrals for a major hunk of his income will find himself out of a job if his perceptions of defendants' mental health differ too much or too often from those of the prosecutor. The same I suppose might be said about the incomes of doctors like Jonathan and me, who frequently work with the defense. But there are important differences. First, we work with many different legal teams and therefore are not beholden to any single one of them. Second, we can be fired. If, as sometimes happens, we find nothing of significance psychiatrically or neurologically, we can be dropped. In most states, our findings, or the lack thereof, are treated as confidential. Defendants cannot be forced to incriminate themselves. Court-appointed psychiatrists, on the other hand, are expected, if not required, to make public their conclusions. Therefore, they are under greater pressure than we are to produce clinical results acceptable to their employer. In short, Jonathan and I are freer to let the chips fall where they may. Of course, no one ever hears about the cases from which we are dropped or those from which we withdraw. Once, when

I flew to Florida to testify in the case of a serial killer, I discovered upon arrival, that the defense had hidden vital information from me regarding the defendant's state of mind. I refused to take the stand. I turned around, and flew home. Needless to say, those defense attorneys never again requested my services.

More recently, I worked on the case of another notorious serial murderer. When the high-profile defendant refused to undergo procedures I recommended, I withdrew from the case. Of note, his own attorney withdrew a few months later. I have learned the hard way the wisdom of pulling out of a case if the defendant or his lawyers decline the kind of evaluation I request. Never was this lesson more painful than in the case of Arthur Shawcross.

Arthur Shawcross was preparing to go to trial in Rochester, New York, for the murder of ten women. Before I even laid eyes on the ill-proportioned, paunchy defendant, his lawyers had obtained a chromosome analysis of his cells and an MRI of his brain. They already knew that instead of the usual XY constellation of chromosomes, he had an extra Y chromosome. More important, the MRI had shown that, nestled at the very tip of his right temporal lobe, was a small, fluid-filled cyst. The brain is a very sensitive organ. The tiniest scar or tumor or cyst can, under certain circumstances, trigger abnormal electrical activity and hence seizures. Here's another scary fact: Abnormal electrical foci at the anterior pole of the temporal lobe have been associated with bizarre, animalistic behaviors. Mr. Shawcross had cut out the vagina of one of his victims and eaten it. A highly regarded forensic psychiatrist, hired by the prosecution, ventured the opinion that he did this to remove traces of semen and thereby hide DNA evidence. I figure there must be an easier way to do that. But I am getting ahead of myself.

Arthur Shawcross had the classic signs and symptoms of temporal lobe seizures—the auras, the stereotyped behaviors for which memory was impaired, the subsequent deep sleep. For example, just prior to a homicidal episode, he would begin to sweat and his world would explode in bright, white light. Moments thereafter his hands would close around the necks of his victims. Then, amazingly, he would fall into a deep, postseizure sleep. When he awakened, the memory of his murderous behavior would be hazy and distorted.

Mr. Shawcross never denied any of the murders to me. He admitted everything. The trouble was, whenever I tried to get a complete account of what he had done, Mr. Shawcross became befuddled. He would repeatedly confuse one murder with another. Finally, in desperation, I asked, "Mr. Shawcross, do you remember what happened?"

"No. Not really."

"Then why did you confess to the police?"

He looked at me as though I were crazy. "Because I was there!"

Several of the murders took place in his car. Following these homicides and after falling into a deep sleep, he would awaken and find a corpse on the seat beside him.

"What would you think when you found the body?" I asked.

He thought a moment or two, then responded, "Uh-oh, I must have done it again." When he realized what he had done, he would scurry to find a place to hide the body. Sometimes, later on, he would return to the body and mutilate it.

After my very first visit to see Mr. Shawcross, it was clear to me that a sophisticated neurologic examination was needed, and I asked the Shawcross attorneys to give Jonathan a call. They refused. They said they had already chosen an eminent Harvard neurosurgeon who had seen the MRI and had recommended that a computerized EEG be performed. After the eminent neurosurgeon received the results, he would examine Mr. Shawcross. For years I had admired the neurosurgeon's work on violence. He and a colleague of his had been among the first to document the association of seizures in the limbic system and violence. If I could not work with Jonathan, then he was probably the next best choice.

Weeks passed, months passed, and still neither the computerized

EEG nor the neurologic examination by the eminent neurosurgeon materialized. Meanwhile the lawyers were pressing me to write a report. It was September and the trial was about to begin. Still the test and examination I had requested had not been done. Time was of the essence. According to the lawyers, if I were to be allowed to testify, I had best produce a psychiatric report immediately. What to do?

Over the weeks and months preceding his trial, I realized that Arthur Shawcross suffered from more than just a seizure disorder. After all, most people in the course of a temporal lobe seizure do no harm. They may pace back and forth, button and unbutton their shirts, but they certainly don't strangle anyone. Not usually. Violence during a seizure is rare. In the course of working with Mr. Shawcross, it became clear that, as a result of early, intolerable abuse, Arthur Shawcross also experienced dissociative states. At these times he would hear his mother in his head, berating him and the women he was seeing. No one was good enough for Arty. They should die. At times he seemed to become his own mother, speaking in a high, feminine, angry voice. "He's got to be punished!" "she" squealed, referring to her son. Once, during a session in which hypnosis was used, Mr. Shawcross relived being sodomized with a broom handle, falling to the floor, and being unable to move. In his ordinary, conscious state he had no memory of this event. Had he really been so traumatized as to induce paralysis? Material produced under hypnosis is always suspect, especially in a court of law.

Consistent with the material produced under hypnosis, medical records from childhood revealed that, at age ten, Arthur Shawcross had been hospitalized at Mercy Hospital for a paralysis from the waist down. The hospital, for want of a better explanation, discharged him with the diagnosis encephalomyelitis. I had interned on the pediatric wards of Yale–New Haven, and I knew that the young Arthur Shawcross had none of the signs or symptoms of the disease: no headache, no fever, no stiff neck. A lumbar puncture had revealed clear, perfectly normal cerebrospinal fluid with no signs of infection. What is more, the ten-year-old recovered swiftly from the paralysis and was sent home. As I pored over the almost illegible photocopy of the microfilmed record, I discovered a doctor's note to the effect that Arthur Shawcross had been hospitalized at age nine for the very same kind of inexplicable symptoms. These episodes were definitely not the result of encephalitis. All evidence pointed to hysterical paralysis, a psychiatric disorder induced by trauma and consistent with his later dissociative states.

I had no question that Mr. Shawcross had been severely abused and suffered from dissociative episodes. Nor did the experts on dissociation with whom I consulted on the case have any doubts. Old school records alluded to suspected parental maltreatment. They described his mother as "punishing and rejecting." In grade school, the young Arthur cowered under radiators while the other children sang songs. When he was seven years old, he frequently ran away from home. Psychological tests performed when he was in grade school revealed a seriously disturbed child, lost in a "fantasy in which he perceived himself a new person." I also knew that a psychiatric defense, especially one based on the diagnosis of a dissociative disorder, would never fly. If for years I had doubted the very existence of the diagnosis, there was no reason to think a judge or jury would buy it. A neurologic defense, however, based not only on clinical findings but also on visible MRI evidence of brain damage, was likely to be far more convincing. Letters and phone calls flew back and forth, as I begged the Shawcross attorneys to obtain the computerized EEG and the specialized neurologic evaluation. If their neurosurgeon would not do it, then call Jonathan. Just get it done!

Here is where I made my first big mistake. I buckled and agreed to write my report in the absence of all of the data I had requested. Therefore, all I could do was describe the dissociative phenomena I saw and hint at the existence of a possible seizure disorder, while I awaited proof of it. To bolster my suspicions, I pored over the old prison records and found references there to seven seizurelike episodes that occurred long before the ten murders. Documented in the prison log were blackouts, fainting spells, episodes of falling to the floor. Once he was found in his cell unconscious. I described these in my psychiatric report. Mr. Shawcross's mother and aunt also reported that Arthur suffered similar episodes of blacking out when he was a child. Even his wives (and he had had several) reported times when he "spaced out" or wandered off and did not know where he had been. Nonetheless, without a sophisticated neurologic evaluation by someone like Jonathan and results of a computerized EEG, the findings were only suggestive of seizures. The lawyers assured me that by the time I came to Rochester to testify, the examinations I requested would be completed.

I arrived in Rochester two days before I was to testify, only to discover that neither the neurologic examination by the eminent neurosurgeon nor the computerized EEG he had recommended had been obtained. Later I was told that moneys supposedly reserved to pay the neurosurgeon had been squandered on the services of a writer-cum-criminologist, Joel Norris. He, with the assistance of defense counsel, conducted videotaped interviews with Mr. Shawcross. Worse, prior to trial, Norris's business partner tried to sell the videos to a local public broadcasting station. In fact, unbeknownst to me, as the trial was set to begin, the local public radio station devoted an entire program to airing these facts. They later sent me the audiotape of their program.

You would think that the exposure of such skulduggery would have given the presiding judge pause. Why, he might ask himself, would a defense attorney allow himself to get into a mess like this? How might it affect the outcome of the trial? I sure would have asked myself that if I were the judge. Well, His Honor didn't ask himself such questions. He was not going to permit these kinds of shenanigans to slow the wheels of justice. The trial must go on. It did.

The eminent neurosurgeon would eventually find himself working with the prosecution. Without ever examining Mr. Shawcross or getting the computerized EEG that he himself had requested, he produced for the prosecutor a signed statement saying that the MRI "showed an absence of the tip of his [Shawcross's] right temporal lobe" but that "there are no pressure effects from this." I wonder what he meant by that. It did not mean that there were no electrophysiologic effects. It did not mean there were no behavioral effects. I know that. He knew that. Why make such a wishy-washy statement? Whom was he trying to please?

One evening about two and a half weeks into my testimony, against the express instructions of the defense attorneys, I picked up the phone and called the eminent neurosurgeon at his home. I got right to the point.

"How could you work for the prosecution when you had been retained by the defense?" I asked.

"I was never retained by the defense," came the self-assured reply.

"How is that possible? They said that you read the MRI. They said you recommended a computerized EEG."

"That's true," he agreed, then continued. "Do you know a Joel Norris?"

"The writer?"

"Yes. Well he's always looking for free advice. He sent me the MRI and we talked on the phone."

"You saw the lesion in the temporal lobe?"

"Of course. I told him to get a computerized EEG. I even gave him the name of the people to do it. But I was never retained by the defense."

To my mind this was a technicality, and I said so. Didn't the ethics of the situation preclude working for the prosecution under these circumstances? The question had crossed the neurosurgeon's mind. When the prosecutor called upon him for assistance, he consulted a lawyer, a close relative, to check out the legality if not the ethics and propriety of furnishing information to the prosecutor after having consulted with the defense. The issue was resolved to his satisfaction when the judge in the case agreed to sign a court order requiring him to provide the prosecutor with a statement.

"But how could you say the cyst in his brain didn't matter?

You never saw the patient. You never got the computerized EEG," I demanded.

"I never said that it didn't matter. I said that the cyst might be significant in terms of the murders themselves, but further tests were indicated. I even told the investigator for the district attorney that whether or not the cyst caused the homicidal behaviors, it would intensify them." But these were verbal communications. Why were they not in his report? I held the phone between my shoulder and ear and struggled to take down his words. This conversation I did not want to forget.

From the day I arrived in Rochester and discovered that the neurologic workup had not been done, I tried to speak with the judge in chambers. Surely if he knew the importance of the neurologic tests he would delay the trial until they could be completed. The judge refused to speak with me. Now, having talked with the neurosurgeon, armed with this new information, it was vital that I talk with the judge and inform him of the truth.

The next morning I again asked to speak with the judge in chambers, in the presence of the defense and prosecution, of course. This time the Shawcross lawyers assured me it had been arranged. Now the prosecutor objected. With hindsight, I can understand why, although at the time I was dumbfounded. Only then, after the judge refused to talk privately in chambers, did I take a deep breath and say in open court, "Your Honor, I have been lied to."

If I were a judge and an expert witness made such a declaration, I would be pretty curious. Certainly I would find a few minutes, maybe cut short my lunch break, to hear what the witness had to say. After all, trials are based on a search for truth, aren't they? The strange thing is, the judge wasn't the least bit curious. Was it the courtroom air that had deadened his curiosity? No, it was not the air. It was as though he knew in advance whatever I had to tell him. The judge admonished me to get on with my testimony. If I really had something I thought he needed to know I should write him a letter when I got back to New Haven.

As I look back, it is clear what I should have done. I should have done what I did in Florida. When I arrived in Rochester and discovered that the neurologic evaluation I had been promised had not been done, I should have turned around and gone home. I should have refused to testify. I didn't. I didn't have the courage. That was my second big mistake, and I paid dearly for it.

To the best of my knowledge, I was the only doctor to testify for the defense. One exchange between me and the prosecutor that occurred during cross-examination stands out in my mind. It went something like this: "Doctor Lewis, could not the interviews with Joel Norris have affected what Mr. Shawcross told you?" At first I said no. When I learned of them, I figured they had occurred after I completed my interviews. They had not. The prosecutor smiled contemptuously as he informed me that five interviews with Norris had taken place during the months I was conducting my evaluation. Under such circumstances I had to admit there was certainly a possibility they had influenced what Mr. Shawcross told me. I did not believe they had, but I never was shown the Norris tapes. How could I be sure?

Not only did the jury not believe me, they hated me. Then again, so did the rest of Rochester. My testimony extended over a three-week period as the prosecutor relished raking me over the coals. During this period my double-locked office at Bellevue was broken into. There's really nothing special about such a break-in; it happens all the time. Computers and videotaping equipment are constantly being ripped off. That's why I had special locks put on my doors. The creepy thing was that in this break-in nothing was taken. My home phone and office phone also started acting up, as though the lines were crossed or someone were listening in. When I mentioned this to a friend of mine whose work involved security in the corporate world, he produced a piece of equipment with tiny red and green lights and told me how to attach it to my home phone. If the green light went on it meant the line was being tapped. It did. I was scared. I wrote to my friend and colleague, Dick Burr, informing him that if anything happened to me he should know that I had not harmed myself. Night after night during the course of my testimony I would return to my hotel, almost punch-drunk from the new information hurled at me in court, information the defense should have shared with me (e.g., the Norris interviews). I would then switch on the news and watch the man (or woman) in the street belittle me and my testimony. Jingles were written about me and played on talk radio. It was a nightmare.

The prosecution had hired one of the most highly regarded forensic psychiatrists in the nation, a man who had been a consultant to the FBI and CIA. He was a handsome, confident man who never appeared hassled. Compared to him I looked clumsy and disorganized. I looked as though the courtroom vapors had gotten to me. In truth I was angry. I had been tricked. I have learned since then that one should never take the stand angry. It wreaks havoc with one's memory and, of course, one's demeanor.

The highly regarded forensic psychiatrist dismissed all of Mr. Shawcross's dissociative symptoms—his amnesias, his hallucinations, his switches of personality state—as malingering. He interpreted Mr. Shawcross's confusion and discrepant accounts as simply lying. In fact, he even dismissed all of his childhood symptoms of psychopathology as insignificant. He concluded: "Mr. Shawcross has never suffered from any mental disease or defect as these terms are ordinarily understood, though he has suffered from less severe mental disorders." What were these "less severe mental disorders"? By now the reader can guess. His report read: "Among criminals, the most common mental disorder is that known as antisocial personality disorder, and that is my primary diagnosis for Mr. Shawcross."

What about the neurologic findings? By the time I took the stand, it was pretty clear that Mr. Shawcross's attorneys were not going to produce a neurologist to present the neurologic findings. They had, however, allowed me to send the MRI to Washington, D.C., for Jonathan to review. I shall not forget our telephone conversation the afternoon he looked at the films.

"Jonathan, did you see the cyst in the temporal lobe?"

"Of course I did. But, Dorothy, what about the scars in both frontal lobes?" He circled the lesions and sent back the film. There they were, plain as day—two straight little scars, one on each side.

Given the fact no neurologist would be testifying, every chance I got I mentioned the clinical indications of a seizure disorder, and I alluded to the scars and the cyst found on the MRI. If the lawyers would not allow a neurologist to show the abnormalities to the jurors, the jurors would at least hear about them from me. I was repeatedly chastised by the judge for not responding directly to questions with a succinct yes or no. Guilty as charged.

The highly regarded forensic psychiatrist gave short shrift to the MRI findings. He also thought nothing of the blackouts and falling episodes documented in the prison chart. The sweating and bright lights? Malingering. The sleep attacks right next to the corpses? Necrophilia! In his words, "Incidental findings of XYY chromosome complement and a benign cyst below one lobe of the brain. Neither of them is of any significance with respect to Shawcross's criminality."

I understand it took the jury less than two hours to find Mr. Shawcross sane and guilty of the murders of ten women. It took me three years to recover from my three weeks on the stand. No one had believed a word I said. Mr. Shawcross was not insane.

The term insanity once had meaning, real meaning. The root of the word is the Latin, *sanus,* healthy, of sound mind. Insane meant the opposite, sick or of unsound mind. In the real world people still use the word insane the old way, as a synonym for crazy, psychotic, not in touch with reality, out of control.

In court insanity has a different meaning; I should say meanings. The legal meanings of insanity differ from state to state. New York State, where Arthur Shawcross was tried, uses a version of the M'Naughten rule, whereby a person is insane only if he does not appreciate the nature of what he is doing or does not appreciate that it is the wrong thing to do. This concept was established in England in the mid-nineteenth century. It is a definition based exclusively on rational understanding and concepts of morality and ignores all psychiatry knows about the neurophysiological, psychological, and environmental forces that influence our behaviors. It also ignores all psychiatry does not know about how to measure the appreciation of wrongfulness. Of course this legal definition of insanity renders the term useless for distinguishing the sick from the well.

About a century after M'Naughten, a group of legal scholars of the American Law Institute formulated a model penal code, containing a broader but, to my mind, more enlightened standard of insanity than M'Naughten. It suggested that a person was not responsible for a criminal act if, by reason of mental disease or defect, he either lacked substantial capacity to appreciate its wrongfulness (i.e., M'Naughten) or lacked substantial capacity to conform his behavior to the requirements of law. This second clause implicitly acknowledges that emotional states and impaired self-control can contribute to violent acts.

Since then, states have wrestled with a variety of other formulations and standards of insanity, including such oxymoronic concepts as "guilty but insane." Civilized societies exonerate the insane from guilt. You can't be insanely guilty or guiltily insane. At least I don't think so. Other states have conceptualized a condition of "diminished capacity," a recognition that all or none standards of sanity and insanity don't do justice to the complexity of human behavior.

The more we understand about the genesis of violence, the harder it is to draw a clear line between guilt and innocence, sanity and insanity. We, as a society of thinking and feeling human beings, struggle within ourselves to cope with competing interests and motivations: the need for protection from dangerous people, sane or insane; the desire for revenge; the knowledge of the psychobiological and environmental influences on violent behavior; and the wish to adapt to evolving standards of decency and morality. Guilt was a lot easier to measure before we recognized that free will, like sanity and insanity, is a constantly fluctuating intellectual and emotional continuum and not a fixed, immutable capacity or state of mind. In response to our struggles to strike balances between what we *feel* we'd like to do to people who commit grotesque acts of violence no matter what their mental state, and what we *think* perhaps we ought to do and ought not to do, jurisdictions have swung back and forth, changing from one definition of insanity to another, then back to the first, often in response to a sensational case of the moment.

Given its etymology, the term insanity by rights should belong to the field of psychiatry, not law. Surely health is more the province of doctors than lawyers (malpractice suits to the contrary notwithstanding). Nonetheless, insanity has become a legal term. It feels as though lawyers and lawmakers whisked the term from our grasp, then batted it around and pummeled it until it took on an almost unrecognizable form. Now, those of us psychiatrists who are asked periodically to testify in court regarding a murderer's mental state are obliged to use the idiosyncratic legal meaning insanity has acquired.

I don't testify in court that often, maybe three or four times a year. A few years ago, by chance, three murder cases I had been working on over the course of several years all came to trial within about a six-week period, one on the West Coast, one in the deep South, and one on the East Coast. I had to work with three different definitions of insanity. When I woke up each morning I felt as though I were in a movie called *If This Is New York It Must Be M'Naughten.*

When angered, legislatures, like individuals, act impulsively. They pass laws that fly in the face of common sense. Under such laws, murderers who are obviously stark raving mad are not legally insane. Everyone knows that a serial killer who eats his victim, even a teensy piece of his victim, is crazy. But somehow, by adopting purely moralistic and unmeasurable definitions of insanity and forcing psychiatrists to make use of them, the legal profession forces us to reach some pretty peculiar conclusions. Was Arthur Shawcross crazy when he murdered his victims and consumed their genitalia? Of course. He had to be. Insane? Not necessarily. Not according to some forensic psychiatrists. I wouldn't be a bit surprised if someday soon a state legislature develops a concept of crazy not insane or psychotic not insane.

My husband, who almost never testifies in court, thinks we psychiatrists should stand on principle, use our own definitions, refuse to be bullied by lawyers. I admire his idealism. But the games are played in their courts by their rules. If we question their terms too strenuously and too often, next time they just might not let us play at all.

And if they kicked people like us out of the game? So what? It would make my life and Jonathan's a bit safer and a lot less stressful. It would also leave some pretty sick defendants high and dry.

Several months after the trial, an investigative reporter contacted me. He had been looking into the Shawcross trial and had discovered a few things he thought I ought to know. In the course of reviewing the evidence, he had come upon several letters written, unbeknownst to me, by the Shawcross lawyers to the prosecutor and to the judge. One was written months before the trial but long after we knew of the cyst and after I had requested the neurologic workup. I gathered from this letter that the prosecutor had gotten wind of the abnormal neurologic findings on the MRI and wanted to see the report. In response to this request, the Shawcross attorneys informed the prosecutor "that there is nothing contained in those records which provide a basis for a psychiatric defense" and that Dr. Lewis would "not in any way rely on them in forming her opinion." This, of course, was not true. In a subsequent letter one of the lawyers informed the prosecutor, "it is my understanding at this time that none of these test results are pertinent to Dr. Lewis' opinion." This was not true. Finally, a letter sent by the defense to the prosecutor just prior to the trial—a period of time when I was pleading with the defense lawyers to obtain the neurologic examination, if not by their eminent neurosurgeon, then by Jonathan—informed the prosecutor that in my opinion none of the neurologic procedures (i.e., the MRI) "demonstrated any abnormalities or evidence of organic brain damage." This was a lie. In retrospect it looks as though Mr. Shawcross's attorneys had never intended to obtain either the computerized EEG or the evaluation by their eminent neurosurgeon.

There was another item the reporter thought would be of interest to me. Mr. Shawcross had been found guilty of the ten murders. He was about to stand trial in another county for an eleventh. In preparation for the upcoming trial, and undoubtedly in response to my testimony regarding the likelihood of a seizure disorder, the lawyers finally obtained the computerized EEG that I and the eminent neurosurgeon had requested. My guess is, they wanted to discredit me once and for all.

The computerized EEG report came back. It read as follows: "Conclusion: EEG/CEEG/Dynamic Brain Mapping is ABNORMAL (sic). It shows paroxysmal irritative patterns bifrontotemporal areas more on the right side." It continued to spell out the importance of the findings: "Sharp waves/spikes=unusually pointed waves=indicate local cerebral irritation. Paroxysmal activity=are bursts of spikes, slow waves or complex of both—associated with SEIZURES (sic)."

Clearly the scars in Mr. Shawcross's frontal lobes and the cyst in his temporal lobe affected the functioning of his brain. One rarely gets such unequivocal evidence of temporal and frontal lobe seizures, not to mention documentation of the brain lesions giving rise to them.

"Well, are they finally going to run with the neurologic defense?" I asked the reporter. I knew that the likelihood of Arthur Shawcross's ever being found not guilty by reason of insanity was small. People were too afraid he might get out of a hospital and kill again. I could understand that. Nevertheless, a new trial in which the neurologic findings would finally be aired would at least teach the public about some of the ingredients that sometimes contribute to the creation of a serial killer. They would learn that serial killers are not born, they are made.

The reporter looked at his feet. Reporters rarely do that. I think he was embarrassed to give me the news. "I guess I didn't tell you. After his lawyer got the results of the computerized EEG, he advised Mr. Shawcross to plead guilty."

"And?"

"He did."

Now, six years later, as I reflect on the Shawcross case from what I hope is the safety of my office, I am intrigued. I keep wondering: Why would the Shawcross lawyers want to ignore, no, hide such extraordinary data that could have helped their client's case? Why did they cooperate so readily with the prosecutor in dismissing such potent neurologic findings? Why, when the prosecutor accused me of springing the neurologic data on him at the last minute, did the defense lawyers not "rehabilitate" me and show in the notes of my first interview my awareness of the temporal lobe cyst and the symptoms of psychomotor seizures? Why did they not produce the letters back and forth discussing the need for a neurologic exam by Jonathan? Why did they let me look so silly? It beats me.

As I think about the Shawcross brain, I think what better way to make a murderer than with an irritable focus in the temporal lobe and the transection of frontal lobe fibers? The person would be left with a limbic system gone haywire, disconnected from the modulating effects of the frontal lobes. If someone wanted to create a killer brain, that's probably the way to do it.

Years and years ago, in the 1950s, 1960s, and 1970s, the military and the CIA were interested in that sort of thing. They were especially interested in mind control, the potential power of hypnosis, drugs, and psychosurgery to destroy memory and mold behavior. Could these methods, alone or in combination, be used to create a killer? That was their question. Reports based on CIA documents indicate that during that period civilian and military prisoners, as well as ordinary citizens, were used in these mind-brain experiments. When I tried to get hold of Mr. Shawcross's army records, I was told that most of them, which were from the Vietnam era, were missing, burned in a fire. Unfortunately Mr. Shawcross could remember almost nothing about his army experiences except for the name of Westmoreland. It was as though his memory had been erased. He had some wild recollections of slaughtering women in Vietnam and cooking and eating their parts.

No one believed him. The prosecutor, who fought the insanity defense tooth and nail, dismissed these bizarre memories as the ravings of a sane man. Since then I have seen two other serial killers with similar memory impairment for their Vietnam years. One of them has only wild, grotesque recollections—half-dreams that no one believes. Their army records have also been destroyed. In my Shawcross workup, had I stumbled on something the Powers That Be were not too eager to reveal? Is that why I was made to look so incompetent, hung out to dry?

Funny thing. According to CIA records, a man of the same name as the prosecutor's, an uncommon name, ran a safe house in New York State in the 1960s where the CIA conducted experiments on mind control. It could, of course, be a coincidence, but I can't help wondering whether the prosecutor and the operator of the safe house are related to each other. Maybe someday another brave investigative reporter will get curious about these cases.

CHAPTER 19

My daughter believes that the judge who sentences a person to death should be responsible for carrying out his sentence. He should spring the trapdoor under the gallows; press the button and deliver the current; inject the poison. She thinks that then there would be fewer executions. Most people, she believes, would have trouble doing those things. I'm not so sure.

She may, of course, be right. After all, most of the murderers Jonathan and I have evaluated, to quote a guard at Starke, "aren't wrapped too tight." They have been raised in such bizarre, abusive, pathological families that they don't think straight. Most of the time it's impossible to figure out just how much of their paranoia and impulsiveness is thanks to a hereditary predisposition to mania or schizophrenia, how much is the result of brain damage from birth trauma or battering, and how much comes from growing up in a violent, crazy household. How does one tease out the psychological consequences of being tortured, or sodomized, or neglected from the physical consequences? What does chronic terror do physiologically to the growing brain? It can't be good.

There is some evidence that severely traumatized animals pour out hormones that actually alter the anatomy of their brains. Too much cortisol seems to damage the hippocampus, that part of the limbic system where scientists think long-term memories are processed and stored. Whatever the combinations of factors that have led our murderers to death row, most of these people are severely damaged, physically and psychologically. Forensic psychiatrists to the contrary notwithstanding, crazy people can plan diabolical acts. In fact, we have found that the grizzliest murders are plotted, planned, and perpetrated by the most psychotic killers. Delusional thoughts and beliefs can give rise to carefully orchestrated homicide. The law does not appreciate this fact; the lay public does. Witness the books and films about killers. Writers and directors are often more sophisticated than lawyers and even forensic psychiatrists when it comes to understanding the psychopathology of murderers. Two of the best books and later films about murderers, *Psycho* and *Silence of the Lambs*, were informed by real cases.

The question in my own mind has long been whether or not recurrent murderous violence can be perpetrated by a relatively normal human being. People have argued that the Holocaust could not have occurred without the willing participation of ordinary German citizens. However, as numerous authors have shown, a variety of factors in German society, including economic decline, social unrest, extremely punitive parenting practices, and a prevailing attitude among Germans that their victims were subhuman made it possible for the Holocaust to happen. Even then, there is evidence that many perpetrators had to block out their murderous acts and dissociate themselves from them in order to function back at home with their wives and children.

My question is different. Within our own society, are there individuals who are able to kill repeatedly and whose only psychopathology, if you could call it that, is a lack of empathy for other human beings? Are there real sociopaths—that is, people who fit the diagnostic criteria for antisocial personality disorder—who simply kill for the fun of it or to make a living? I have never seen one. Then again, lawyers probably don't call upon Jonathan and me in such cases.

My curiosity to see a pure sociopath led me to make an offer to the psychiatry residents working on the forensic service at Bellevue. Many years ago I offered ten dollars to anyone who could find me a recurrently violent offender who had no signs of psychotic thinking or organic impairment. No one took me up on my offer, though once I had a nibble. A forensic psychiatry trainee was convinced he had found just the sort of man I was looking for. We set up an appointment for me to meet him. On the morning of the scheduled appointment, the trainee cancelled. He discovered that his patient was paranoid. Another time a doctor on the forensic service alerted me to the admission of a hit man. Here was my chance. I would finally see a cool, competent killer—someone for whom killing was a way of life, a job.

My heart fell the minute I set eyes on the scruffy fellow. After speaking with him for an hour, it seemed most unlikely to me that the dull-witted, uncoordinated bungler before me could possibly have been entrusted by others to carry out murders. I would not have trusted him to go to the store for me for a loaf of bread. As for the twelve "hits" he claimed to have made, they seemed to me to be elements of an elaborate delusional system. I suspect that successful hit men, if they exist, are more adept at eluding police and rarely land on the psychiatry wards of Bellevue. Some years ago I had a terrible time trying to find Robert De Niro a diabolical model on which to base his portrayal of the villain in the remake of *Cape Fear*. Forensic psychiatry services like Bellevue's just don't attract a dashing clientele.

Jonathan says he once evaluated an assassin. That's what Jonathan called him. According to Jonathan, the man had, coolly and without qualms, "offed" fourteen victims, collecting between one and ten thousand dollars for each hit. However, Jonathan's assassin did have his principles. He refused to kill a high school classmate. He paid someone else to do it.

"So Jonathan, the guy was perfectly normal. No psychosis? No brain damage? Just no conscience?"

"I didn't say that. He had been horribly abused as a child. There were soft signs and he had frontal lobe damage."

"And psychosis?"

"He was paranoid." Jonathan thought for a few seconds. "Then again, if he shot fourteen people, he must have had a few enemies."

Perhaps the incentive to find me a pure sociopath was insufficient. I upped the ante to one hundred dollars. Still no one produced a recurrently violent person who lacked psychotic symptoms, neurologic impairment, and a conscience.

Then one day in 1991 the occasion to see such a person presented itself. I was being interviewed by a Spanish film crew, doing a documentary on death row in the United States. They were interested in hearing firsthand about the study Jonathan and I had done of juveniles on death row. The crew had been traveling around the country, interviewing condemned prisoners, defense lawyers, prosecutors, prison wardens, and the like. Mine was to be their final interview before returning to Madrid. In the course of our conversation, they mentioned the fact that they had just come from the Deep South, where they had filmed an interview with an executioner. That's my man, I thought, and promptly put in a call and arranged to meet him. I shall call him Bob Smith. I never did learn his real name. He wouldn't tell me.

As I said at the start of this book, the art of working with people who kill other people includes never being locked up with them alone. I therefore prevailed on Catherine Yeager, my colleague and dear friend, to accompany me to the interview. Because I expected this to be a unique experience, I also invited George Billard, a filmmaker I had met while taping a deposition, to come along and document the interview on film. Cathi brought along our own video camera as a backup. If this person had really executed nineteen people, and if he could perform his job with equanimity, surely this would be an interview worth studying in the years to come. In fact, it is now five years since I spoke with Bob Smith, and each time I watch the tapes of our meeting, I discover something new and fascinating that I missed during the hours we talked face-to-face.

It was nightfall by the time we found the trailer park that Bob Smith called home. Because his own trailer was too small to accommodate all of us and our equipment, he had arranged to borrow the larger trailer of a friend for the interview. Nonetheless, it was a tight squeeze. As I recall, by the time the two tripods and cameras were set up, there was little room for George, who had either to stand or half-sit on a bookshelf. Bob Smith and I sat perpendicular to each other at the corner of a rectangular table.

What do you ask a man who has caused the death of so many human beings? As I said, Jonathan and I have examined about a dozen serial murderers. One of them, William Bonin, had murdered fifteen boys. Now I found myself in a trailer park in the Deep South, seated at a table with a man who had ended the life of nineteen human beings. The only person I had ever met who had killed more people than Bob Smith was Ted Bundy.

Bob Smith was a good-looking man, tall, full bearded, muscular— nothing like the scrawny Johnny Garrett or the pudgy William Bonin. I imagine Lucky Larson might have looked like him had he not severed his right facial nerve in the car accident when he was seventeen. This man seated so close to me in the tiny trailer would have been handsome, were it not for his slightly flattened nose. I would learn that Bob Smith, like so many of the men Jonathan and I had interviewed during our research on violence, had experienced his share of barroom brawls; the bridge of his nose had taken the brunt of several of them. Still, he projected a combination of strength and charm. He was obviously at ease as he popped open a can of beer from his six-pack and handed it to me. He then opened a can for himself and settled into his chair.

I began. "How does what you do affect you?" The response was quick and sure.

"It don't. In no way."

I was speechless. What he said didn't make sense. I thought back to my husband's question to the serial killer, William Bonin, a man who had tortured and killed more than a dozen young boys. My husband had listened for two hours as I interviewed Bonin. Just before ending the session, I turned to Mel, who was seated behind me, and asked if he had any questions.

"As a matter of fact I do," Mel answered in his elegant, soft-spoken English way. "What are your feelings when you do those things?" (My husband was referring to the torture and murder of the young boys.)

Bonin paused. He thought and thought, then asked, warily, "Is that a trick question?"

But that was different. Bonin was a serial murderer, a man who picked up unsuspecting young boys on the highway, squeezed their genitals, raped them, and strangled them. Bonin remembered nothing of the sexual perversions to which he had been subjected as a boy. We had to rely on his mother's memory and on the records of orphanages and hospitals and correctional schools to learn what had happened to him. That he had blocked out all memory of his childhood, as well as all feelings relating to his atrocious acts, was not all that surprising. Killers do that. But I expected Bob Smith to be different. He had nothing to hide, nothing to forget. It was inconceivable to me that Bob Smith was untouched by his job.

I paused, thinking of the other man I had known who had killed that many people and more, Ted Bundy. Ted Bundy told me that for a time he was able to satisfy his violent, sexual impulses by looking at pictures, reading books, and masturbating. Then for a period of years he abducted and raped young women. In the beginning he did not kill. However, once he murdered—once he crossed that boundary, violated that taboo—killing got easier and easier. I remember asking him, "Why didn't you get help? See a psychiatrist?"

"I thought about it. But by then it was too late. They would have told," he answered. He knew there was something wrong with him. He had some feelings about what he did; he just couldn't stop. The man talking with me professed to no feelings at all about what he did. Could it be true? Had I at last encountered a person who had neither psychotic nor neurologic symptoms, who simply killed for a living?

"Do you know why I wanted to talk to you?" I asked.

"No."

"Let me explain. I do research on violence, on people who do violent things. I have talked with people on death row. I've heard things from that point of view." I was obviously struggling to word my question inoffensively and felt I was doing a pretty lousy job of it. "I wanted to know what it's like for you to do this kind of work."

"It's just a job I do," came the matter-of-fact reply. "I don't wear a mask and I don't have no nightmares."

Was that true? Is it possible for a man to lack all feeling for those whose lives he takes? And, if so, how does a person get that way? "Tell me about your childhood."

His answer was quick, as if he'd been asked the same question dozens of times. "I was drug up. We was so poor we had to knock on doors for food. That's why I got no sympathy for those who make excuses, who say they was poor or they was abused and that's why they did what they did."

"Tell me about your dad."

"My dad was a redneck."

"Where was his family from originally?"

"Germany."

"What did he do for a living?"

"The old man was a construction worker. We had to go where there was work. Clearfield, Pennsylvania; Rapid City, South Dakota; Cheyenne, Wyoming; New Mexico. I've been to all forty-eight states. There was no welfare or food stamps in those days."

"Did you have enough to eat?"

"Yes." I could have sworn that he just said he went door to door begging for food. Perhaps over time the inconsistency would clarify itself. As in other interviews, I chose, for the moment, to avoid confrontation. "And your mom? Tell me about her."

"She was from the North." That was it. Next question?

"Do you have brothers and sisters?"

"Two brothers and a sister." Then, for a few moments, he became pensive, and the slightly hard, defensive edge to his voice that I had detected earlier disappeared. "I lost one brother. Just before I was born he died of an ear infection. He was three. They say I replaced him." Then, in a twinkling, the almost wistful tone was gone, and he changed the subject. I, on the other hand, was reluctant to abandon the topic of childhood.

I decided to take a slightly different tack, one Jonathan and I have often found useful. I would frame my questions about childhood in a medical context. Psychiatrists could learn a whole lot more than they do about patients if they only asked doctor-type questions; if instead of saying, "Do you see things no one else sees?" they first asked about visual acuity or eye infections, if they asked about earaches before they asked about hearing voices.

"Let me ask you some medical questions," I began, and printed "Medical History" on my pad in such a way that he could read it easily upside down. "Do you know anything about your birth?"

"I was born at 4:23 A.M. and I weighed nine pounds."

"Was your mother's delivery hard?"

"No."

"How about her pregnancy?"

"It was fine."

"Any other problems?"

"The navel chord got infected. They thought I was gonna die." So Bob Smith's introduction to the world was not all that different from Lucky Larson's or Lee Anne Jameson's. He continued. "They told me how hard it was on Mama, seeing as she had just lost a baby."

"What happened?"

"They put her on Quaaludes. She was on that three, four years." Without my asking, Bob Smith was providing me with a family psychiatric history.

"Did she need any other treatment?"

"She was in and out of the mental hospital. She was brought to the hospital five or six times. They just kept giving her Quaaludes."

"Anyone else have trouble with their nerves?"

"I had a friend once who killed himself."

"Oh?"

"His old lady was fucking around, so he killed himself."

"How about you? What are your moods like?" I was delighted at the easy segue into questions about his own mental health.

"I'm moody."

"Ever get depressed?"

"Looking at bills."

"Who doesn't? I mean really depressed. Like not wanting to get up in the morning?"

"Every morning! I've heard people say 'Quit your job. Do what you want to do.' "

"Have you ever felt so sad you thought of suicide?"

"Never. What's that gonna solve?" Then he turned to me and asked, "Have you ever thought of suicide?"

"Sure," I answered. It was true. I had thought about it so often as a child that I even wrote a story about watching my own funeral.

Bob Smith looked at me in amazement. "You're the last one I'd think would consider suicide."

"I did."

"Well, not me. I wouldn't allow anyone to make me feel that way. I'd kill them, not me." How does one respond to that? I didn't. I pretended to ignore it.

"You don't like your work?" Bob Smith was not a full-time executioner. He had told the Spanish film crew that he was also a master electrician.

"It's survival," came the response.

"What would you do if you could do anything you wanted to do?"

"I don't know. Work outdoors. Be a park ranger. They're in control of their life."

"Why didn't you become a park ranger?"

"I didn't go to college. You have to graduate college to be a park ranger."

"What grade did you go to?"

"Eighth."

"Did you ever repeat a grade?"

"Seventh. I had to go to remedial classes."

"How come you stopped in eighth grade?" It was clear to me that Bob Smith was intelligent.

"It was my fault. I felt trapped. I wanted to roam."

"Any special problems at school?"

"English. It was hard for me. I could never get the nouns and pronouns straight. But I do like to read. My brother told me by reading you could travel the world and never leave home." Then he added, "My English teacher started us collecting stamps. I gave them to a little girl I know."

As I listened, in spite of the prejudices with which I had come to this interview, I found myself almost liking Bob Smith.

"Do you have a temper?" I asked.

"Not a temper. I don't bother anybody 'less they bother me. I'm hard to get riled, but when I do. . . . Things happen in life you have no control over."

"What can get you mad?"

"People can say something to upset you. If a person wants to get you mad he can." He continued, "Anytime you meet this individual, they gonna keep on, keep on, keep on."

"Did you ever go further than you meant to?" That's a favorite question of mine. It's not just good with violent inmates. It's good with abusive parents. It helps them let you know what they've done to their kids without making them feel too guilty.

"I never deliberately hurt anyone."

"Ever knock anyone out?"

"Sure, I hit sometimes and they didn't get up. Men get to drinking. You get a few drinks in you and you think you're ten feet tall and bulletproof. You're not."

"What's the worst that's ever happened to you?"

"Had my nose punched, busted. Had it broke once or twice. Had my ribs kicked in, my hand smashed. I busted it."

I wondered silently what his MRI looked like.

"How'd that happen?"

"People's heads are harder than you think." So much for his never deliberately hurting anyone. Again, I ignored the inconsistencies.

"Ever punched a wall?"

"Yes. I've done that."

"Ever been in trouble with the law?" I ventured. "Ever been in jail?" I tried to sound casual.

"I sure have!" The words were boastful, not apologetic.

"What for?"

"Assault and battery. Getting in fights."

"Any scars?" That's another question I really like. The people Jonathan and I evaluate behind bars have their histories of fights and beatings written all over their faces, heads, bodies, arms, and legs. In response to my question, Bob Smith extended his right hand.

"What's that?" I asked, looking at a small round scar.

"A scar from a twenty-two magnum."

"How'd that happen?"

"I happened to be in the right place at the wrong time."

Sometimes Bob Smith got things backwards. I chose not to point out his confusion and to go with the flow. "Tell me about it."

"Just the wrong place at the wrong time. I told them at the hospital I was cleaning my gun. I checked myself out after four days. Things happen in life you have no control over."

"What's that?" I pointed to a tattoo I could not quite make out.

"That's the Grim Reaper. My brother did it for me when I was a kid."

I must have seen one version or another of that tattoo on at least ten different death row inmates. "Are there any scars I can't see?"

That's another good question for violent people. If someone were to ask me that question I would talk about the pain of lost friendships or the death of my mother or something like that. But people on death row—murderers—answer it quite literally, which is exactly how I meant it. You can learn a lot from those hidden scars.

"I was stabbed in the back in a bar," he declared, as though this were an everyday occurrence. "You know, I never found out who did it. I figure I was dancing with some dude's wife. I drove myself to the hospital." He pulled up his shirt and displayed the scar.

"How about accidents? Like bike accidents, or car accidents?"

"I don't remember any." Then, oblivious to what he had just said, he continued, "I've had a lot of car accidents, head-on collisions. I never was hurt. Got my nose busted. Once rolled over on the Interstate. I've been knocked goofy. You get into arguments. Sucker punches."

By this time I felt as though I had wandered into a hall of mirrors or the middle of Chapter Seven of the *Interpretation of Dreams*, the chapter that describes the way in dreams opposites can exist simultaneously. For Bob Smith, yes was no and no was yes. Yes, he had to beg for food; no, he was never hungry. No, he never deliberately hurt someone; yes, he nearly broke his fist punching it into other people's heads. No, he was never in a car accident; yes he had lots of head-on collisions. Psychotic people think that way. I kept my peace. Confrontation, I knew, would shut him up, and that was the last thing I wanted to do.

Bob Smith paused and looked me in the eye. "I know what you're getting at. No, I ain't had no brain damage." I was not completely convinced, but kept these reservations to myself. If not brain damage, what did account for Bob Smith's peculiar way of thinking? He did not always make sense.

"I want to ask you some more medical-type questions. How are your eyes? Do you wear glasses?"

"Just for reading."

"Have your eyes ever played tricks on you?"

"You know about peripheral vision. You're always going to see what you didn't see," came the response. I nodded. I hadn't the foggiest idea what he meant.

"How about your ears? Ever had an ear infection?"

"I got scars in my ears."

"Did your ears ever play tricks on you?"

"Oh sure. I'm not gonna tell you I haven't heard something."

"Have you ever had the experience of thinking someone called you or your mother a bad name and you turned around and you were mistaken?"

"I don't have to worry. People do call me bad names. I got into fights 'cause of people picking on me." Bob Smith was as paranoid as the other killers Jonathan and I had evaluated.

"Who hassled you?"

"Other kids. Seniors always hassle juniors. Didn't you?"

I was startled again at his directness. He had not been trained in patient etiquette. Patients aren't supposed to ask psychiatrists questions like that. I had to remind myself that he was not my patient and I was not his doctor.

"Didn't you?" he repeated.

"No. I was perfect." My god, I was actually bantering with an executioner!

"You were telling me before about your mom and dad. Did either of them have a temper? How were you disciplined?"

"I had damn good beatings."

"Tell me about them."

"My dad, he'd come in and Mama would tell him we did something."

"Like what?"

"Talking back to Mom. Skipping school."

"What would he do?"

"He'd tell us Monday we were gonna get a whipping Friday. He said the waiting was worse than the whipping. He was right. If one of us screwed up, we all three got a whipping. We were supposed to watch each other."

"What did he hit you with?"

"Most of the time his hand. Now when he wanted to . . ." his voice trailed off. Then he resumed, "I'd rather *he* whipped us than my mom."

"How come?"

"She was sneaky. She'd tell you everything was all right. She'd say, 'Go inside and take a bath.'" He paused and looked directly into my eyes. "You ever been beat with a pussy willow club?" he asked.

"A what?"

"With a switch from a willow tree?"

I confessed I had not. My parents did not cross Central Park West to cut switches from the shrubbery in the park. Nor did they send me to do it.

"You ever been whipped when you was wet?"

Again, I had to admit I had not. I recall once being spanked by my father. I must have been about six or seven years old. A friend and I had hidden together under the skirt of a dressing table when it was time for her to go home, and my parents couldn't find us. In New York City, that's a pretty scary situation for parents. Even then I wasn't hurt, just humiliated. But my Long Lane delinquents had taught me that being beaten when you are wet is especially painful. The little boy who burned down the administration building of his treatment center had been wetted down and beaten by his psychotic aunt.

Bob Smith continued to reminisce. "If you cut one too small, she'd send you out again." Jonathan and I have heard that many times; at Long Lane, on death row, we have heard it again and again.

I took a break while George changed the roll of film. I needed some time to collect my thoughts. We had been talking for a couple of hours, during which Bob Smith had consumed five beers of a six-pack. I, in contrast, was still nursing my first. By then I could have used another, but I deliberately limited myself to one. Making sense of Bob Smith's words while struggling to keep things moving was challenging enough without alcohol. I needed a clear head. In all likelihood, this would be my only chance to talk face-to-face with an executioner. I did not want to miss anything. It probably sounds odd, but I regarded talking with Bob Smith as a privilege, one few psychiatrists ever have. I was determined to use the time well.

George signaled that the film was rolling. I took a swig of my remaining beer and began. (When my English husband saw the tape of me guzzling beer with an executioner, he was appalled.) "How did you get into this line of work?"

"My brother told me about it. He saw an ad in the paper. It said the state executioner had died. My brother knew I was a strong believer in the death penalty. So I made some phone calls. I got a civil service application and applied for it. The person who interviewed me told me later on I was the most aggressive one who applied." Then, he added, "I was the only one turned in an application." As usual, I let this contradiction pass. By now I was used to them. For Bob Smith, realities shifted from minute to minute. In time I simply learned to shift with them. It was like getting my sea legs on a rocky boat. After a while, nothing makes you woozy and the nausea subsides.

"And then what happened?"

"I got a call from a warden. Six months later I executed my first one."

First one. Not first person. Not first man. Not even first murderer. First one. It sounded like shooting one's first deer or scoring with a woman for the first time. But when teenagers talk about those kinds of firsts, they describe them with some feeling, with pride or sheepishness. Bob Smith spoke of his "first" without a trace of affect.

"Who was it?"

"He was a black dude. He killed a black security guard for no reason."

"What was he like, the first man you executed?"

At this point Bob Smith's voice changed as he tried to imitate a whiny child. "He said he had a bad childhood. He was mistreated." Then, with contempt, he snarled, "That's how he got all those stays."

"So you think he was no different from you, I mean his upbringing?"

"It's a crock of shit. I told you I was drug up. I got in every trouble you could get." And you didn't kill anybody, did you? That's what I wanted to say, but I didn't. Clearly it was on my mind as I asked my next question.

"The first time you did it, an execution, what was it like?"

"I was nervous. I didn't know what would happen. I didn't know what to expect. Like you go to a party with someone. You don't know if they're gonna pull their pants down and urinate in a flower bowl."

"Huh?"

Now there was an analogy! Execution: it was just one big party. When he talked about urinating, was Bob Smith talking about himself? The condemned? I had heard that condemned men often lose control of their bowels and bladders. Maybe executioners do, too. Bob Smith continued, "Once I did that one, it was over with. There was nothing to it."

"What is it like? I've never seen an execution. I've seen the electric chair in Florida." I was not sure I was ready to hear the answer, but some long hidden curiosity from the Rosenberg days pushed me to probe more. I don't think Dick Burr, the public defender, ever recovered from witnessing an execution. He never seemed the same afterward. It took Jim Coleman, Ted Bundy's chief lawyer, a long time to get over watching that execution. Afterwards he locked himself in his hotel room and never even said good-bye when I left the motel and returned to Connecticut. Twice I had witnessed what witnessing an execution did to defense attorneys. Now I was asking what execution did to the executioner.

Bob Smith began. "I'm at a location. I'm not gonna say where for security. They tell me a certain time. I'm not gonna tell you what time. We go to the death house."

"How long in advance do you know?"

"Thirty minutes. I'm a matter of minutes away." Then came a typical Bob Smith contradiction. "I know the date. If it's Friday, I have to be there Thursday night."

"What happens if you have the flu?"

"Never happened. I've never been sick."

"You don't have an understudy?"

"I have no knowledge of it."

"You mean you could be dying and you'd be there?"

"I could be dying." A civil servant devoted to his job, I thought, a good soldier. He continued, "You'd be amazed what the state wants to charge. . . ." He hesitated and this time he caught himself, "I mean pay somebody to take someone's life. A hundred and fifty dollars! And they want you to pay your own expenses." Bob Smith was not, as he implied, a hop, skip, and a jump from the prison. Although he lived in a trailer camp in Tennessee, he was the executioner for a neighboring state. He needed more than a half-hour's notice.

Bob Smith continued to grumble about the conditions of his job. "They want you to lose money, to lose work. If they contact me, I expect them to at least cover my expenses. They won't even do that. I've paid over eight hundred dollars to get four hundred. The money means nothing." A hundred and fifty. Four hundred. Whatever Bob Smith was paid for the executions he performed, he obviously felt undervalued.

"Why do it?"

"I agreed on a certain price. I made a commitment. I've asked them to pay my expenses. If it's cancelled I get my plane trip and expenses and a hundred and fifty dollars. If the execution goes down, I get four hundred dollars. That's all." He looked at me for some sign of compassion. The most I could manage was, "Why do it?"

" 'Cause of my convictions."

The time seemed right to ask what was really on my mind. "Do you ever empathize?"

He looked blank, the William Bonin look. I tried again. "Do you ever put yourself in the person's place?"

He paused, somewhat taken aback. "I've never been asked exactly that before."

I explained, "When I was a kid, I remember the Rosenbergs. I remember the way they were executed. I remember putting myself in their place." As a child, I was fascinated by the Rosenbergs. Sometimes I imagined myself Ethel, strapped to the chair; other times I felt like one of their children, suddenly motherless and fatherless. I couldn't decide which felt worse—being killed or being orphaned.

"Do you ever put yourself in their place?" I tried again.

"Never," came the response.

"You think people are born evil?"

"Yes. You're evil. You're gonna die evil. You could take them off death row. They'd do it again. Evil's gonna float back."

"You feel it's genetic?"

"No, it's not genetic. People are bad. People are mean. You have animal instincts. Most of us control our rage." Then, to my amazement, he added, "I have never found no reason to take a human life." I must have looked puzzled because he immediately said, "You find that weird 'cause I'm an executioner." I did.

Now it was his turn to explain. "There's no reason for me to go to a convenience store and shoot someone. Now, taking that low-life sonofabitch and zapping him, that I can understand." I still didn't get it. Fortunately it didn't matter. Bob Smith had warmed to his topic and continued with minimal encouragement.

"I'm not saying I couldn't hit someone and kill them. Not 'cause I'm out of control. . . . I got to be in control. Not gonna lose your cool. If I hit you and you die, I go to jail for manslaughter. That's different from holding up someone." The nuances of his argument escaped me. What I did understand was that the man sitting next to me was filled with such rage that it clouded his reasoning. This rage fueled his barroom brawls, the shootings, the knifings, the arrests for assault and battery. Any line I may have drawn in my mind between Bob Smith and Lucky Larson had blurred completely. They were indistinguishable.

Our very expensive film was rolling and rolling, and still Bob Smith had not really told me what it was like to execute a man. I looked down at my notes, then up again.

"I was asking you about what it was like to execute someone." Bob Smith looked puzzled. He had been interviewed many times, or so he said. Something about this interview intrigued him.

"You know, you're the only one who's come to interview me who brought notes. Or maybe you're the only one who shows them. You're bringing out a lot. The others beat around the bush."

"I try to ask what I want to know. Do you think you got the job 'cause you're an electrician?"

"I'm sure that's why they picked me."

"Do you have to check things out beforehand?"

"No." His response suggested that he had not been hired for his electrical expertise.

"So what's it like?"

He started to cough. I waited for the coughing to subside.

"I know what you're getting at. I'll answer anything you ask," he assured me.

I decided to pose my question concretely. "Do you see the person in the chair?"

"No, I don't see the person . . . I see the person. I don't even see the person when they're making their final statement. I hear it so many times it means nothing to me." For a meaningless event, it sure confused him. He paused. I waited.

"They bring him in. The prison guards strap him in. Then they got to step aside so the witnesses can see. They lower a flap over the face. Before that, the witnesses can see who they're executing. Then they lower the flap." As he spoke he seemed to visualize the entire ceremony, to see what he swore he did not see.

"The warden nods. I press the button. I have a timer who stands behind me. Timer says, 'Now.' I press. For ten seconds it hits two thousand volts. He says, 'Stop.' I lower the voltage. The timer says, 'Now.' I press the button for twenty seconds."

"It's not the warden who times it?"

"No. It's an employee of the prison. It's a volunteer. Nobody's asked to do it. It's been the same employee for nineteen executions." Then, just to make sure I got it down right, he reviewed the lesson. "First ten seconds at two thousand volts. Then I switch to five hundred volts. That's for twenty seconds. Then I go up to two thousand volts."

"How come they messed up in Florida last time?" I asked. There had been an execution in which the head of the condemned man had caught fire, but the man had not died immediately. Another series of shocks were required.

"It wasn't in Florida," he corrected me. "It was Alabama. I know why. I'm not gonna say. Total stupidity. Using people who was incompetent."

"Was it the first time they did it?"

"I don't know. I'm like Schultz. You know, from *Hogan's Heroes*. I know nahthink," he joked, imitating the German accent of the Nazi prison camp guard of the T.V. series.

When I watch the videotape of this interview I am taken aback as much by my own demeanor as by Bob Smith's. From time to time I see us laugh together. I watch the camaraderie build between us. Every so often I admire the way I phrase a question. I am subtle, disarming. I am Diane Sawyer. I am Barbara Walters. (As my Uncle Arnold would have said, "You'll break your arm patting yourself on the back.") More often, I see on that tape the cagey inquiring reporter of the tabloids. How much of what I am doing is really research? How much is just morbid curiosity? Whatever my motivation was that evening, I just kept on asking questions.

"You told me you were considered for the position of executioner in a state up north. You said you were on their 'A' list. Would you really consider learning a new procedure like lethal injection?" George had wanted me to ask that.

"I already know how."

"How come?"

"I seen it done." He paused for a moment, as if deciding whether or not to share his knowledge. Then he bragged, "I could perform any execution required."

"Do you have any feeling about it? I mean what kind you perform?"

"I'd rather lethal injection."

"Why?"

"It's easier on me."

"I guess it's also more humane," I suggested.

"Why worry what's humane? No one worries what's humane for the victim."

"What do you know about the people you execute?" This question was not asked out of idle curiosity. Bob Smith did not know it, but I had worked briefly on the case of his last client. The condemned was a minor when he killed a state trooper and was sentenced to death. The boy was not executed for several years, by which time he was well into adulthood. Nevertheless, when I spoke to the young man several weeks before his execution, he sounded to me like a kid. He was just like dozens of the adolescents Jonathan and I had examined at Long Lane. I have no idea what he was like when he murdered his victim. He may have been hard as nails. But death row for certain juveniles can have a paradoxical effect. It softens them. Juveniles condemned to death are usually secluded from the regular prison population. What is more, for the first time in their lives, if they are lucky, they receive some attention from intelligent, caring adults—public defenders, paralegals, investigators. In response, these youngsters often mellow. They let the chip drop from their shoulders and learn to trust a little. I am not saying that they necessarily become safe to walk the streets. But they do change, and the person executed five or ten years after a murder is not the same person who committed the crime. One person committed a murder, another dies for it. That's how it is.

That phenomenon should not surprise anyone. We all change. When I think of the ways I have matured over the past decade, just in terms of my knowledge and skills, not to mention my temperament, I am astounded. I have fantasies of calling up certain patients I saw, say, fifteen years ago and saying, "Hey, I think I may have made a mistake. I think I understand now what you were trying to tell me. I think I know what was wrong. Today I would treat your symptoms differently. Come see me. I won't charge." I am a much better psychiatrist now than I was then. And, of course, I am forever apologizing to my children, Gillian and Eric, for losing my cool when they were small; for yelling at them over things that fifteen years ago infuriated me but that today I realize didn't matter much. Whenever I do this, Gillian says, "Don't worry about it, Mom. You weren't so bad," and Eric reassures me that he was not permanently traumatized. But both of my children see that I have changed. The justice system is less wise and charitable than my children. It has trouble with concepts like maturation and change. The system acts as though a twenty-seven-year-old inmate who has not committed an aggressive act in ten years was just as violent and unthinking as he was at seventeen when he killed someone.

"What do you know about the people you electrocute?" I asked again.

"I don't know nothing about them. Not what race, not what crime. Nothing." Then he added, "I don't even read newspapers."

Bob Smith just did his job. He adjusted the voltage and pushed the buttons. Whoever happened to be seated in the chair, as he put it, "got zapped." It was as impersonal as that. I figured it had to be. Otherwise he would not be able to do it. Nobody would.

"I paint a picture after each execution," he volunteered.

"What do you paint?"

"Nothing. I just paint on canvas. Some people say it's gross. Some say it's hideous."

"What do the pictures represent?"

"I told that bunch from Spain that I captured their souls on canvas, the ones I electrocuted. But that's not true. To me it's just paint on canvas."

"What are you feeling when you paint those pictures?"

"Nothing."

"When you were a kid, did you paint or draw?"

"Just military planes and tanks. I used to do a lot of abstract things." He thereupon picked up a ballpoint and made a scribble.

"A free picture from Bob Smith," he crowed, and handed me the scrap of paper, as though he were Picasso, doodling on and signing a restaurant check that never would be cashed.

"Draw any other stuff as a kid?" I asked.

"My childhood is all gone," he replied, thus ending definitively any discussion of childhood.

"May I see your paintings?"

Bob Smith had anticipated my request. "You can see number one and number nineteen and one more."

Number one, an explosion of blacks and reds and yellows, had no discernible form. Streaks of paint shot outward from a central void. After a while he set it aside and placed another picture before me. A dark haunted face of grays and blues stared at me from the second canvas, forcing me to stare back. I looked at it for a minute or two and nodded. He reached for the third canvas. "This one's number nineteen. It's my last one." He thereupon placed before me the picture he had painted just after electrocuting my patient. A one-dimensional white face, shaped like an upside-down pear, spun toward me out of a vortex of dark, frantic brush strokes. Blobs of black paint designated eyes, nose, and mouth. "Everybody wants this painting," he exclaimed. It was hard for me to take my eyes from it. No one spoke—we all just stared at the canvas. Finally I broke the silence. "How do you feel after an execution?"

"I block it out of my mind. It don't exist. It's there but it's not there. It's stored away." The face on the canvas told a different story. Something did happen to Bob Smith each time he pressed that button.

"And after you paint the pictures? How do you feel then?"

"Nothing. I block it out. Anything I don't want to remember I block it out." Did Bob Smith dissociate after an execution? Was he like Johnny Garrett? Could he make himself believe he hadn't done it? Was that why he could say, "I never killed no one"?

"What about pain?" Did he block that out? Johnny could.

"I can do that, too."

Little time and little film remained.

"What's that?" I asked, pointing to a rather bulky book.

"That's my scrapbook. Want to see it?" I nodded yes.

Together we sat, side by side, and turned the pages.

"Is that your first execution?" I pointed to a newspaper clipping on the first page.

"That's my little chair," he tapped the clipping. "I've slept in that chair." Cathi told me later that I looked appalled. "It was the only chair available," he explained. Prior to one execution there had been some sort of delay, perhaps a brief stay of execution. Whatever the reason may have been, Bob Smith came early to the event. Tired from his day job and finding nowhere else to get comfortable, he relaxed and caught forty winks in the chair. What else was an exhausted executioner to do? I stared at the newspaper clipping of Bob Smith's "little chair." It looked just like Old Sparky.

"Did you wire it?" Perhaps that accounted for the fondness in his voice when he spoke of it.

"No." He turned the page of the scrapbook.

"That's the warden. He killed a prisoner." I did not ask why. Bob Smith turned the page.

"Now this guy," he said, pointing to a newspaper clipping, "this guy was humongous! We had to use double straps. He beat a man to death with his fists, then stuck him in his car." He turned the page.

"This one sat outside a trailer and shot the guy who was fooling around with his girlfriend." He turned to the next page.

"This one beat a kid to death." Then, with contempt, "This is what they want to turn back to civilization." He flipped to the next page.

"This sonofabitch killed two kids, this piece of shit right here." He pointed to a picture on the opposite page. "This is the two fathers of the kids. . . . This piece of shit and his brother tied the boy to a tree and molested the girl. Then they laid them down next to each other and shot them in the head." For someone who claimed to know nothing of the people he executed or their crimes, he had a rather extensive dossier on each. What is more, he never needed to look at the text of the clippings. He had committed the facts to memory.

"And this," he said, pointing to the picture of a young black boy, "is the piece of shit they wanted to save. Somebody should have been skinned alive." Somebody? Did he mean the boy? Did he mean the boy's lawyer? I said nothing. He continued.

"You know what pissed me off? They had one of these Catholic bitches in there. One of these sisters. She kept saying, 'I love you. I love you.' If she'd 'a been there they'd 'a laid her down and shot her." Bob Smith could not stop; he was flooded with memories of events he claimed never to have seen. "She was squealing, 'I love you.' She kept falling out. She went into the witness booth." Then he mumbled, almost to himself, "The bitch should have been killed with them."

"Who?" Had I heard him correctly?

"That old Catholic sister." I had.

For the first time I confronted Bob Smith with one of his inconsistencies. "You told me you don't see them. You don't see the man being executed."

His response was instantaneous. "Yes. He's right there!" Then, to make sure I understood, he drew me a diagram of the death chamber. He saw. On to the next page.

"This is a little girl. They raped her and murdered her and threw her in a field and run her over with a tractor. They're just sexual goddamn perverts." Flip. Another page.

"I executed that one. You know he had a goddamn root canal that morning. That's something the newspapers don't know."

Bob Smith's knowledge of the condemned was not limited to newspaper accounts. He had inside information. He knew a thing or two about his clients before they sat down in his little chair. Now he picked up steam.

"I executed these two, but I don't remember them." Flip.

"I executed him." Flip.

"I executed him."

"Who's that?" I asked, pointing to a picture that looked familiar.

"That's the last one I did." Then I knew why the face looked familiar. I had worked on the case.

"How do you feel about executing kids?" I tried to sound casual, offhand, indifferent.

"I don't feel a damn thing about it. How many people do you think he killed?"

"Two or three."

"Two." Then Bob Smith surprised me. "Some people has got to be institutionalized," he declared. "They can't function outside."

"There are people who need to be in an institution," I agreed. It was true.

"You're one of them in your profession who helps get them out. Some people have got to be in an institution. Never let loose."

"Right. What about retarded people?" I asked.

"I never executed no retarded people." I wondered if he knew his last client's I.Q. I did. As I recall, it hovered in the seventies.

"Would you? Kill a retarded person, that is?"

"Yes. It would never happen." Another Bob Smith paradox. I must have shown my discomfort.

"What do you call retarded?" he challenged. "Somebody picks his nose? Someone who goes to special class? To remedial? Well I had to go to remedial classes."

So Bob Smith, like Lucky Larson and Johnny Garrett and Lee Anne Jameson, had been in "Special Ed."

"Do you consider me retarded?"

"No." Bob Smith was not retarded.

"How about killing women?" I asked.

"I don't have no qualms about it. Sex, race, religion got nothing to do with it. . . . I don't have no pity for nobody." The phrase rang in my ears. "I don't have no pity for nobody."

I came to Tennessee to interview a sociopath, someone without a trace of psychopathology other than an inability to empathize with his fellow man. Now I had met someone who told me he had "no qualms" about killing anyone—man, woman, or child. But had I found what I was looking for? Had I finally met a sociopath? Was Bob Smith the character I had been seeking for years—the cool premeditated killer without a trace of psychosis or brain damage? Obviously not.

Bob Smith was as confused and muddleheaded, as battered and beaten, as the violent men Jonathan and I had interviewed on death row. And by his own admission, he had a violent past. His serial executions were but the latest manifestations of his paranoid rage. The line that separated him from Lucky Larson and Johnny Garrett was thin indeed. Like Lucky Larson and the rest, Bob Smith had had more than his share of brawls; his body, when I examined it, bore scars from bullets and knives. That he had served time only for assault and battery, whereas they had been condemned to death for murder, seemed more the luck of the draw than a reflection of either character strength or mental health. Bob Smith insisted, "You gotta have control"; but in the next breath he declared, in his own inimitable way, "Sometimes you got no control over what happens."

Bob Smith insisted that he had no pity for anyone. I think that he probably once did. Execution is not a benign procedure, not for any of the participants. The explosion of pain and confusion let loose in Bob Smith's brain each time he did his job was splattered and scrawled in paint on the canvases he produced immediately after each execution. Then all was forgotten. "I block it out," he said.

I doubt that Bob Smith was always that good at blocking out pain. When he responded to the ad, he must have had some capacity to do that or he would not have applied for the job of executioner in the first place. But by the fifty-seventh time he pressed the button and activated his "little chair," (three times for each of his nineteen executions), he had had a lot of experience. I suspect that each press of the button further inured him, making it easier and easier over time to do his job.

Could anybody do it? Could just about any of us press that button? If the state's attorney who prosecuted a capital murder case or the judge who handed down the death sentence knew it would fall to him to carry it out, would he do it? Could he do it? I doubt it. I think my daughter is probably right. If that task came with the territory, most of those prosecutors and judges would not even apply for their jobs. Normal people can't do things like that. Most of us are much too squeamish to kill another human being except in self-defense. It seems to take intense, repeated, intolerable pain early in life, and some sort of organic impairment or psychotic thinking to overcome that taboo.

Mel, my husband, constantly cautions me against generalizing from a single case. Generally I don't. But Bob Smith is the only executioner I have ever met or expect to meet; therefore, I must speculate on the only data I have and am likely to get. The way I figure it, most of the prosecutors who seek the death penalty, and most of the judges who condemn murderers to death, rely on the fact that our society will always produce enough people who were so brutalized during their own childhoods, so muddleheaded and paranoid, that they are more than willing to perform the grisly jobs that ordinary people would not dream of taking.

"I don't have no pity for nobody." The words hung in the air. There wasn't a whole lot more to say. George turned off the movie camera and started to pack away the equipment. Cathi finished up the roll of videotape with some clips of Bob Smith's scrapbook and some shots of his canvases. The videotape was still rolling when she asked, off-handedly, "How does your family feel about what you do?" We already knew that Bob Smith's brother had found him the job. Bob Smith said that he wasn't certain just how his sister felt. She did let him stay over at her house those nights he was on call and needed to be near the prison.

Bob Smith had been married a couple of times. The first time, he ran off with a thirteen-year-old. He had a son from that marriage. In fact, he was already a grandfather.

The videotape continued to roll.

"How would you feel about your son or your grandson going into the same line of work?" Cathi asked.

"It's fine with me," Bob Smith responded. Then he added, "I know how my grandson feels."

"How's that?" I asked.

"He says 'zap 'em, Granddaddy.' "

EPILOGUE

Ted Bundy, Johnny Garrett, Marie Moore, Jonathan, me. Could any one of us become a murderer? Could anyone in the world become a murderer? Probably—at least I think so. Given certain kinds of neurologic and psychiatric problems, and being raised by violent, abusive parents, just about any of us could be turned into a killer. And you don't need to be born with those problems; they can be acquired. The brain is not as resilient as we might wish. It's not just the batterings that take their toll, or the car accidents and brain infections. We now know that intense, ongoing emotional stress can change the very structure of our brain, much less its function. No one is immune. It could happen to any of us.

Most people find that hard to believe. They can't imagine that they could commit murder. Certainly all those people who stood outside the prison at Starke just before Ted Bundy's execution, chanting, "Burn, Bundy, Burn!" never for a moment thought that they could murder. Only now, as I reread the earlier chapters of this book and seek the words to bring it to a close, am I struck by the irony of that scene. There, as I drove through the gates to meet with Mr. Bundy for the last time, I saw a hoard of citizens, confident that they could never become killers, clamoring for death.

How much do we know about what makes us violent? A better question: How much do we want to know? How curious are we? Sometimes we act as though we haven't the faintest idea why people become murderers. But, in truth, we know a lot more about what makes for violence than we often care to admit. So we play dumb. To understand sometimes means to forgive, and these days people aren't in a very forgiving mood. For example, we know that, for the most part, murderers are made, not born. Many of the genetic theories entertained in the 1970s, like the XYY syndrome, have been called into question. Recently scientists in the Netherlands identified a family in which several of the males behaved in wildly aberrant ways. These males, they discovered, carried a mutant gene that affected the way they metabolized certain neurotransmitters in the brain. Neurotransmitters are the chemical messengers that transmit impulses from one nerve cell to the next. To me, the most interesting finding of that study was that not all of the affected males were aggressive. The question remains: Why did some of the men with the genetic mutation rape and assault while others did not? What made the difference?

At this time it is safe to say that there is no known genetic abnormality associated specifically with violent crime. No particular national or ethnic or racial or religious group has proved itself to be innately and enduringly more violent than another. That is not to say that from time to time one or another group has not tried to so distinguish itself. There is, of course, a normal genetic condition, characteristic of about 50 percent of the human population, that is associated with violent crime: the XY syndrome, or being male. One can't simply blame male violence on social conditioning. In almost every animal species—bears, chimpanzees, even fish and lizards—males are more aggressive than females. Male hormones, androgens, must have something to do with this phenomenon. If male animals are deprived of androgens at crucial stages in their development, they will not develop normal male aggressiveness.

However, although men in our society commit about nine times as many murders as women, most men are not violent. Neither having a masculinized brain nor having lots of androgen pouring through one's bloodstream is sufficient to create a violent man. Nevertheless, it seems somewhat more difficult for men than for women to control their violent impulses. Perhaps, in murder cases, being male should be considered a mitigating circumstance. It's a thought. I should mention it to Dick Burr—it could make for an interesting defense.

What else do we know about the genesis of violence? We know that our basic aggressive and sexual instincts, and our pleasurable feelings, spring from what we currently call the limbic system—those deep, primitive brain structures we discussed earlier that have widespread connections to the rest of the brain. We know that our sense of fear is localized predominantly in the amygdala, a nucleus of cells hidden within each temporal lobe. We know that destruction of these nuclei eradicates fear, whereas stimulation of them can induce it. We cannot do without the amygdala. But fear is often the nidus for paranoia. A certain amount of fear is necessary for survival. On the other hand, too much can make us dangerous.

There is also evidence that the primitive urges springing from the limbic system are modulated or controlled by our frontal lobes. When we disconnect the pathways between our reptilian brain and our frontal cortex, we no longer have good control of our urges. Accidents and injuries often do just that kind of damage. If the connections between our frontal lobes and limbic system are disrupted, how responsible are we for flying off the handle? It's a hard call. How responsible is a truck driver for a crash if his brakes are worn? We also know that diffuse damage to our brains, a common consequence of batterings, tends to make us more irritable and impulsive. Damage to just about any part of our brain makes self-control problematic, and repeatedly violent individuals have had more than their share of hard knocks, literally and figuratively.

We are beginning to understand the brain's neurochemistry and the effects of specific neurotransmitters on behavior. Neurotransmitters such as norepinephrine, dopamine, and serotonin affect our thinking, our emotions, and our moods. Take serotonin, for instance. We know that by lowering the serotonin levels in animals we can make them more aggressive. We also know that by increasing serotonin levels we can make them gentler. Certain members of monkey colonies are naturally endowed with high concentrations of brain serotonin. These serotonin-rich monkeys are a whole lot nicer to each other than their less well-endowed peers. They are more likely to groom one another and to share their food. It looks to humans as though a certain type of morality comes more easily to them. I wonder if human beings are like that. From the start, is doing the right thing easier for some of us than for others? Studies on human beings have shown that extremely violent men may have lower concentrations of brain serotonin than gentler men. Did they start out that way or did something happen to them to decrease their stores? Whatever the explanation, law-abiding, moral behavior may be especially hard for them.

What fascinates me most is the fact that brain concentrations of substances like serotonin are not immutable. They are not simply genetic givens—experience affects them. Certain kinds of stressors can decrease brain serotonin levels and thereby change behavior. For example, if you isolate animals at crucial developmental stages, if you keep them caged all alone, their serotonin drops. What is more, when you then release them and put them in contact with other animals, they are fiercely aggressive. Pain and fear also reduce serotonin levels and promote aggression. That's how pit bulls are trained to fight. Heat, crowding, discomfort, and upbringing by aggressive members of a species also increase animal aggressiveness. Now there are a few basic research findings it might make sense to share with the deputy warden at Starke. I could write to him, but would he read my note?

Sometimes, when I have a really bad day, it looks to me as if we, like the deputy warden, are not much interested in understanding violence. It may look as though we are. Those seven Bundy books would seem proof of our curiosity to learn what makes people like Theodore Bundy violent. But think about it: If we really wanted to know what made him violent, would we have killed him? He died with so many questions left unanswered. I never even saw an MRI of his brain. A week or two after his death, I got a couple of calls from the FBI agent who had gotten close to Mr. Bundy while he was in prison and had picked his brain. Now he wanted to pick mine. He kept me on the phone quite a while. We played a game of cat and mouse, each of us trying to find out what the other knew. I knew about the knives Ted Bundy placed in his aunt's bed when he was only three years old. He knew what Ted Bundy said about the sexual uses of decapitated heads and why their front teeth were often missing. Obviously a lot remained to be discovered about Ted Bundy and his family. By killing him, we blew our chance to learn more.

How curious were people about Mark David Chapman, the man who shot John Lennon? Jonathan and I were in the midst of examining him in preparation for a possible insanity defense when an epiphany convinced Mr. Chapman to plead guilty. Did God speak to him and show him the way? Did someone else get to him and convince him to keep quiet? Or did a group of neurons in his limbic system fire off and give rise to his sudden enlightenment? Was it a seizure? A hallucination? A manic moment? A dissociative episode? We shall probably never know for sure. One thing we do know is that Mark David Chapman's decision to plead guilty and forgo a trial did not seem a reasonable decision, either to me or to his lawyer. It still doesn't. In fact, his lawyer begged the judge to obtain an independent competency evaluation to assess Chapman's ability to make such a plea. The judge thought he knew better: he, like the judge in Heath Wilkins's case, recognized a competent defendant when he saw one. He refused to order the evaluation and accepted the guilty plea.

Prior to sentencing, Mr. Chapman's lawyer made one final attempt to bring to light some of our psychiatric and neurologic findings. The data might at least influence the kind of sentence he received. However, when I took the stand and started to respond to the lawyer's first question, the judge cut me off. He was not interested. He wasn't the least bit curious.

Judges are not the only ones who sometimes find it easier not to know. I think of Velma Barfield. She was a serial murderer. She was also the first and only woman to be executed in the United States in the last quarter-century. Shortly before her scheduled execution, Dick Burr, who was assisting the local attorney on her case, called me and asked me to examine her. There were no funds for the examination. I'm not sure if the court refused them or if the local attorney did not ask for them. I know he was not all that enthusiastic about my coming. It was, therefore, a freebie. This did not please me. At Bellevue, I rely almost entirely on funds from these kinds of evaluations to keep our office running and do our violence research. Getting money from the government to do clinical research on violence is next to impossible. I am still trying unsuccessfully to convince the Office of Juvenile Justice to help me study the children of the hundred or so violent delinquents Jonathan and I studied in the late 1970s. The study just might give us a window on the intergenerational transmission of violence. Given the level of violence in our country, you would think the government would be interested in this topic. Not so.

My department chairman at N.Y.U. wishes I'd find something biochemical or physiological to study so I could pull in some big grant money. But if I did that, who would talk to the murderers and their kin and find out what sorts of experiences had lowered their serotonin levels or why their frontal lobes didn't communicate well with their limbic systems? Besides, most people agree that the most important influence on how we treat others as adults is how we were treated as children.

Dick Burr accompanied me to the prison and sat in on the psychiatric examination of Velma Barfield. What I remember most clearly is that, in order to get to the small courtroom set aside for our interview, we had to pass by the gas chamber. I shall never forget a gauge I saw on the wall of the outside corridor. "That measures the level of cyanide gas that escapes so they don't poison any of the witnesses," Dick explained.

"Thanks for sharing that."

We learned lots about Velma Barfield that day, Dick Burr and I. I was pretty sure much of what we learned could have been used in a clemency appeal to the governor. When I left North Carolina, I was optimistic.

A few days later Dick Burr called to tell me that Velma Barfield and her lawyer had decided not to reveal the most crucial psychiatric findings. Velma was afraid of upsetting her folks and losing their support during what might be her final days. To my mind, these definitely would be her final days if she refused to allow disclosure. What got me was that her lawyer took the same position she did. He worried about embarrassing her family. He had grown to like them.

I offered to return to North Carolina and talk with Velma again. I was pretty sure that I could convince her to change her mind. I thought that if she realized how much her story might help people understand what kinds of experiences could drive a woman to murder, she would relent and allow her full story to be told. But her attorney was adamant—just let things be. He would not even allow me to speak with her on the phone.

Velma Barfield was executed in a new, modern death chamber in North Carolina. The gas chamber remained empty and the corridor safe. She was put to death by lethal injection. A couple of years later, when I went to North Carolina's death row to examine a couple of juveniles, a guard insisted on showing me the anteroom where Velma Barfield awaited death and the room with the gurney on which she died. It looked pretty sterile compared to Old Sparky. Such is the progress of justice.

I can't really say that Velma Barfield's secrets died with her. Like

Dick Burr and her local attorney, I am not allowed to reveal them and her folks aren't likely to spill the beans, so I guess they will die with us. It's hard to play by those rules. Just before her execution I fantasized calling the governor or Gloria Steinem or going to the newspapers with Velma's story. I didn't; I'm not allowed to.

Now, as I think back about Ted Bundy and Mark David Chapman and Velma Barfield—in fact, as I think back about Johnny Garrett and the clemency board that confirmed his death sentence without even reading the materials that his superb court-appointed defense attorneys so diligently provided them, or looking at the videotapes I had made of his madness, I think I understand what's happening. Ever since 1976, when the Supreme Court mandated separate sentencing phases in capital cases, juries have been obliged to consider the mitigating as well as the aggravating circumstances of a murder. Aggravating circumstances focus for the most part on the grotesqueness of the crime or crimes: Was the victim tortured or raped or mutilated? Was there more than one victim? Then there are the mitigating circumstances. These often focus on the defendant's abusive childhood and on issues of mental health. Herein lies the contradiction. Another mathematical formula comes to mind: The gruesomeness of a murder is directly proportional to the craziness of the murderer. That's just the way it is. Now ask a jury to wrestle with that equation and come up with the right answer. It can't be done.

And our own lack of curiosity? How is it that we pour millions of dollars into Bundy books and the like, but are, nevertheless, willing to sacrifice further knowledge about him and his ilk in the interest of doing away with them? Maybe Ted Bundy was right. I suspect we are all far more curious about what the murderer did—the gory details of the crime—than about why he did it. It's the act of murder that fascinates us and tickles our own limbic systems. No wonder people fight for seats at executions. Is that, at least in part, why I do the work I do? Maybe. I wouldn't be surprised.

A final word for my tweedy professor in the back row of the auditorium, whose question I have tried hard to answer; it is a corollary of the last equation: In a given murder, our desire to learn its causes, and the time we are willing to spend doing that, are inversely proportional to the grisliness of the crime and the pleasure we anticipate deriving from the execution.

INDEX